YORK NOTES COMPANIONS

This book is to be returned on or before
the last date stamped below.

Education

Library Service

11 JUN 2012

Harlow, England • London • New York • Boston • San Francis
Sydney • Tokyo • Singapore • Hong Kong • Seoul • Taipei •
Cape Town • Madrid • Mexico City • Amsterdam • Munich • F

D1339173

YORK PRESS
322 Old Brompton Road
London
SW5 9JH

PEARSON EDUCATION LIMITED
Edinburgh Gate
Harlow CM20 2JE
United Kingdom
Tel: +44 (0)1279 623623
Fax: +44 (0)1279 431059
Website: www.pearsoned.co.uk

First edition published in Great Britain in 2010
© Librairie du Liban *Publishers* 2010

The right of William May to be identified as author
of this work has been asserted by him in accordance
with the Copyright, Designs and Patents Act 1988.

ISBN 978–1–4082–0474–0

British Library Cataloguing in Publication Data
A CIP catalogue record for this book can be obtained from the British Library

Library of Congress Cataloging in Publication Data
May, William, 1982-
  Postwar literature, 1950 to 1990 / William May.
    p. cm. -- (York notes companions)
  Includes bibliographical references and index.
  ISBN 978-1-4082-0474-0 (alk. paper)
1. English literature--20th century--History and criticism--Handbooks,
manuals, etc. 2. Literature and society--Great Britain--History--20th
century. 3. Great Britain--Civilization--1945- I. Title.
  PR478.S57M39 2010
  820.9'358--dc22
                                2010008348

10 9 8 7 6 5 4 3 2 1
14 13 12 11 10

Phototypeset by Pantek Arts Ltd, Maidstone, Kent
Printed in Malaysia, CTP-KHL

Contents

Contents

Part One
Introduction

The world appears
as a very dull novel in which the characters –
Edwin, Wanda, Septimus and Moira,
are constantly looking out of the windows to observe,
bleakly or with sighs, that it is raining again.

John Ash, 'Some Boys
(or The English Poem circa 1978)' (1981)[1]

John Ash's description of the English poem circa 1978 as 'a very dull novel' is a damning but self-aware indictment of the literary climate. His mocking verse suggests a form so moribund, housebound, and tedious that the only point of comparison is to a novel, that form which promised innovation two hundred years ago, but now seemed destined only to repeat itself, a temporary panacea for a literature doomed to perpetual decline. The reading of the postwar period as a time of diminishing literary returns is not limited to John Ash's poem. The elderly sisters in Barbara Pym's novel *Less than Angels* (1955) take comfort from a radio play about people like themselves that they have already heard before 'but neither could remember exactly how it ended … so life seemed to go round in a circle'.[2] The playwright Braham in Christopher Hampton's *The Philanthropist* (1970) is happy to pen works that pass the time rather than aspire to art, boasting of his God-given ability to 'create essentially frivolous entertainments' enjoyed by enough frivolous people for him 'to amble comfortably through life'.³ Postwar literature is so self-effacing it often convinces critics of the qualified nature of its success.

Studies of twentieth-century British literature have tended to privilege the modernist experiments of the 1920s or the 'revival' of the British novel in the 1980s and 1990s over the amorphous and messy years in between. For some commentators, the British novel seems to go missing in action between Virginia Woolf's *Between the Acts* (1941) and Angela Carter's *Nights at the Circus* (1984). For these literary historians, although the 1950s give us the poems of Philip Larkin and the plays of John Osborne, subsequent decades are mostly a waiting game until postmodernism reinvigorates the stale world of British literature. The Romantic lyric or the industrial novel of the Victorian period present us with discrete literary forms and genres, whereas the postwar period, they might argue, offers only anomalies and long novels by Iris Murdoch.

This study of British literature from 1950 to 1990 works against that assumption, finding in the fiction, poetry, and drama of the period an unparalleled richness of voice, method, and matter.

While the first three decades of the twentieth century argued for the novel as an art form through writers such as Joyce and Conrad, it was the postwar period that had to arbitrate between the formal and moral expectations of the genre. If the final decades of the century saw a cautious embrace of postmodern play and experimentation, it was the immediate postwar period which gave us a novel entirely imagined by a protagonist who is in fact dead (William Golding, *Pincher Martin*, 1956), a novel published with separate bound chapters to be read in any order (B. S. Johnson, *The Unfortunates*, 1969), or a poetic drama written in an invented language (Ted Hughes, *Orghast*, 1971). These examples should serve as a corrective; two of them are explored in detail in Part Three (Hughes and Golding). Although this was a period often defined, politically, by consensus, its literature is marked by a new diversity. The diversity of the postwar period comes, in part, through state intervention, something that would have been unthinkable by the modernists with their emphasis on creative autonomy. The expansion of secondary education after the war and the creation of the Welfare

State didn't just create more readers and writers, as we explore in the 'Class and Education' chapter in Part Four, but different kinds of reading and writing. The literature of the period is at once emboldened by the new cross-currents and social transformations and anxiously shackled by them. If modernism is often associated with elitism, this was a literature stimulated by a new audience, but also mindful of its responsibilities towards that same audience. The apparently conservative rejection of modernist experiment in the postwar period can also be read as a liberal gesture, widening the net of literary debate and participation.

Critical approaches to literature itself were similarly varied. The immediate postwar period found New Criticism taking centre stage, an approach which classified texts by genre or type, and subjected them to empirical scrutiny. In part, this is the method used in Part Three of this study, which considers the generic categories that defined the literature of the period – from the lyric to the postmodern novel – but combines this with a focus on individual texts, offering an extended commentary on six indicative plays, poems, and novels. Yet the 1970s and 1980s also saw the rise of theoretical approaches to literature in English Studies. It is with a particular historical pertinence, then, that Part Four of this study combines contextual and historical readings of texts with the insights offered by Marxism, feminism, or postcolonial theory.

It was not only in education that literature responded directly to the changed Britain of the postwar era. The period begins with Indian Independence in 1947 and ends with the destruction of the Berlin Wall in 1989; between those two events we find Britain losing its Empire and attempting to reconfigure its sense of national identity. At the same time, the world at large attempts to move towards concord and collaboration. For this very reason, Britishness itself becomes a contested category. The collapse of the Empire and the increasingly international world of literature means that British is often a nominal, unhelpful, and sometimes hostile term for the writers included in this volume. Although Sylvia Plath was American, her influence on British poetry begs her inclusion; her poetics are explored in depth in Part Three alongside the work of Stevie Smith and Philip Larkin. While John Osborne's *Look Back in Anger* (1956) is often seen as rejuvenating the British stage, the most influential play of the postwar period was Samuel Beckett's *Waiting for Godot* (1955), originally written in French, premiered in Paris, and penned by an Irishman. Beckett, too, provides a key context for postwar drama – his work is explored alongside Harold Pinter and Tom Stoppard in 'New Stages' in Part Three. For Irish poet Seamus Heaney, who wrote a poem in protest when included in a 1980s British poetry anthology, the term 'British' is politically insensitive as well as inaccurate. The novelist Salman Rushdie, author of *The Satanic Verses* (1988), fiercely rejected the term British or Commonwealth arguing that during the late 1980s Britain was harbour but not home. Many writers look to the United States, either for a home, as with Thom Gunn or Christopher Isherwood, or a literary starting point, as in the modernist poetry of Basil Bunting. The inclusion of all these writers in the present volume says as much about the contested term of Britishness and nationality in the postwar period as it does about the pragmatics of compiling a useful survey of that period.

For this reason, nationality and nationhood are recurring themes in this study, particularly in the chapters 'Immigrants and Exiles' and 'Nostalgia and National Identity' in Part Four. Postwar immigration from the Caribbean to Britain saw a new awareness of race and cosmopolitanism in British culture, and also provided an invigorating alternative to the apparent consensus of the 1950s. Samuel Selvon's *The Lonely Londoners* (1956), which traces the fortunes of Moses Aloetta and a group of West Indian and African immigrants in London, is clear-eyed if comic about the hardships and prejudices they encounter. There is an argument that this period is defined, for all its variety, by the concerns of the outsider, to borrow the title of Colin Wilson's 1956 philosophical work, rather than the comforts of consensus. Many of Iris Murdoch's characters sit smugly in middle-class contentment at the outset of her novels, but few remain there for long; we frequently see the university campus in the postwar period, but usually through the eyes of the bewildered scholarship boy, as in Kingsley Amis's *Lucky Jim* (1954); even the apparently permissive liberation of the 1960s is often depicted by the sceptical observer or the onlookers. The invention of sex famously comes too late for Philip Larkin's disgruntled speaker in 'Annus Mirabilis' (1973).

Sex, while not, as Larkin's poem suggests, invented in the postwar period, was marked by a sea change in attitudes during the 1950s and 1960s. One way of reading the period might track the change from the buttoned-up conservatism of the immediate postwar period, with its austerity and baby boom, to the promise of legal abortion, free birth control, and the decriminalising of homosexuality in the 1960s. Yet the literature does not always correspond to the history, as the chapters in Part Four suggest; while the Lady Chatterley trial of 1960* and the overhaul of theatre censorship laws in 1968 both point to increasingly liberal attitudes to what is read and by whom, writers as diverse as Joe Orton, Margaret Drabble, and David Edgar remain ambivalent about the new world of permissiveness. We might also note that while the postwar period gave birth to the 'teenager', and was the first to recognise the adolescent as someone with economic and cultural significance, it also brought the retirement home.

In the same way that the nationality of writers included in the book is worthy of investigation, the dividing lines between pre- and post-1990 might, too, seem arbitrary. The timeline in Part Five presents a neat journey from the Coronation to the end of the Cold War, yet history, as so many writers from the period show, is contingent, relative, and more often dictated by what is convenient. For many, the rise of Thatcherism in the 1980s, the break-up of the Trade Unions, and the abandoning of the principles of the Welfare State for a free market economy might seem to make the world after 1979 seem much closer to our own than to that of the Suez Crisis or the Coronation. The rise of novelists such as Martin Amis, Angela Carter, and Julian Barnes has prompted many commentators to curtain off the final two decades of the twentieth century as 'contemporary'. Yet, throughout this volume, readers will hopefully come to realise how much the literary and cultural debates of the postwar period continue to define our lives. Terms such as meritocracy, ecology, immigration, assimilation, and social mobility were not just part of the cultural debate, as now, but were, in some cases, being used for the very first time.

* In 1960, Penguin were taken to court for publishing D. H. Lawrence's novel *Lady Chatterley's Lover*, and successfully defended the work from charges of obscenity. For a fuller discussion of the trial and its implications, see the section on 'Permissiveness and Censorship' in Part Four: 'Sex and Identity'.

Throughout this volume and the *York Notes Companions* series, there has been a deliberate attempt to focus debate on new voices or neglected works from each period alongside the more obvious choices. As Part Two: 'A Cultural Overview' notes, literary critics of the 1950s and 1960s were quick to offer terms such as 'Angry Young Man' and 'The Movement' to define current trends, but contemporary readers might do well to question the efficacy of these labels and their implicit policy of exclusion. While no postwar study can ignore Kingsley Amis or Philip Larkin, it would do just as well to consider Penelope Fitzgerald or Michael Hofmann. If Angela Carter seems ubiquitous in the postwar literary landscape, Christine Brooke-Rose can tell us just as much about experimental feminist fiction. The changing fashions of critics over the last thirty years has offered a number of competing 'postwars'; if anything this volume should provoke further debate in its inclusions as well as its inevitable omissions. It is expansive and suggestive rather than exhaustive, as the further reading sections in Part Five suggest. If the postwar period is a time of consensus, there is a healthy absence of consensus about what authors the term postwar may in fact denote.

William May

Notes

1   John Ash, 'Some Boys (or The English Poem circa 1978)', *Collected Poems* (Manchester: Carcanet, 1996), p. 20, ll. 4–8.
2   Barbara Pym, *Less than Angels* (London: Granada, 1980), p. 39.
3   Christopher Hampton, *The Philanthropist, Plays: One* (London: Faber, 1997), p. 122.

Part Two
A Cultural Overview

What can history tell us about literature, and vice versa? What are the ethics of using one to read the other? These are questions that fiction, poetry, and drama from the postwar period ask with unfailing regularity. In Penelope Lively's *Moon Tiger* (1987), the protagonist Claudia attempts to write the history of the world on her death-bed, but comes to realise it is comprised of millions of unreliable memories. As a character notes in *The Satanic Verses* (1988), 'the trouble with the English is that their history happened overseas, so they don't know what it means.'[1] The decades after the Second World War saw curious disparities between the nation's sense of itself at home and abroad. The coronation of Elizabeth II in 1953 was both an expression of patriotic tradition and the first modern television event. Many thought, as with Elizabeth I's reign, the new monarch would usher in a period of national cultural revival. Yet as late as the Coronation, food rationing was still in place, a lingering legacy from the Second World War. The USA's Marshall plan had pledged millions to rebuild Britain's bombed cities and collapsed economy, but had placed the country in debt, both financially and politically, to the United States, as the political crisis that erupted in 1956 was to demonstrate. For nearly one hundred years, Britain had assumed control of the Suez Canal in Egypt, using it as a strategic access point to colonies in the Far

East, India, and Australia. When the Egyptian president, Colonel Nasser, attempted to regain control of the canal, Britain launched a tripartite attack with France and Israel in 1956. Yet the United States refused to co-operate with the invasion and threatened to withdraw financial support for Britain; troops were forced to leave Egypt within a week. This humiliating defeat caused the then Prime Minister, Anthony Eden, to resign. Britain's presence on the international stage during the 1950s suggested a nation unsure of its position in a new world order, even if the name of its ruling monarch suggested the glories of the past. United States Secretary of State Dean Acheson famously declared that Great Britain had 'lost an Empire and not yet found a role' in December 1962.[2] Although he was speaking in the context of EEC membership, it seemed all too easy to apply his comment to the nation at large.

This anxiety about a post-Empire Britain defines the social and cultural movements of the period; Suez became both a national embarrassment and a literary motif. P. H. Newby's novel *Something to Answer For* (1969) places the blame for the Suez Crisis at the feet of the unfortunate character Mrs Khoury, determined to take her husband's body back to the Lebanon to be buried. In 1978, Anthony Burgess penned *1985*, a futuristic dystopian novel set in the year of the title, but makes it unclear whether history begins with man's fall or with Anthony Eden's resignation: 'history was a record of the long slow trek from Eden towards the land of Nod, with nothing but the deserts of injustice on the way'.[3] Harold Macmillan's granting of independence to colonies including Sierra Leone, Nigeria, Cyprus, and Malta in the early 1960s on the one hand suggests a freedom and unshackling, yet the ever decreasing influence of Britain and its marginal status in the Cold War suggests a narrative of decline. Perhaps inevitably, this narrative has an appeal for literary commentators, who are quick to announce the death of the novel, the cul-de-sac of modern poetry, or the moribund nature of theatre. Yet this critical death knell has its expedient advantages for authors, too: the age is as full of revivals as it is of dead ends.

Affluence or Austerity?

The move from postwar austerity to affluence, as suggested by J. K. Galbraith's *The Affluent Society* (1958), also makes an appealing story. The creation of the Welfare State, ushered in by the Beveridge Report in 1947, gave Britain the National Health Service, its first form of social security, and saw the mass expansion of secondary and tertiary education. The baby boom and the drive towards efficiency and economic recovery creates an image of 1950s Britain as prosperous, comfortable, and homogenous. This was the era of political consensus, where ideological as well as practical agreement between Labour and the Conservatives briefly removed the notion of 'opposition'. Yet, as Robert Hewison has noted, 'without insisting on uniformity, consensus encourages conformity'.[4] The late 1950s also saw a rise in disposable income and an explosion in cheap, mass-produced goods. Yet this journey to prosperity worked both ways. In the late 1960s, under Harold Wilson, the pound was devalued, and finally floated against the dollar in 1971. In 1979, the 'Winter of Discontent' saw poorly paid employees go on strike, and by the early 1980s unemployment had topped five million. Like the Queen's coronation some thirty years earlier, the wedding of Prince Charles and Lady Diana Spencer found the nation at their television sets in 1981, but one in three of those watching were now without work.

The dominance of Thatcherism in the 1980s did not halt unemployment, but rather redefined it as a strategic tool for moving British workers from manufacturing to service industries. The railways, broadcasters, and many utility services were privatised. The Welfare State notion of society was abandoned in favour of individuals and families. Even the family itself seemed to be under attack. A character in Mike Leigh's *High Hopes* (1988) shrugs off Thatcher's Britain with a resigned: 'They're out of date, families; they ain't no use any more.'[5] Unsurprisingly, Thatcher was sceptical of the benefits of consensus, glossing the term as 'the process of abandoning all beliefs, principles, values and policies in search of something which no one believes in, but to which no one objects'.[6] Yet if she made it her goal to be effective rather than popular, the Conservative drive to modernise Britain was also sold to the public as a nostalgic gesture. Never was Thatcher's popularity higher than when she launched a military offensive against Argentina in 1982 after they invaded the Falkland Islands. This was an Empire that was apparently worth fighting for, even if nobody could point to it on a map.

Literature and Politics

The disparity between public and private histories also highlights the limitations of making literature into a timeline. The early 1960s are often seen as a time of increased permissiveness, a move away from the stifling conformity of public life in the 1950s. In 1960, for example, Penguin was taken to court for publishing the allegedly obscene *Lady Chatterley's Lover* by D. H. Lawrence, and emerged victorious. In 1963, President Kennedy was assassinated in the USA, and Britain saw the Profumo Affair, its first MP sex scandal. In 1968, perhaps the most iconic year of the postwar period, widespread student rioting occurred throughout Europe, with counter-cultural protests against the Vietnam War. Yet Gabriel A. Almond and Sidney Verba's *The Civic Culture* (1963) surveyed the British public only to find they had 'a highly developed sense of loyalty to their system of government, a strong sense of deference to the independent authority of government and state, attitudes of trust and confidence, and a deep commitment to moderation in politics'.[7] Meanwhile, the protagonist of Penelope Fitzgerald's *At Freddie's* (1989) breezily informs us 'it must have been 1963, because the musical of *Dombey & Son* was running at the Alexandra'.[8] The earth-shattering events of contemporary politics are irrelevant in a world which measures time by the local theatre programme.

Other writers are less wary about setting up their characters under the long shadows of history. Margaret Drabble's *The Ice Age* (1977) uses the mass unemployment of the period as a barometer for measuring her own fictive world. The growing power of the Trade Unions combined with the economic downturn at the time meant that poorly paid workers went on strike, bringing the nation to a standstill. Yet Drabble uses the world around her metaphorically rather than seeking out documentary realism: the crippling strikes of the 1970s are metamorphosed into the central conceit of the book as 'a huge icy fist, with large cold fingers … squeezing and chilling the people of Britain.'[9] The cracking, glacial world of the novel divides its characters by income or residence. Whether they live in a caravan or a rented flat, their lives are equally 'condemned' by the financial necessities of that moment in history and the pragmatics of writing a state-of-the-nation novel. No individuals are able to remove themselves from the engine of society. Her subsequent novel, *The Radiant Way* (1987), trades in 1970s unemployment for end-of-the-decade optimism, as Liz Headland throws a 1979 New Year's Eve party where intellectuals and journalists come to gabble and drink as 'old opinions were shed, stuffy woolly shabby old liberal vests and comforters were left piled on the floor.'[10] Yet here, too, their lives are imperilled by uncertain futures. A theatre director worries about her Arts Council funding while epidemiologist Ted Stennett puzzles over the 'science-fiction disease of AIDS' (p. 32). The 1980s reader, with the benefit of hindsight, would have found something cruelly inevitable about their trajectories as Thatcher slashed arts subsidies and AIDS became a global epidemic.

Hugo Williams's 1994 poem 'Post-war British' finds the speaker looking at an old family photograph at the beach from 1948. In the background, a dog fetches a stick which, in the speaker's mind, comes to be the photo itself, thrown out with the express purpose of being retrieved at a later date. The space separating the speaker from his own image is that forty-year span often known as the postwar period; in returning to it, we notice how much it has shaped the subsequent decades:

> And here we all are at last –
> our faces coming up tired but satisfied
> at the other end of our lives,
> our knitted bathing-trunks falling down.[11]

The comic, seaside image of the postwar period suggests a refusal to take things too seriously. The Cuban Missile Crisis in 1962 or the threat of the H-bomb haunted the children of the 1960s. However, the small-scale civil unrest in Britain in 1968 compared to, say, that in Paris, where anti-Vietnam protests brought revolutionary anarchy to the city, highlights a pragmatic, empirical scepticism. Tellingly, the first author to be taken seriously as a cultural voice in the postwar period was Kingsley Amis, who played the part of a Socialist reformer very reluctantly, and scoffed at the notion that literature might enact political change. Yet it is his comic creation Jim Dixon who is heralded as the future of Britain by the *Universities & Left Review* in 1957, not because he ushers in a revolution, but because his irritation with complacency reminds us it is 'on this pitiful, trivial, level that people live'.[12]

The Movement

The troubles and agitations of the everyday define many of the key movements of the period. Perhaps the most mythologised is The Movement itself, a confusing term for a group of writers drawn to stasis and conservatism. The term describes writers from the 1950s who rejected the neo-Romantic excess of Dylan Thomas or the modernist elusiveness of Ezra Pound for colloquial language, traditional forms, and a qualified suspicion of the sentimental. Many of these writers, including Kingsley Amis, Thom Gunn, and Philip Larkin, had benefited from a grammar school education, and found themselves striking awkward anti-intellectual poses amid the traditional universities they went on to attend. For Larkin, famously, modernism was an elitist cul-de-sac, and he longed for a literature that 'used language in the way we all use it';[13] the use of the plural pronoun makes striking links between Larkin as a poet and his readership. An article in *Britain Today* was proudly able to assert that 'the Victorian age has come into its own again'.[14] In practice, this meant poetry in iambic pentameter or with a clear rhythmic structure; works that rejected obscurity or classical references; cultural references to jazz trumpeters rather than the *Odyssey*; a landscape that was defiantly provincial. The Movement's aesthetic was codified through the publication of the two *New Lines* anthologies in 1956 and 1963, which included poets such as Elizabeth Jennings, Donald Davie, Robert Conquest, and D. J. Enright and, later, Hugo Williams and Anthony Thwaite. Yet, as Blake Morrison argues in *The Movement* (1980), the term can be usefully extended to fiction of the period too; as with the poetry, we find everyday speech, realist techniques, and scepticism of emotional excess. When someone finally prompts Jim Dixon in *Lucky Jim* (1954) to hold forth on the nature of love, his musings are heavily qualified by colloquial equivocation. The avant-garde novelist B. S. Johnson declared in 1973 that the traditions of the nineteenth-century prose narrative were 'anachronistic, invalid, irrelevant, and perverse',[15] yet his comments are perhaps more an expression of frustration than usefully diagnostic.

The Angry Young Man

Closely related to The Movement, though more diffuse and less well defined, is the term Angry Young Man, which was first applied to John Osborne in the wake of his play *Look Back in Anger* (1956). The Angry Young Man was anti-establishment, working or middle class, and sharply critical of consensus and complacency. With no war to fight to define his ideals, he became the English equivalent of the rebel without a cause, that angry and confused American white male epitomised by James Dean.* Kingsley Amis, too, made an easy fit here, although Jim Dixon was more anxious than angry. Throughout the late 1950s, the term gained currency in critical studies and the popular press, and was even extended to women – both the playwright Shelagh Delaney and the novelist Doris Lessing were dubbed 'AYMs'. While few of those labelled as angry young men welcomed or understood the term, Tom Maschler's *Declaration* (1957) collected together mission statements from several writers associated with the movement, including Alan Sillitoe, John Osborne, Arnold Wesker, John Braine, and Harold Pinter. Here they laid

---

* James Dean (1930–55) was an American actor as famous for his tragic death in a car accident as his iconic role in the 1955 film *Rebel Without A Cause*, where he played a misunderstood and melancholy teenager.

out often conflicting programmes of a new literature. If contributors such as Doris Lessing were angry, they were also sceptical, like Larkin, of the benefits of literary experiment. As she argues pointedly in her essay, 'The Small Personal Voice' (1957) the realist story is 'the highest form of prose writing; higher than and out of the reach of any comparison with expressionism, symbolism, naturalism, or any other ism'.[16] These were manifestoes, like those of The Movement, which often urged writers to replace one recycled form with another, or to distrust modish innovation.

While the poetry and fiction of the period set itself up against the supposed excesses of 1940s writers such as Dylan Thomas, the work of playwrights such as John Osborne is often read as a reaction against the genteel theatrical comedies of Noel Coward and Terence Rattigan. Postwar theatre, more than fiction or poetry of the period, was effective in convincing its audience of a revolution. In 1956, George Devine formed the English Stage Company, which would go on to produce over a hundred new plays in the subsequent decade. The National Theatre, based at the Old Vic until 1988, interspersed its seasons of classics with new works by Tom Stoppard and Peter Shaffer. Drama received a particular boost from its association with television and film; it was often linked with the British New Wave cinema of the period, which drew heavily on French influences. These films, like the plays or novels they were based on, were pseudo-documentary in style, often using untrained actors and run-down urban locations to effect a new sort of realism. This style, often referred to as kitchen-sink realism, defined the scope of the postwar theatrical language. The plays of Osborne, Pinter, and Delaney take place in bedsits and neglected city parks; denouements are played out by disused canals. The spaces are rented, dilapidated, and often contested. The language, too, steps outside the prewar repartee of Coward for the demotic (everyday speech) of the working class. Like Larkin, these playwrights were using language the way they spoke it, although the theatre audience, which remained largely middle and upper class, were perhaps less used to the vocabulary. However, when these works found their way into people's front rooms, the results were often unprecedented. *Cathy Come Home* (1966), a BBC drama directed by Ken Loach, showed a young mother suffering the ignominy of unemployment, homelessness, and finally the removal of her child by the social services. Watched by a quarter of the British population, it did more than any government White Paper to begin the public debate which would ultimately lead to the Homeless Persons Act in 1977.

Reactions and Reactionaries

Meanwhile, the poetry of the 1960s and 1970s staged a reaction against the perceived conservatism of The Movement. The influence of experimental American verse, in particular Black Mountain poets such as Robert Creeley, led to a reassessment of modernist form and innovations. Basil Bunting, the British Objectivist poet who had been living in the USA since the war, returned to his native Northumbria in the 1960s and published *Briggflats* (1966), the most successful long poem of the postwar period. In 1965, Britain saw its first 'happening',* when Allen Ginsberg joined Michael Horovitz and poets such as Adrian Mitchell on stage for the International Poetry Incarnation at the Royal Albert Hall, to the delight of more than 7,000 spectators. An interest in performance poetry united many voices from the 1960s and 1970s, from Denise Levertov's anti-Vietnam protest poetry to the Liverpool poets immortalised in the anthology *The Mersey Sound* (1967), still the most successful poetry anthology ever published with over a million copies sold. The immense popular success of this Penguin anthology, which featured works by Brian Patten, Adrian Henri, and Roger McGough, prompted some sniffy critical responses – Philip Larkin declared that the fashion for poetry readings had created a facile genre of 'easy rhythms, easy emotions, easy syntax,'[17] while Peter Porter remarked wearily 'there's a tremendous fondness for anything soft and squashy'.[18] Yet its popularity also cleared the way for other approaches. Small poetry presses such as the Fulcrum Press, the Ferry Press, and Writers Forum offered outlets for more experimental poetry and, in 1971, the new British avant-garde launched a full-throttled assault on conservative British

---

* The term 'happening' was first coined in 1957 by Allan Kaprow to describe events, situations or performances which might be considered artworks. However, by the mid-sixties, the term was being used more generally to describe any gathering of people for an improvised, informal event.

poetry by effectively taking over the Poetry Society. Under the editorship of Eric Mottram, the society's publications prioritised experimental works by poets such as J. H. Prynne, Maggie O'Sullivan, Andrew Crozier, Sean Bonney, and Ken Edwards. If Mottram's controversial departure from the editorial board in 1977 sent the avant-garde underground again, the tussle between Movement- and modernist-inspired poetry reveals an energetic literary debate that belies a narrative of literary decline. The flourishing of Afro-Caribbean poetry in the period – from John Agard and James Berry to the dub poetry* of Linton Kwesi Johnson – also saw an alternative emerge to the studied white male cynicism of The Movement. If jazz and rock music helped popularise the Mersey Poets, it was rap and ska that would bring second-generation immigrant poets to the attention of the more general reader.

The novel, too, though it retreated from formal experimentation, was far from the clapped-out genre commentators of the period had prophesied. Novelists such as Muriel Spark, William Golding, and Iris Murdoch asked serious ethical questions of the form; for these writers, allegory or satire always served a moral purpose. Although, as Raymond Williams's study of the contemporary novel had concluded in 1961, 'in the overwhelming majority of modern novels, including those novels we continue to regard as literature, the ordinary criteria of realism still hold',[19] the expansive landscape also saw writers working across genres in challenging ways. Doris Lessing's early novels centre on female experience, the injustices of apartheid, and socialist ideals, drawing on her upbringing in Rhodesia. Yet, while many critics would point to *The Grass is Singing* (1950) or *The Golden Notebook* (1962) as her most significant works, Lessing's own preference is for her science fiction series *Canopus in Argos* (1979–83). In these works, Lessing explores forced evolution in an imagined future society.

The work of J. G. Ballard and Anthony Burgess also made a convincing case for dystopian writing and science fiction, offering as much incisive social commentary as the grittiest of kitchen-sink dramas. In a period that saw the world's first test-tube baby, and a generation brought up under the threat of nuclear annihilation, novels dealing with apocalypse, eugenics, and genetic modification were exploring the

---

* Dub poetry is West Indian in origin, and is usually spoken over reggae music with a heavy bass line.

possible, rather than the improbable. Realism itself was being challenged as a genre by the ever expanding potential of scientific discovery; as Bryan Appleyard notes in *The Pleasures of Peace* (1989), 'fiction needed to encompass entirely new forms of human organization'.[20] Appropriately, Ballard's novels are as much concerned with moral and social questions as scientific ones. In Ballard's fictional world, the only means of uniting a divided society is through the shared struggle of ecological armageddon (*The Drowned World*, 1962; *Hello America*, 1981); he shifts the science fiction plausibility debate from his novels' matter to their narrators, who turn in a series of unreliable performances, from the delusional Blake in *The Unlimited Dream Company* (1979) to the insane Robert Maitland in *Concrete Island* (1974). Meanwhile, Burgess's *A Clockwork Orange* (1962) imagines futuristic languages as well as worlds; the Anglo-Russian youth slang of his homicidal protagonist Alex taps into the societal fear of the teenager as alien delinquent. Science fiction writers were not alone in questioning the efficacy of traditional narration. Authors of the 1980s such as Graham Swift, Martin Amis, Salman Rushdie, or Julian Barnes did not abandon the postwar commitment to sceptical comedy, but used intrusive authorial voices (Martin Amis, *Money*, 1984), magic realism* (Salman Rushdie, *Midnight's Children*, 1981), or essayistic collage (Julian Barnes, *A History of the World in 10 ½ Chapters*, 1989) to complicate their response to the novel form.

In tandem, the publishing industry found new ways to promote its authors that resisted the journalistic convenience of tags like the Angry Young Man. The increasing prominence of the Booker Prize, established in 1969, offered shortlisted authors greater sales and critical assessment. In 1983, the journal *Granta* published a list of twenty young authors on the rise. Its prophetic canonisation of names like William Boyd, Rose Tremain, and Graham Swift proved so effective it has repeated the exercise twice since. Yet if critics were quick to herald the regeneration of British fiction, they were happy to gloss over works by those same authors that offered no such breaks from convention.

---

* Magic realism describes literature that combines a realist framework with fantastical elements. *Midnight's Children*, for example, centres around a protagonist who is telepathetic and has an enormous nose, but these characteristics are explained in the narrative by political and historical events, rather than the supernatural.

Culture Wars

Unlike the literary landscape, which was marked by violent movements between conservatism and innovation and back again, the cultural and critical context for reading literature in the period underwent perhaps the greatest and most irrevocable of changes. The early 1950s found New Criticism still holding sway over the establishment, defined by works such as Wimsatt and Beardsley's *The Intentional Fallacy* (1946; revised 1954). Critics such as I. A. Richards, William Empson, and Cleanth Brooks had promulgated literary study as a rigorous, objective process. This is best exemplified by close reading or practical criticism, which involved giving students a short literary extract with the author's name removed and asking them to analyse it. The possible intentions of authors or their biographical histories were deemed irrelevant; emotive responses to the texts were equally unwelcome. In place of these, neat, structural analyses of the words on the page came to typify the work of the literary critic. This was an approach which looked for typologies and systems, and privileged the professional reader.

Yet the dominance of New Criticism, particularly in Cambridge, seemed under attack from all sides in the postwar period. C. P. Snow was invited to give the annual Rede Lecture at Cambridge in 1959, later published as *The Two Cultures and the Scientific Revolution* (1960). This lecture criticised the literary establishment for blinding itself to new technology and science; the gulf between the humanities and science, Snow argued, meant that literature was much the poorer and worse equipped to solve the world's problems. Although Snow's book prompted furious debate, even opponents like the critic F. R. Leavis were establishing their own alternatives to the New Critical approach. For Leavis, whose 1930s journal *Scrutiny* had helped define his position, literature was a moral programme, and authors were to be ranked in terms of their didactic qualities. As he argued in *Education and the University* (1943), language was a product of culture, rather than a separate entity, and entrance to the English canon required a moral seriousness which, in his opinion, authors such as Laurence Sterne or Thomas Hardy lacked. The criticism of his wife,

Q. D. Leavis, was equally influential in the postwar period. The anxieties about mass readerships and declining cultural standards expressed in her *Fiction and the Reading Public* (1932) established a sociological approach to literary study that would define the concerns of the 1950s and 1960s.

For postwar critics such as Richard Hoggart and Raymond Williams, literature needed to be read as an expression of the culture that produced it. What would come to be known as cultural studies saw a film, a television programme, or an advert as equally worthy of investigation as a cultural 'text'. For Hoggart in *The Uses of Literacy* (1957), for example, the anxious heroes of postwar fiction could be explained by the advent of the scholarship boy, the grammar school-educated student who becomes the first member of his family to go to university. For Williams in *The Long Revolution* (1961), the novel's commitment to realism was as much to do with the Welfare State as an aesthetic programme of reform. By the 1980s, the work of Stuart Hall had defined Cultural Studies as a subject of study in itself.

Theories and Revisions

The continued influence of the Swiss linguist Ferdinand de Saussure (1857–1913) on literary culture was also seen in the development of structuralism which saw literary texts as complex systems of interrelated parts. Like the New Critics, the structuralists were interested in close readings, but the purpose behind these readings was to identify the various structures which governed human behaviour rather than to elucidate a particular work. For Jacques Lacan, structural readings of psychoanalysis could separate human behaviour into a series of codified patterns. The work of Roland Barthes and Jacques Derrida applied structural principles to literature, often finding in the essential ambiguity of language a literature which deconstructed itself. This distrust of language, not least as a form of propaganda, finds its way into much poetry and fiction of the period, too: the narrator of John Fowles's *The Magus* (1965; rev. 1977) describes a mid-century Britain where 'words had lost their power, either for good or evil; still hung, like a mist, over the reality of action, distorting, misleading, castrating; but at least since Hitler and Hiroshima they were seen to be a mist, a flimsy superstructure'.[21] Despite the apparent ahistoricism of structuralist approaches, they may well have been inspired by the history their techniques disavowed, as Fowles suggests here.

In the 1970s and 1980s, academics from many British universities abandoned Leavis's notion of the canon, drawing instead on the possibilities of continental theory. These institutional schisms were dubbed the 'theory wars', comically recalled in campus fictions by David Lodge and Malcolm Bradbury. The influx of theoretical positions which followed in the wake of Derrida's and Barthes's work transformed the study of English literature. The arrival of literary theory onto British campuses in the 1970s and 1980s not only caused heated debates, but also prompted a rediscovery of forgotten or neglected works from the past and a reassessment of identity politics. Yet, at their centre, many of these theories were far from academic, and were anchored to current political debates and problems. The national liberation movements in many former colonies prompted works such as Frantz Fanon's *Black Skin, White Masks* (1952), which saw the black psyche as self-divided, forced to live in a white world and imitate the behaviour of the coloniser. Consequently, postcolonial approaches to the canon found that Joseph Conrad's *Heart of Darkness* (1899) had much to tell modern readers that the formalists* had left out.

Likewise, feminism produced literary criticism as well as sociology and psychoanalysis. The influential *Madwoman in the Attic* (1979) by Sandra Gilbert and Susan Gubar examines the binaries that limited Victorian woman novelists, whereas Elaine Showalter's *A Literature of Their Own: British Women Novelists from Brontë to Lessing* (1978) offers an alternative British literary history. These works not only reassessed the canon, but reconfigured it: among others, Showalter's work helped to rejuvenate the critical standing of Virginia Woolf, who in the mid-1970s remained a relatively minor literary figure. Much literary theory aimed at decentring and undermining the authority of the written word as well as the literary canon, as in Roland Barthes's famous pronouncement of the death of the author in a 1968 essay of the same title. As a harassed

---

* Formalist approaches to literature, such as New Criticism or Russian Formalism, focus on the inherent structures of a text, such as tropes, metaphors, or linguistic patterns, as opposed to historical, biographical, or cultural considerations.

substitute teacher tells his wide-eyed class in B. S. Johnson's *Albert Angelo* (1964), '*omniscient* is the word we use to mean "knows everything" … but does God know everything? *Everything*? … and why should he be interested, anyway?'.[22] Here, the perceived indifference of God combines a deconstructionist approach to literature with a Movementish disregard for authority. This was an intellectual programme infused with revolutionary potential. Yet, perhaps inevitably, new canons of theorists reared up in place of the Great Tradition they rejected.* Ironically, given that Roland Barthes's essay proclaims the death of the author, it did much to make him an unimpeachable authority on literary theory. The destruction of the canon in favour of neglected voices has also instituted a familiar diet of substitutes on the university syllabus.

Television and the Arts

Outside the academy, parallel debates were taking place about mass culture and the place of literature in society. Marshall McLuhan's *Understanding Media* (1964) saw television as a newly democratic medium which, in its immediacy and popular appeal, broke down conventional hierarchies and social divisions. Yet literature from the period finds television a malevolent spectator of domestic life. John Wain remarks ominously in 1963, 'for two hundred years the novelist had held the attention of the great mass of readers with no serious competition';[23] now everywhere it looked were distractions, substitutes, and faddish alternatives. In Muriel Spark's *The Ballad of Peckham Rye* (1960), television is a prelude to loneliness and a poor substitute for thoughtful solitude. For the impoverished characters in Edward Bond's *Saved* (1965), the onstage broken television mocks their attempts at family life, 'like one a them daft mirrors at a circus'.[24] Yet these responses are perhaps anxious rather than accurate: the postwar period saw the flourishing of public service broadcasting. In 1964 the BBC received a second channel, after the 1962

---

* F. R. Leavis's influential work *The Great Tradition* (1948) offered a fixed canon of morally improving literature, which for him included Jane Austen, Joseph Conrad, George Eliot, and Henry James.

Pilkington Report praised its cultural output. Series such as *Play for Today* prompted new writing by Dennis Potter, John Osborne, and Mike Leigh, and offered important showcases for young writers. However, the sense that television was providing an alternative rather than a supplement to other cultural activities stubbornly persists in literature and sociological commentary of the period.

The establishment of a national council for arts funding in the 1940s also elided culture with Welfare State provision. The council began life as the Council for the Encouragement of Music and the Arts (CEMA), a wartime initiative spearheaded by economist John Maynard Keynes, and was renamed the Arts Council of Great Britain soon after. Its changing fortunes from 1950 to 1990 provide a telling cultural and political barometer of the period. Its first large scale project was the 1951 Festival of Britain, which attempted to give the nation a sense of recovery and confidence in a country still shattered by the Blitz. Architects unveiled a series of new buildings on London's South Bank drawing heavily on the International Modernist style; exhibits included sculptures by Barbara Hepworth and murals by John Tunnard. While the Festival was well attended, its aim to inspire the creative rebuilding of Britain was largely forgotten. Churchill's 1953 government destroyed all the new buildings save for the Royal Festival Hall. Modernism seemed a legacy Britain was reluctant to embrace either in its buildings or its fiction. Some projects were more successful, such as the opening of the Hayward Gallery in 1968, but the political attacks that continued to dog the Arts Council throughout the 1970s and 1980s testified to a larger unease about the role art played in society.

Hoggart's *The Uses of Literacy*, for example, worried that the increased wealth and leisure time of the working class would see them become targets of crude entertainments and cynical marketing. Yet other commercial ventures proved as democratic as they were financially successful. In 1935, Allen Lane had found himself at a provincial railway station and without anything to read. His answer was to establish Penguin Books, a company founded on the principle that cheap, widely available, and high quality fiction would sell in sufficient numbers to make it commercially viable. The phenomenal success of his publishing house, which sold its wares in corner shops and at railway stations as well as through more conventional outlets, made the best fiction, poetry, and criticism available to a much wider reading public than ever before. Like the BBC, Penguin styled itself as a company keen to widen the tastes of its market. By the time Hoggart came to write *The Uses of Literacy*, he was able to use Allen Lane's publishing house to profile the class he wanted to address:

> They own the Penguin selection from Eliot, as well as some other Penguins and Pelicans; they used to take *Penguin New Writing* and now subscribe to *Encounter*. They know a little, but often only from reviews and articles, about Frazer and Marx; they probably own a copy of the Pelican edition of Freud's *Psychopathology of Everyday Life*.[25]

As Hoggart's profile suggests, much of the new cultural debate is centred on class, 'that topic all-absorbing' in Arthur Marwick's study *British Society since 1945*.[26] Much literature from the period follows similar lines, or worries at the impossibility of reducing Britain's messy hierarchy into fiction – 'intricacies of social life made English habits unyielding to simplification', concludes the writer Jenkins in Anthony Powell's *The Acceptance World* (1955).[27] The effects of the Butler Education Act, as explored in Part Four: 'Class and Education', would have a profound impact on the social make-up of Britain's intelligentsia, but sometimes only served to highlight, rather than collapse, class differences. The working-class voice is heard with renewed acuteness in literature from the period, both on the stage and the page, but it is also appropriated and ventriloquised.

The years 1950 to 1990 do not form an impermeable or discrete historical unit. However, literature from those years is mindful of common historical reference points. When the playwright Howard Brenton imagines a dystopian future in his 1974 play, he does so by re-examining the past. *The Churchill Play* fictionalises a Britain ten years in the future, and follows internees of a concentration camp who are putting on a play about Winston Churchill. Churchill's legacy is both acknowledged and attacked, as the prisoners hover between portrayals of the myth and the man. Meanwhile, his later work *Greenland* (1988) opens with the current Labour political campaign before moving to an apocalyptic wasteland from the future where nuclear survivors try to construct the history of the twentieth century from dug-up rubble. Their increasingly ridiculous attempts to explain what a washing-up bottle might have been used for point up our own fallacious proclamations on the past. Alan Brownjohn's 'Scene from the Fifties' also balances carefully between the knowingly idealised and the ominous:

> The daughter in the kitchen daintily
> Prepares an England to receive them all;
> The pile of 45s in Mary's room
> Is not seen as something doing any harm.[28]

The action seems to centre on the obedient daughter in the kitchen, but the time bomb of the teenager and the social revolutions associated with it lie unnoticed upstairs. These warnings, or rereadings of the past, make the years still so close to our own always open to reconsideration.

Notes

1   Salman Rushdie, *The Satanic Verses* (London: Viking, 1988), p. 336.
2   Address to the Atlantic Alliance at the United States Military Academy, December 1962, as quoted in Douglas Brinkley, *Dean Acheson: The Cold War Years, 1953–1971* (New Haven: Yale University Press, 1992), p. 167.
3   Anthony Burgess, *Future Imperfect: The Wanting Seed & 1985* (London: Vintage, 1997), p. 497.
4   Robert Hewison, *Culture and Consensus: England, Art and Politics Since 1940* (London: Methuen, 1995), p. 75.
5   Mike Leigh, *High Hopes*, in *Naked and Other Screenplays* (London: Faber,

1995), p. 231.

6   Margaret Thatcher, *The Downing Street Years* (London: Harper Collins, 1993), p. 167.

7   Gabriel A. Almond and Sidney Verba, *The Civic Culture: Political Attitudes and Democracy in Five Nations* (London: Sage, 1989), p. 243.

8   Penelope Fitzgerald, *At Freddie's* (London: Duckworth, 1989), p. 7.

9   Margaret Drabble, *The Ice Age* (London: Weidenfeld and Nicholson, 1977), p. 65.

10   Margaret Drabble, *The Radiant Way* (London: Weidenfeld and Nicolson, 1987), pp. 32–3.

11   Hugo Williams, 'Post-war British', *Collected Poems* (London: Faber, 2002), p. 195, ll. 25–8.

12   David Marquand, 'Lucky Jim and the Labour Party', *Universities & Left Review*, 1:1 (Spring 1957), p. 2.

13   'Philip Larkin interviewed by Robert Philips', *Paris Review*, 84 (Summer 1982), p. 34.

14   Benjamin Ivor Evans, 'The Victorian Revival', *Britain Today*, February 1948, p. 20.

15   B. S. Johnson, *Aren't You Rather Young to be Writing Your Memoirs?* (London: Hutchison, 1973), p. 32.

16   Doris Lessing, 'A Small Personal Voice', in Tom Maschler (ed.), *Declaration* (London: MacGibbon and Kee, 1957), p. 56.

17   Philip Larkin, 'Masters' Voices', *Required Writing: Miscellaneous Pieces 1955–1982* (London: Faber, 1983), p. 136.

18   Peter Porter, 'The Poet in the Sixties: Vices and Virtues', in Grevel Lindop and Michael Schmidt (eds), *British Poetry Since 1960* (London: Carcanet, 1970), p. 78.

19   Raymond Williams, 'Realism and the Contemporary Novel', *The Long Revolution* (London: Chatto & Windus, 1961), p. 102.

20   Bryan Appleyard, *The Pleasures of Peace: Art and Imagination in Postwar Britain* (London: Faber, 1989), p. 253.

21   John Fowles, *The Magus* (London: Jonathan Cape, 1977), p. 190.

22   B. S. Johnson, *Albert Angelo*, in *Omnibus* (London: Vintage, 2005), p. 55.

23   John Wain, 'The Conflict of Forms in Contemporary English Literature', *Essays on Literature and Ideas* (London: Macmillan, 1963), p. 32.

24   Edward Bond, *Saved* (London: Methuen, 1969), p. 34.

25   Richard Hoggart, *The Uses of Literacy* (Harmondsworth: Penguin, 1957), p. 257.

26   Arthur Marwick, *British Society since 1945* (Harmondsworth: Penguin, 1990), p. 34.

27   Anthony Powell, *The Acceptance World* (London: Hutchinson, 1955), p. 32.

28   Alan Brownjohn, 'Scene from the Fifties', *Collected Poems* (London: Hutchinson, 1988), p. 264, ll. 21–4.

Part Three
Texts, Writers and Contexts

The Moral Novel: Golding, Murdoch and Spark

> The connection between art and the moral life has languished because we are losing our sense of form and structure in the moral world itself … we need a new vocabulary of attention.
>
> Iris Murdoch, 'Against Dryness' (1961)[1]

A narrative of the twentieth-century British novel might divide its development into three discrete stages. It begins with a break away from the painstaking Georgian realism of Arnold Bennett and John Galsworthy to embrace the 1920s modernist experiments of Virginia Woolf and James Joyce; it stutters into a sceptical conservatism with the postwar fictions of Kingsley Amis and Alan Sillitoe; it makes its peace with postmodernism via the playful narratives of Julian Barnes and Angela Carter in the 1980s. The structural neatness of this model, which moves from radical innovation then cautious retraction to a final assimilation, is seductive. Yet it glosses over the fact that contemporary writing has retained a stubborn attraction to realism, which remains the dominant mode of the modern novel. Similarly, it suffers from a sort of formal hindsight. While the anti-modernist tendencies of The Movement and the Angry Young Man in the 1950s were seen then, and often retrospectively, as anxious and reactionary, their concerns about the efficacies of experimental fiction need to be understood amid wider debates about society and ethics in the period.

Commentators on the contemporary British novel throughout the 1950s, 1960s, and 1970s remarked on its sense of moribund stagnation. David Lodge was appropriately polite yet unmistakable in his implication when, in 1977, he noted: 'reviewing the English novel in the twentieth century it is difficult to avoid associating the restoration of traditional literary realism with a perceptible decline in artistic achievement.'[2] For Lodge, as the title of his study, 'The Novelist at the Crossroads', makes clear, the English novelist was now faced with a stark choice between innovation and incremental deterioration. Bernard Bergonzi sounded a similar note of concern in *The Situation of the Novel* (1970):

> the novel seems to have lost its newness, to be no longer novel. Once, of course, the form of the novel and the sensibility that went with it were radical, even subversive, projecting a bourgeois and individualistic attack on aristocratic values and traditional sanctities … but over a couple of centuries the novel's radical role has been changed into a moderately conservative one, and the technology with which it is involved, instead of being revolutionary, has now become slightly old-fashioned.[3]

These statements, while often couched in the language of objective diagnosis, still characterise the postwar novel as being in crisis. It is a popular teleological (i.e. defined by endings or final outcomes) reading of the form which in the eighteenth century offered everything that was modish and radical and now offered only realist reiteration. Like the conformist world it depicted, the postwar novel rejected the obscurity, ambivalence, fragmentation, and innovation of the modernist text for a return to the comforts of nineteenth-century realism. Yet the work of William Golding, Iris Murdoch, and Muriel Spark suggests that if the novel was at a crossroads after the war, the roads leading it onwards were not, in fact, formal, but moral. The dilemma was not one of aesthetics, but one of conscience. The three novelists seemingly share little in the way of technique or genre, yet a comparative study of their work suggests that they all found themselves positioned at similar crossroads, even if the individual choices they made were often conflicting.

Morality, Allegory and Satire

One way of explaining the conservative trend of postwar fiction is by pointing to the democratising process of the Welfare State; since literature was no longer the preserve of the elite, it could no longer afford to alienate or challenge its readers. Yet the novelist and philosopher Iris Murdoch offers a rethinking of this position. Although she would agree with Bergonzi's and Lodge's summations of the contemporary novel being in anxious freefall, the causes she outlines are not to do with a burdensome modernist inheritance or the reading taste of the grammar school boys. The Welfare State changes the course of novel-writing not, for Murdoch, because its radical expansion of secondary education alters the number and social make-up of people reading and writing fiction, but because the political system it sets up suffocates its citizens' sense of independent moral judgement. In her 1961 essay 'Against Dryness', Murdoch argues:

> The Welfare State is the reward of 'empiricism in politics'. It has represented to us a set of thoroughly desirable but limited ends, which could be conceived in *non-theoretical terms*; and in pursuing it, in allowing the idea of it to dominate the more naturally theoretical wing of our political scene, we have to a large extent lost our theories. (p. 26)

For Murdoch, pragmatic postwar Britain with its love of efficiency and economy threatened the development of ethics or morality. Continuing to fashion the novel in this climate was necessarily difficult; tellingly, the hero of her first novel, *Under the Net* (1954), opens his narrative by declaring 'the present age was not one in which it was possible to write a novel'.[4] The novelist's responsibility is then to reject narrative as an aesthetic concern in favour of it as a tool for moral exploration. The novel must build itself from what Murdoch's essay defines as a new 'vocabulary of attention' (p. 31), refinding its form and structure by reacquainting itself with the forms and structures governing the moral world.

Crafting a moral novel in an increasingly secular Britain carried its own particular difficulties. Though this was an age of consensus, consistent moral positions were not something that could be taken for granted. As critic Helen Gardner noted in a 1960s lecture on 'Religion and Tragedy':

> However much the 'world views' or 'world pictures' that have been constructed for earlier ages simplify what men actually thought and felt, it is difficult to believe that any future scholars will ever attempt to construct such a systematic picture of common beliefs and assumptions for the twentieth century.[5]

Critical practice was also beginning to question humanist responses to fiction. Ian Watt's influential study *The Rise of the Novel* (1957) argued that the genre marked a transition in society from the objective and social world of classical literature to the 'subjective, individualist and private orientation'[6] of modern life, making it ill-suited for didacticism. While in 1987 J. Hillis Miller argued that universal moral law itself was intrinsically linked to storytelling,[7] many postwar literary critics, shying away from the prescriptive moral readings of literature by F. R. Leavis which had dominated literary debate, seemed increasingly unsure that reading could make us better.

Murdoch, too, while able to offer an acute summation of the contemporary novel's purpose, was less clear about how this should be followed through at the level of form, content, and narrative. Her argument assesses the beleaguered modern novel in terms of its literary-historical trajectory. While in the eighteenth century the notion of human nature was 'unitary and single', and in the nineteenth-century novel we saw 'real various individuals struggling in society', the modern novel:

> is usually either crystalline or journalistic; that is, it is either a small quasi-allegorical object portraying the human condition and not containing 'characters' in the nineteenth-century sense, or else it is a large shapeless quasi-documentary object, the degenerate descendant of the nineteenth-century novel, telling, with pale conventional characters, some straightforward story enlivened with empirical facts. (p. 27)

Here she rejects the kitchen-sink realism of Alan Sillitoe or Kingsley Amis as 'journalistic', while the hermetic moral conundrums of novels by William Golding are 'crystalline', forgoing character in the interest of abstract ideas expressed through allegory. Yet how might the contemporary modern novel avoid both the trappings of empiricism (the documentary-style of the New Realism) and the evasions of allegory?

In Murdoch's own fiction, the formal solution comes through her narrative voice. Her novels are predominantly first-person narrative, with almost exclusively male protagonists. As Wayne Booth argues in *The Rhetoric of Fiction* (1961), 'impersonal narration has raised moral difficulties too often for us to dismiss moral questions as irrelevant to technique'.[8] Here, Murdoch hedges her bets. Her own concerns about the ethical dimension of fiction are solved by making these narrator-protagonists predisposed towards reflection, whether they are pompous actors removed from the distracting pettiness of the stage (Charles Arrowby in *The Sea, The Sea*, 1978) or linguists who battle with the moral purposes of language (Hilary Burde in *A Word Child*, 1975). Her settings, while never straining for documentary detail, are usually modern day; her characters' moral dilemmas are played out at the top of London's BT tower (then the Post Office Tower) or in an Oxford quadrangle. Her characters' tendency towards the upper class and Oxbridge-educated sits uneasily with the postwar shift towards a more democratic literature, but also reveals her disregard for period details. Her settings are predominantly postwar Britain by default rather than design. Structure follows voice in bending to Murdoch's moral imperative; her fictions avoid dense parallel plotting or neat Dickensian coincidence for roaming, reiterative narratives that stumble towards philosophical truths through a mixture of ethical reasoning and self-indulgent fantasising. From Bradley Pearson in *The Black Prince* (1973) to the fantastical world of Bruno Greensleave in *Bruno's Dream* (1968), her protagonists are never at the mercy of formal constraints imposed by their author. Rather, the text is completely at their disposal, and any repetitions, digressions, or evasions are justified as being part of their own moral consciousness.

Meanwhile William Golding, in Murdoch's two-tiered system, is the crystalline novelist par excellence. Allegory and fable are intrinsic to many of his novels, from the exploration of mob mentality via the marooned schoolboys of *Lord of the Flies* (1954) to the castaway protagonist *Pincher Martin* (1956); the bustle of the modern world with all its objects, facts, and details rarely intrudes. While both of these novels are set in the modern day, they shipwreck their protagonists as a way of avoiding the world they have left behind. More typically of his oeuvre, *The Spire* (1964) focuses on the life of a medieval cleric, while *The Inheritors* (1955) depicts early man through the eyes of the Neanderthals. As Golding admitted in interview, 'I wouldn't know how to begin to write about contemporary society';[9] his novels, like Murdoch's, investigate moral perception and issues of free will, but unlike Murdoch, he does this always within the vacuum of an ordered novelistic world. An image from his novel *Free Fall* (1959) is the closest Golding comes to describing the relationship between the contemporary author and his audience. The writer's typewriter gropes in the dark whilst the reader grasps the finished book with hands like tongs. Here the acts of reading and writing are gestures towards moral consciousness from two individuals full of darkness and self-deceit. Language, style, and the physical fact of the book itself threaten to get in the way of any such meaningful exchange. As his narrator states, 'to communicate is our passion and our despair'.[10] For Golding, individual human character itself is a direct consequence of the Fall; to become conscious of ourselves is to make us culpable.

Muriel Spark offers a further complication to Murdoch's sober request for a morally cognisant fiction, less, as in Golding's work, through the form of her novels but rather through the mode. Spark is both a moralist and a satirist, who offers concision and wit as her tools for deflating moral hypocrisy. In crisp, tightly woven sentences she crafts acerbic and deft comedy; her novels are as brief as Murdoch's are baggy. Spark's Catholicism also adds another territory to the map of postwar moral fiction. Like her predecessor Evelyn Waugh, she mocks her characters and their ambitions less to jettison them into a more meaningful existence by the conclusion of her novels than to point up the banality of their corporeal lives. Her satiric targets are notable only for their variety of purpose and misdemeanour; the power-hungry Abbess (*The Abbess of*

Crewe, 1974), the officious factory manager (*The Ballad of Peckham Rye*, 1960), the religious convert (*The Mandelbaum Gate*, 1965), or even the amateur biographer (*Loitering With Intent*, 1981). All find their desires eventually revealed as squalid, self-serving, or short-sighted.

Spark's own scepticism about holding forth – pomposity is one of her most frequent targets – means her novelistic practice is largely expressed through her fiction itself rather than expository essays. One exception, her 1971 essay, 'The Desegregation of Art', is typically pithy. Exposing the flaws of what she describes as social realism, Spark attacks the literature of 'sentiment and emotion';[11] works that make sympathetic appeals to our social conscience, for Spark, score their points too easily. A piece of earnest kitchen-sink drama, for example, offers a bourgeois audience the sense that they have understood the working class, and reassures them they need not show any interest in them outside the theatre. In place of a self-righteous and socially aware art, Spark argues, writers should return to 'the art of ridicule' (p. 35), which replaces emotion with intelligence, and sentiment with satire. Moral perception is sharpened not through a literature of indignant protest but one of 'deliberate cunning'; while Spark might share Murdoch's concern about the moral necessity of art, for Spark it is only achieved through 'the satirical, the harsh and witty, the ironic and derisive' (p. 37). So while the novels of Spark, Murdoch, and Golding are full of structural and thematic parallels, their formal and stylistic choices show a range of responses to shaping the modern novel.

The Problem of Evil

The moral concerns of the postwar novel were largely related to the problem of evil. As Europe came to learn the horrific truths of the Holocaust and the Nazi genocide, the safe ballasts of humanism or religious consolation looked increasingly fragile. Campanati in Anthony Burgess's *Earthly Powers* (1980) maintains that Hitler was a 'moral virus'[12] that infected the twentieth century rather than an embodiment of man's inherent tendency towards evil; other fictional characters remain less sure. It is no coincidence that both Murdoch and Spark mention

Hitler in their programme for the modern novel. Murdoch rails at 'our inability to imagine evil'; despite Hitler, we retain a 'facile, dramatic and … optimistic' picture of human nature in art ('Against Dryness', p. 30). The modern liberal consensus is reluctant to acknowledge something it knows to exist but cannot account for. Similarly, the penitential Hilary Burde in Murdoch's *A Word Child* gloomily admits that the world is quick to overlook wrong-doing; 'even Hitler is being forgotten at last'[13] he notes, suggesting that real evil is something we would rather avoid discussing. In Spark's essay, characteristically, Hitler is invoked to show the necessity of derision. Imagining a 1930s documentary of the 'goose-stepping' Hitler, Spark argues that 'if the massed populations of those times and in those countries had been moved to break up into helpless laughter at the sight, those tyrants wouldn't have had a chance' (p. 36). Spark's position is extreme, and perhaps glib, but it suggests satire is a moral imperative rather than an aesthetic choice.

All three novelists preoccupy themselves with the ever-present evil in mankind; three of their works show a further connection by making use of a diabolic intruder. In each plot, a suspicious outsider infiltrates a community, wreaking havoc with its traditions and moral codes before mysteriously disappearing. In Iris Murdoch's *A Fairly Honourable Defeat* (1970), the Machiavellian Julius unravels a quartet of happy couples, puncturing their self-satisfied happiness by forcing them to acknowledge their baser desires. Julius's significance in Murdoch's novel is both moral and structural; he is the catalyst for uprooting the well-meaning charitable donations and complacent champagne-drinking of Hilda and Rupert Foster's married life. Morgan describes her infatuation with him in a way that situates him both as problem and solution:

> 'Julius is *in* me. I haven't solved Julius. All my moods have been modes of consciousness of him. First ecstasy, then misery, then cynicism. Now this new sense of possible enlargement.'[14]

Julius, the missing problem of evil, stalks in often comic scenarios through Murdoch's novel, offering self-realisation as well as chaos. Only the opening conversation – his name is the first word uttered in the book –

hints at a possible allegorical significance behind his elusive malevolence. Hilda and Rupert discuss his character, repeatedly reminding each other that 'he's not a saint'. Hilda mentions Julius's involvement in biological warfare research and questions his moral make-up, only to be reminded by her husband that: 'You have to investigate the stuff in order to find the antidotes.' Hilda replies: 'I hate that old argument. All evil lives on it' (p. 4).

Omission is evasion, but to call evil into being is also to have your moral compass threatened. The self-satisfied couple of the novel's opening scene nevertheless play out Murdoch's own philosophical debate here: in order to find a way of dealing with evil, it must be present in all the art we produce. To banish it is not to extinguish it.

Golding's *Darkness Visible* (1980) complicates this pattern, offering two separate narratives of wholly 'good' and 'bad' characters before offering a final section which brings them together in a way which undermines easy moral binaries. The first section presents us with the schoolboy Matty. His inexplicably mutilated face, in contrast to his innate goodness, casts him as the postwar child, scarred by the wrongdoings of others. Feared and misunderstood by his schoolmates and by his paedophilic teacher Mr Pedigree, who sits the boys in order of physical beauty, he is only redeemed by the allegoric voice of the narrator, who reminds us 'the sun shone from one side of his face'.[15] Mr Pedigree, under increasing suspicion from colleagues over his relationship with his students, uses Matty as a scapegoat when a boy leaps to his death. When questioned, Matty speaks only the word 'evil', like an Old Testament figure resurrected to provide moral succour to the modern Godless world. In contrast, the protagonist of the second section, Sophy, defined by the quasi-incestuous relationship with her father, is explored through her moral tendency towards evil. As a child, she masters the arc of the circle her arm needs to make to throw stones at dabchicks; only once she has perfected this power does she decide not to use it. Similarly, her life of crime and sexual excess suggests an embodiment of the 'evil' Matty names when questioned by the police. Yet such demarcations become increasingly difficult in the third section, which brings together their two narratives. The final section, 'One is One', ends with a dying Mr

Pedigree, haunted by thoughts of Matty's honesty. Golding's novel of perception and moral relativism suggests that innate human goodness is no more explicable or easy to navigate than pure evil.

In Spark's *The Ballad of Peckham Rye*, the Scottish graduate Dougal Douglas stirs up a cocktail of extra-marital sex, rioting, and murder amid a closely knit working-class community in South London. Frequent playful references to two lumps on his head tempt readers to identify him with the devil, yet these hints of diabolism are hard to take seriously. Douglas is a surreal, protean character, able to take on whatever shape his current confidante desires. He hardly functions as an embodiment of earthly evil; the novel suggests that human evil is a relative term defined by communities and institutions. Only in the petty banality of factory routine and business speak do Spark's true satiric targets emerge: prudence, small-mindedness, and the inability to see outside one's narrow surroundings. For Spark, the 'evil' character is as much a scapegoat for the novel's misdeeds as the blameless Matty is in *Darkness Visible*. The notion of evil as an intrusion on the lives of these mild-mannered characters only serves to reinforce how far each individual suppresses his or her tendencies towards chaos, anarchy, and darkness. *The Ballad of Peckham Rye*'s narrative suggests 'a desire to show a pattern larger than individual purpose', as Peter J. Conradi remarks more widely of Murdoch and Spark.[16] True self-knowledge, these novels suggest, is an acceptance of transgression rather than a path to rectitude. The evil intruder functions as a symbolic figure, drawing the reader's attention to the everyday deviancies of the fallen human heart.

The Other World

The fascination with embodied evil is matched by fleeting glimpses of the nonsecular world. In Spark's *The Ballad of Peckham Rye*, the final scene finds the beleaguered Humphrey looking up at the sky after a walk in the park to suddenly catch a glimpse of 'another world'.[17] Here, hidden in a concluding paragraph, lies the hint that all our earthly performances and interactions are insignificant when considered in terms of the world beyond. There is little in addition to this passing mention: Humphrey's vision may be celestial or simply a view of another South London borough. Yet this embedded and structurally significant reference to the afterlife points to the wider treatment of religion in the period. Faced with a sceptical and increasingly secular Britain, these three novelists all chose to explore doctrine, dogma, and orthodoxy through closed religious communities. A debate about religious practice in a realist postwar setting seems to take some justifying, as if novelists acknowledged the impossibility of subsuming theological debate into the drab practicalities of the postwar period.

In Golding's *The Spire*, the author retreats to the fourteenth century, and follows the doomed narrative of Jocelin, the Dean of Barchester Cathedral, who believes he has been chosen by God to build a 400-foot spire on the top of the cathedral. There is a clear echo of the Babel story here, in which man attempts to build a tower that will reach heaven. God punishes man by scattering him all over the earth and condemning him to speak many languages. In Golding's novel, Jocelin defies architectural possibility by constructing a spire that does not topple, but there are other, more human costs: its building inadvertently causes the death of the deformed cathedral factotum, Pagnall, and his wife, Goody. Jocelin justifies his project to the sceptical and increasingly irascible builders by explaining it as God's folly. Rational man is interrupted when 'out of some deep place comes the command to do what makes no sense at all'.[18] Here God is a sort of authorial intruder. Yet Jocelin's subservient adherence to God's word also comes with a sense of self-righteousness and overweening pride. His own narrative celebrates the church and its spire as the one gesture towards goodness in the depraved city he sees around him (see pp. 106–7). Yet while the church is described here as an ark-like refuge, it is the catalyst for all the novel's evil. There is allegorical significance in the fact that the spire remains standing at the end of the novel even though it outflanks the structural supports of the existing building, yet Jocelin himself as is left broken and morally riven, like 'a building about to fall' (p. 222). As Gabriel Josipovici points out, the book, too, stands up 'free of the man who built it';[19] our own reading of *The Spire* re-enacts that same process of building.

Equally, Murdoch's early novel *The Bell* (1958) finds the parameters of the secular and the devout blurring throughout the narrative. The novel follows a troubled couple who come to stay in a religious lay community attached to an abbey. The members of this community are in a sort of gestural purgatory or, as the Abbess tells the wife, Dora:

> they are a kind of sick people, whose desire for God makes them unsatisfactory citizens of an ordinary life, but whose strength or temperament fails them to surrender the world completely; and present day society, with its hurried pace and its mechanical and technical structure, offers no homes to these unhappy souls.[20]

Neither in nor outside the secular postwar world, the community welcomes the London couple, who only further the moral and extramarital complications, from Dora's seduction of the boy Tobey to the pastor Michael's acknowledgement of his homosexuality. Much of the plot focuses on the Abbey's missing bell. As if reversing the iconographic centre of Golding's novel, Murdoch's is haunted by rumours that a nun drowned herself after taking a lover, and that the Abbey's bell fell into the depths of the lake as if in moral response. The plan to rescue the bell is prompted here more by jocular amusement than religious imperative, but, like Jocelin's building of the spire, has an equally catastrophic human cost. In the end, the sexual criss-crossing of the characters unravels the society: Michael's feelings for Tobey are discovered and lead to suicide, and the lay community is taken over by the Abbey. The halfway world of moral possibility is closed, and even as it shrinks before Dora as she rows away, she considers the scurrilous possibility of it as a subsequent anecdote for her London friends: 'Tonight she would be telling the whole story to Sally' (p. 320).

The gossipy response to religious crisis is further emphasised in Muriel Spark's *The Abbess of Crewe*. Like the lay community in *The Bell*, which hovers half way between the secular and the sacred, the world of the Catholic convent finds its doors rarely closed. The comedy centres around the election of a new Abbess at Crewe, which collapses into a media circus after her defeated rival hints at a rigged election. On the defensive, the new Abbess surveys and records the private world of the Abbey in order to 'master' the invasive press who might otherwise make this world into a public scandal. Although Spark would hesitate to offer herself up as an allegorist, there are clear echoes here of the Christine Keeler scandal, which in the early 1960s saw a Conservative MP sacked over his politically explosive relationship with a call girl who was also involved with a Russian spy. Spark takes on the hypocrisy of private institutions, whether those that would insulate themselves from the outside world or those, like the upper echelons of government, that attempt to control the world from within their chambers. As the Abbess sighs:

> 'This is a sad hour for England in these, the days of her decline. All this public uproar over a silver thimble, mounting as it has over the months. Such a scandal could never arise in the United States of America. They have a sense of proportion and they understand Human Nature over there; it's the secret of their success.'[21]

Far from using the closed world of a religious community to discuss theological issues or to consider moral abstractions, all three novelists suggest how permeable the barriers are between the public and private, the sacred and the secular, or the selfless and the self-serving. The 'other world' that Humphrey glimpses in the park at Peckham is no more visible to the Catholic father than the factory girl.

The Perceiving Subject

Murdoch's notion of the novel having lost its way was, as we have seen, quick to shift the blame from its formal to its moral weakness. Yet for all Murdoch's distrust of the well-made art object or the self-contained and comforting world of fictive narrative, it is difficult to isolate moral perception from issues of language and representation. All three novelists, in their different ways, relate moments of moral epiphany or heightened awareness to the acquisition of language. In doing so, their texts become preoccupied by the aesthetic considerations Murdoch would apparently renounce. This is particularly true of William Golding's *The Inheritors* (1955), which narrates the gradual dominance of the New Men (*Homo sapiens*) over The People (the Neanderthals); they eventually kill and eat their evolutionary ancestors. The majority of the novel is told through the perspective of Lok, the last remaining Neanderthal. Golding's use of a small, controlled vocabulary and a limited perspective for his narration means readers must puzzle out the rational explanation for his often perplexing descriptions. When the New Men launch arrows at Lok, he is able neither to identify them as such nor to read their violent intent. When he is nearly hit by one, he 'has a confused idea that someone was trying to give him a present'.[22] Through this alienating narrative technique, the reader is invited to feel a great sympathy for him, not least because of his limited awareness that he is the last of his species. Yet as Lok's death draws near, Golding switches to omniscient narration, describing Lok's last moments with the disregard of the evolved species: 'the red creature stood on the edge of the terrace and did nothing' (p. 216). Having been at pains to humanise him through our reading, Golding now invites us to see him for the alien forefather he really is. Golding's narrative device puts language itself under the microscope, constructing a style that is difficult not because it is cryptic, but because it is shortsighted. Lok's gradual awareness of the new species strains the boundaries of his own forms of knowledge and perception. He is described as 'beginning to know that other without understanding how it was that he knew' (p. 77). Only retrospectively do readers come to doubt their own knowledge and understanding, as the closing narrative shifts to a final pragmatism which prompts the reader to see Lok's death as a necessary process of evolution.

The narrator-protagonist of Murdoch's novel *A Word Child* (1975) is a contemporary version of the faltering, fallible Lok. Yet far from being limited by his fragile grasp of language, Hilary Burde is undone by its mastery. Hugo in Murdoch's *Under the Net* reminds us that 'language is a machine for making falsehoods' (p. 68). Burde begins his narrative convinced of the opposite; he is a brilliant and conscientious linguist, and his deprived and unhappy childhood finds its only refuge in the world of words:

> Grammar books were my books of prayer. Looking up words in the dictionary was for me an image of goodness. The endless task of learning new words was for me an image of life.
>
> *A Word Child*, p. 22

As the quasi-biblical language suggests here, Burde constructs language as a form of divinity. Yet his reverence for language as something connected only arbitrarily with reality leads to dangerous and sometimes deadly decisions; this is a religion founded on false idols. The conclusion of the novel finds him desperately penitent about his actions yet all too aware of how close penitence is to violence, hatred, and resentment. Given that language has proved his undoing and is also the material of his own narrative, there is space here for a metafictional reading. Yet this is a paradox which Burde does not perceive, and the text itself seems reluctant to consider. Instead, Burde, and Murdoch herself, are keen to stress the everyday nature of the story. Anxious lest this novel might be read, like Golding's, as a self-reflexive allegory on form and language, the conclusion asserts that 'tragedy belongs in art. Life has no tragedies' (p. 383). Murdoch's broken hero is not allowed the consolation of being absorbed into a literary archetype. He remains, stubbornly, normalised.

While both Golding and Murdoch offer protagonists whose language has failed them, in *Loitering With Intent* (1981) Spark purposefully distorts the boundaries between biography, fiction, and transcript. The writer-protagonist who gradually becomes aware of the frailties and evasions of language does so in an increasingly metafictional world. The narrator, Fleur Talbot, describes her involvement with the Autobiographical Association in Northumberland. The Association, run by Sir Quentin Oliver, employs Fleur to take dictation of and organise the memoirs of its members who regularly meet to share their life histories. Despairing of their literary merit, Talbot nevertheless resolves to use these experiences for her first novel *Warrender Chase*. However, as those around her begin to imitate portions of her novel, she begins to wonder whether she is creating the text or vice versa. The literary pretensions of the memoir club become awkwardly intertwined with the writing of her own story:

While I recount what happened to me and what I did in 1949, it strikes me how much easier it is with characters in a novel than in real life. In a novel the author invents characters and arranges them in convenient order. Now that I come to write biographically I have to tell of whatever actually happened and whoever naturally turns up. The story of a life is a very informal party; there are no rules of precedence and hospitality, no invitations.[23]

While Murdoch's narrative is at pains to limit its readings to the world of the text, Spark plays provocatively with the intrusions of autobiography. There are unsettling ironies in a novel in which the narrator decries the difficulty of writing 'real' life rather than settling for the easy convenience of fiction, but they are ironies that Spark chooses to unleash as quickly as Murdoch seeks to contain them. What look initially like conservative realist trends in the postwar novel, are also points at which it delves, often inadvertently, into self-conscious narrative play. Like Lok, the last of his species, who becomes possessed of the sense that something significant is happening, the attempts to close down the reflexive uncertainties of the modern novel also signal, albeit obliquely, its future development.

Moral Tones

The strains of preserving the realist tenets of the modern novel are shown in a series of works by Murdoch, Golding, and Spark that fuse genres with a self-conscious sense of experimentation. While these innovations are often introduced in the interests of moral dimensions rather than formal ones, the end result is often a text that hovers provocatively between a variety of modes. Spark's *The Girls of Slender Means* (1963), from its opening paragraphs onwards, offers a setting that is at once meticulously realised and surrealist in its overall effect:

Some bomb-ripped buildings looked like the ruins of ancient castles until, at a closer view, the wallpapers of various quite normal rooms would be visible, room above room, exposed, as on a stage, with one wall missing; sometimes a lavatory chain would dangle over nothing from a fourth or fifth-floor ceiling; most of all the staircases survived, like a new art-form, leading up and up to an unspecified destination that made unusual demands on the mind's eye.[24]

The narrative here makes its subject the contingencies of perception as much as the war-torn buildings the girls inhabit. The voice offers the possibility of symbol – the buildings 'looked like the ruins of ancient castles' – but soon erases its deviance from documentary realism. As with the tone, so with the content of Spark's novel, which continually offers gestures towards the fabular, the surreal, or the allegorical while always finding its generous roots in the everyday. This space is at once theatrical, with its exposed rooms, and 'quite normal', dogged by its utter banality. The 'unusual demands' this opening scene makes on the eye mirror Spark's narratorial perspective throughout; the tendencies towards the other-worldly, the epic, the moral, or the symbolic only come via the quest for realism. Only the exceptional circumstances of the postwar period permit this intrusion of the surreal into the ordinary world her characters inhabit.

The men who are drawn into the mercurial and chaotic world of the May of Teck Club, where the eponymous girls lodge, are similarly unable to tell whether they are attracted by the pragmatic common sense of these girls of slender means or their beatific attitudes. In one scene, Nicholas listens to Joanna reciting a poem, and the narrative confesses he is enamoured of the May of Teck Club but has 'an aesthetic and ethical conception of it, lovely frozen image that it was' (p. 108). The narrator both colludes with and slyly critiques Nicholas's position, leaving the reader unsure as to whether these female figures are exceptional or mundane. The first scene of a girl looking out of a window finds her eyes giving out a light that 'resemble[s] near-genius, but was youth merely' (p. 4). Similarly, Nicholas will later sit in the club, while the narrator turns his idle thoughts between apparitions and narrative facts:

A girl in a long evening dress slid in the doorway, furtively. Her hair fell round her shoulders in a brown curl. Through the bemused mind of the loitering, listening man went the fact of a girl slipping furtively into the hall; she had a meaning, even if she had no meaningful intention. (p. 110)

Nicholas perceives the girl to have some 'meaning', but no 'meaningful intention'; this tension, or limitation, suggests that the purgatorial, earthly world we inhabit will remain ultimately frivolous to a Catholic novelist. Actions are stripped of context to become either loaded with unspecified significance or comically banal.

The prevailing tone of Murdoch's novels, by contrast, is expansive, nomadic, and apparently unplanned. Her narrators are careful to give no outward signs of grand design. In this respect Charles Arrowby, the protagonist of her Booker Prize-winning *The Sea, The Sea* (1978), is archetypal. Retiring to a remote house on the coast after a career on the London stage, his own process of recording events determines our sense of the novel's aesthetic decisions. The novel is made up of his own journal, beginning the text with an assertion that:

> It is necessary to write, that much is clear, and to write in a way quite unlike any way which I have employed before. ... This is for permanence, something which cannot help hoping to endure ... I must make no attempt at 'fine writing' however, that would be to spoil my enterprise. Besides, I should merely make a fool of myself. ... Of course there is no need to separate 'memoir' from 'diary' or 'philosophical journal'. I can tell you, reader, about my past life and about my 'world-view' also, as I ramble along. Why not? It can all come out naturally as I reflect. Thus unanxiously (for am I not now leaving anxiety behind?) I shall discover my 'literary form'.[25]

For Arrowby, the compulsion to tell and record is greater than the need to form a pattern. His literary form is serendipitous, improvised, and consciously 'unanxious', with its disavowal of 'fine writing'. Yet even as he lays out the apparently open gestures of his journal, his own neologism 'unanxiously' prompts him to rhetorical, self-conscious asides. To announce a conscious disregard for form is no more to leave it behind than to surrender to its need for principles and aesthetics.

While Charles Arrowby's narrative in *The Sea, The Sea* suggests an unresolved tension between form and memory, Golding's *Pincher Martin* (1956) unravels its implications. Here, the narrative is given over to the titular protagonist who is apparently the lone survivor of a shipwreck. After swimming to safety on a deserted island, he undergoes a familiar Robinson Crusoe journey, reaping the benefits of the island's natural resources. As readers follow this narrative, they learn retrospectively of Martin's former life, and his self-serving past. Yet when the novel reaches its conclusion, the voice of God, or perhaps the author, intervenes, revealing to Martin that he was, in fact, killed instantly during the shipwreck. His own egotism has constructed a narrative of spectacular survival, meaning we have been reading a story that, in the novel's world, never happened. Even after death, the selfishness of man seeks to construct ways out of his own mortality. In *Pincher Martin*, tone quite literally becomes the means to evade the blunt truth of death.

Forms of Debate

The unravelling narrative of *Pincher Martin*, which turns from journal on the first reading to psychic hallucination on the second, highlights an aspect of all three novelists' work which seems far from the formal conservatism we might expect. The diffident Catholic girl Caroline at the centre of Spark's first novel *The Comforters* (1957) flees London after breaking up with her partner Laurence. Yet this period of reflection is interrupted when she begins to hear the sound of typewriters in her head. At first suspecting intruders, she gradually comes to believe that she is overhearing her own life being made into a story:

> *Caroline wondered. But what worried her were the words they had used, coinciding so exactly with her own thoughts.*
> And then the typewriter again: tap-tap-tap. She was rooted. 'My God!' she cried aloud. 'Am I going mad?'
> As soon as she had said it, and with the sound of her own voice, her mind was filled with an imperative need to retain her

sanity. It was the phrase 'Caroline wondered' which arrested her. Immediately then, shaken as she was, Caroline began to consider the possibilities, whether the sounds she heard were real or illusory.[26]

Her conviction worries her friends and family, believers and non-believers alike. Both rational and doctrinal arguments are put before her to convince her otherwise. Yet she trains the voice by following its own instructions; Caroline goes on to become a novelist, using the very narrative of her life to construct her world. The moral backlash her actions provoke raises questions about the act of writing itself. Figured in the fearful Catholic world of the novel, the desire to create and fictionalise is dangerously irreverent. To write is not to enforce a moral code but rather to transgress one. In one of Spark's most playfully experimental works, she suggests that narrative must follow the founding impulse of artistic creation itself in flirting with the unorthodox.

Golding's *Free Fall* (1959) is similarly mindful of the evasions of chronological narrative. The narrator-protagonist is Samuel Mountjoy, a painter preoccupied with the patterns and geometries of the world around him. He offers us a nonchronological series of memories of life in order to assess the point at which he ceased to have free will. Like an internalised version of Caroline, who begins to suspect her life is simply fodder for an unnamed novelist in a parallel dimension, Mountjoy recognises that narrative offers neither catharsis nor confession but gestures to a hidden moral vacuum that cannot be unlocked. The novel asks whether the way we organise and narrate lives is a consequence of our moral failure or the cause of it. In setting out the problem, Mountjoy offers a manifesto of the nonlinear that seems closer to the modernist entreaties of Virginia Woolf than the conservative tenets of the postwar novel (see p. 6). He argues that time is always split between perception and memory, and that life cannot be placed in sequence like a row of bricks. Like Murdoch's Charles Arrowby in *The Sea, The Sea*, Mountjoy's retrospective narrative rejects the trappings of traditional chronology, less in the interests of 'honest' form than in the language of aesthetic imperatives. Perception and memory are ever at odds in Golding's novel. Narrative only offers readers the truth in as far as they might speculate how far it deviates from it. Yet for all of Spark's and Golding's forays into metafictional texts, intrusive authors, inverted narratives, and unravelling characters, perhaps Murdoch's use of multiple narrators in *The Black Prince* is the most striking, and the most apposite for exploring the tensions between moral and formal impulses in postwar fiction.

Extended Commentary: Murdoch, *The Black Prince* (1973)

As we have seen, Murdoch stubbornly adheres to the first-person form. Yet her 1973 novel *The Black Prince* is particularly pointed in its undermining of narrative authority. As with many of Murdoch's novels, the narrative hinges on the revelation and subsequent complications of love, here between the self-satisfied Bradley Pearson and the young girl Julian Belling. Yet here, more than ever before, love is discussed in the language of reality and illusion. Its ability to transform the real into the fictive, to offer both moments of clarity and collective hallucination means that any treatment of love must reflect those opposing modes. In this context the novel's subtitle, 'A Celebration of Love', suggests that narrative order or realist representation will come second to the dizzying demands of love itself. For here, unusually, in addition to the searching first-person, we are offered a series of interlocking narratives and a final editor's postscript. The novel concludes with a series of contesting documents; an envoy* by Bradley's friend Francis Marloe, which claims Bradley was homosexual and reinterprets several events in the novel to support his case; Julian's letter which looks back on their relationship as one which 'words cannot describe' and 'certainly his words' cannot, and brandishes the text that precedes her envoy 'a literary failure'.[27] Rarely does Murdoch's work contain or invite a discussion of literary aesthetics.

---

* Envoy refers to the concluding words of a poem or piece of prose, literally the section that 'sends forth' the writing.

Meanwhile, the editor's postscript further tugs away at the realist contract: 'I hear it has even been suggested that Bradley Pearson and myself are both simply fictions, the invention of a minor novelist. Fear will inspire any hypothesis' (p. 362). In these closing lines, we glimpse another Murdoch, a philosopher and moralist prepared to use the internal contradictions of the novel form itself to further complicate our ethical response. So what is at stake in this complication of her aesthetic?

The novel's title, *The Black Prince*, points us to Shakespeare's *Hamlet*, and the narrator-writer Bradley offers a series of digressions and speeches on the play throughout. The quasi-soliloquy, of Bradley's narrative suggests his affinity with the relentlessly conflicted tragic hero. The competing perspectives of other characters echo the complex context in which we encounter Hamlet's soliloquies. As Bradley says of *Hamlet*, the soliloquy shows him speaking to his audience 'as few artists can speak, in the first person yet at the pinnacle of artifice' (p. 199). Yet *Hamlet* is a less useful reference point for understanding the characters and their actions than for considering Murdoch's own art. Bradley praises Shakespeare for having created, in *Hamlet*, a work that is 'endlessly reflecting upon itself, not discursively but in its very substance' (p. 199), and so gestures at its appeal to Murdoch. The novel's own self-reflection is not limited to its postscripts; its three protagonists, Bradley, Julian, and her father Arnold, are all novelists, and their debate about the purpose and possibility of art is a key concern within the novel. Bradley's competitive relationship with Arnold leads to a dismissive summary of his writing as 'inquisitive chatter' (p. 49). At the opening of the narrative Bradley compares his own rigid puritanism and sense of meticulous structure to the formless works of his nemesis. Yet by falling in love with Arnold's daughter, Bradley loses the framing control of his story: life becomes derailed and messy. He neglects his suicidal sister, Priscilla, and vows to keep his love for Julian secret only to abduct her. By the novel's conclusion, he celebrates Shakespeare instead because, like all good art, his work is a 'jumble in the end' (p. 240).

The narrative voice hovers between deliberate design and arbitrary incident. The novel is full of mythic and structural patterning: it begins with Arnold phoning Bradley to confess he may have killed his wife, Rachel, and ends with Rachel killing Arnold. Bradley's posthumous editor makes reference to the classical story of Marsyas, who was flayed by the god Apollo when he claimed to be a better musician. Here, the allusion presents Bradley's story as an allegory about artistic overreaching. Only after having been punished is Bradley, the writer, able to complete his narrative. Yet, elsewhere, the novel is more casual. Bradley begins his story of artistic envy and transformative love only to break off and confess 'it might be more dramatically effective to begin the tale at the moment when Arnold Baffin rang me up', before going on to offer a third possible opening to the novel which would engage with the 'deeper structure' of events (p. 22). Here, Murdoch positions herself somewhere between her contemporary John Fowles, who unpicks the certainties of the Victorian novel by giving two alternative endings to his nineteenth-century parody *The French Lieutenant's Woman* (1969), and the transitional modernism of E. M. Forster, who starts *Howards End* (1911) with the equivalent of a narrative shoulder-shrug: 'one may as well begin with a letter.'[28] Like Forster, Murdoch's exploration of liberal humanism continually threatens to unpick the certainties of form itself.

Murdoch in interview was quick to dismiss the apparent gestures towards postmodernism and deconstructionist readings of *The Black Prince*. For her, the postscripts were merely 'play', and a careful reader of the novel would quickly navigate the narrator's evasions and petty deceits.[29] This was not a novel, in her view, that veered into dangerous moral relativism or undermined its own structure. Yet her creation of two opposing writers in the novel – each one geared, as A. S. Byatt has pointed out, towards the 'crystalline' and 'journalistic' excesses she lays out in her essay 'Against Dryness'[30] – hints at self-reflective critique. Bradley Pearson becomes, then, the archetypal figure of the conservative postwar novelist; his own aesthetic demands ultimately become subsumed by the process of the novel itself, which ends up writing him.

Notes

1   Iris Murdoch, 'Against Dryness', in Malcolm Bradbury (ed.), *The Novel Today: Contemporary Writers on Modern Fiction* (Manchester: Manchester University Press, 1977), pp. 23–31, pp. 29–30.

2   David Lodge 'The Novelist at the Crossroads', in Malcolm Bradbury (ed.), *The Novel Today: Contemporary Writers on Modern Fiction* (Manchester: Manchester University Press, 1977), pp. 84–110, p. 88.

3   Bernard Bergonzi, *The Situation of the Novel* (London: Macmillan, 1979), 2nd edn, pp. 26–7.

4   Iris Murdoch, *Under the Net* (London: Chatto & Windus, 1955), p. 21.

5   Helen Gardner, 'Religion and Tragedy', *Religion and Literature* (London: Faber, 1971), p. 116.

6   Ian Watt, *The Rise of the Novel* (Berkeley: University of California Press, 1957), p. 177.

7   J. Hillis Miller, *The Ethics of Reading* (New York: Columbia University Press, 1987), p. 2.

8   Wayne Booth, *The Rhetoric of Fiction* (London: University of Chicago Press, 1961), p. 378.

9   William Golding in interview with James Woods in the *Guardian*, as quoted in Kevin McCarron, *William Golding* (Plymouth: Northcote House, 1994), p. 41.

10 William Golding, *Free Fall* (London: Faber, 1991), p. 8.

11 Muriel Spark, 'The Desegregation of Art', in Joseph Hynes (ed.), *Critical Essays on Muriel Spark* (Oxford: G.K. Hall, 1992), pp. 33–7, p. 34.

12 Anthony Burgess, *Earthly Powers* (London: Hutchinson, 1980), p. 546.

13 Iris Murdoch, *A Word Child* (London: Chatto & Windus, 1975), p. 127.

14 Iris Murdoch, *A Fairly Honourable Defeat* (London: Chatto & Windus, 1970), p. 207.

15 William Golding, *Darkness Visible* (London: Faber, 1980), p. 32.

16 Peter J. Conradi, *The Saint and the Artist: a study of the fiction of Iris Murdoch* (London: HarperCollins, 2001), p. 121.

17 Muriel Spark, *The Ballad of Peckham Rye* (London: Penguin, 1999), p. 143.

18 William Golding, *The Spire* (London: Faber, 1964), p. 121.

19 Gabriel Josipovici, *The World and the Book* (Basingstoke: Macmillan, 1994), p. 256.

20 Iris Murdoch, *The Bell* (London: Chatto & Windus, 1958), p. 82.

21 Muriel Spark, *The Abbess of Crewe* (London: Macmillan, 1974), p. 22.

22 William Golding, *The Inheritors* (London: Faber, 1965), p. 110.

23 Muriel Spark, *Loitering With Intent* (London: Bodley Head, 1981), p. 59.

24 Muriel Spark, *The Girls of Slender Means* (London: Macmillan, 1963), p. 1.

25 Iris Murdoch, *The Sea, The Sea* (London: Chatto & Windus, 1978), p. 2.

26 Muriel Spark, *The Comforters* (Harmondsworth: Penguin, 1964), p. 50.

27 Iris Murdoch, *The Black Prince* (London: Chatto & Windus, 1973), p. 360.

28 E. M. Forster, *Howards End* (Harmondsworth: Penguin, 1972), p. 6.

29 C. W. E. Bigsby, 'An Interview with Iris Murdoch', *The Radical Imagination and the Liberal Tradition: Interviews with English and American Novelists* (London: Methuen, 1982), pp. 129–30, p. 130.

30 See A. S. Byatt, 'People in Paper Houses: Attitudes to "Realism" and "Experiment" in English Postwar Fiction', in Malcolm Bradbury and David Palmer (eds), *The Contemporary English Novel* (London: Penguin, 1979), pp. 19–41.

The Postmodern Novel: Barnes, Carter and Swift

The opening of Angela Carter's 1971 novel *Love* presents us with a protagonist, Annabel, who 'had no instinct for self-preservation if she was confronted by ambiguities'.[1] It is tempting to draw an analogy between Annabel and the postwar novel itself which, as we have seen, often seemed determined to return to realism in the face of a society which seemed increasingly unsure about its new-found security and supposed political consensus. The 1950s, 1960s, and 1970s found few British novelists besides B. S. Johnson, Christine Brooke-Rose, or John Fowles who were eager to respond to the sense of intellectual revolution and cultural upheaval embodied by the Paris riots of 1968 or the French poststructural theories that followed in its wake. In 1969, Fowles had asked what relevance the realist novel had in the age of Alain Robbe-Grillet or Roland Barthes,[2] but his question had gone largely unanswered in British fiction. Only in the final two decades of the twentieth century did mainstream writing begin to respond to the threatening 'ambiguities' which so terrify Carter's protagonist.

The term postmodernism, first used to discuss architecture in the 1950s, offered itself up to literature with renewed fervour in the 1970s and 1980s, spearheaded by critical works such as Hayden White's *Metahistory* (1973), or Patricia Waugh's *Metafiction* (1984)* which both

---

* The prefix 'meta' derives from the Greek word meaning 'after', 'beyond', or 'with'. It is usually used as a prefix in English to mean 'about', e.g. 'metahistory' concerns history itself as a branch of knowledge.

noted a turn towards the deconstructionist in contemporary history and literature. Truth seemed contingent; artworks increasingly turned to parody, pastiche, and ironic modes; omniscience and the notion of the grand narrative were, in Jean-Francois Lyotard's view, abandoned for the free play of competing voices and reader-orientated meanings.[3] Techniques of collage dominated all forms of art, while art in turn came to question and self-consciously explore its own representative techniques.* David Lodge noted that the open endings of modernist fiction had turned to the 'multiple ending, the mock ending, or the parody ending'.[4] Mikhail Bakhtin developed a theory of the novel based on the notion of 'heteroglossia', arguing that single narratives were breaking up into comic, anarchic, and pluralist texts built of 'a diversity of individual voices'.[5] Roland Barthes famously declared the death of the author in his influential essay of the same name in 1968, arguing that author-centred responses to a novel closed off their interpretative possibilities.[6] As with Bakhtin, the emphasis was on decentring meaning, or creating a range of subjective responses. While the postwar moral novel responded directly to the suffocating impositions of the Welfare State, the postmodern novel was more often read as a by-product of capitalism, exemplified by theorist Frederic Jameson's *Postmodernism, or the Cultural Logic of Late Capitalism* (1991). Jameson argued that irony and pastiche were the only possible response to a society that prized the corporation over the individual and the commercial over the cultural. This was a world where depth was replaced by surface, or by multiple surfaces.

America had been producing self-reflexive work for decades in the cut-ups of William Burroughs, the metafictions of Thomas Pynchon, and the theoretically engaged writing of Donald Barthelme, but the embrace of postmodern practice in Britain remained at once more cautious, and more pedestrian. In texts such as Graham Swift's *Waterland* (1983), as Linda Hutcheon notes, we find novels that attempt 'a problematized inscribing of subjectivity into history'.[7] In other words, the individual consciousness interrupts the grand historical narrative, revealing that the narrative itself is subjective. Swift's novel even begins with a dictionary definition of his own neologism, 'historia', a word which permits the

---

* See, for example, Andy Warhol's *Campbell's Soup Cans* (1962), which foregrounds mechanical reproduction and commercial advertising over the artist's craft or vision.

personal, the local, and the provisional into the authoritarian tradition of history. From the late 1970s onwards, the British novel explored with increasing confidence the ambivalent narrator, the nonchronological narrative, and the self-reflexive text. It began to combine 'high' and 'low' forms, and to question moral instruction as a legitimate function of the contemporary novel. Late capitalism already told us what to think; the role of the novel was to make us sceptical of what we were told to think. Many postmodern narratives question empirical knowledge, whether via the bemused journalist in Angela Carter's *Nights at the Circus* (1984), who cannot compress the fantastical story of his subject, Fevvers, into the banality of a factual report, or the games-within-games of John Fowles's *The Magus* (1965; rev. 1977), which puts its protagonist Nicholas D'Urfe through an impossible series of intellectual riddles only to undermine the efficacy of rational reasoning altogether.

Although scepticism was a defining feature of the postmodern novel, it combined with the pragmatism of British culture to produce a hybridised form. Compared to the works of contemporary American authors such as Don DeLillo or Toni Morrison, British authors tended to view it with the same caution that postmodernism itself applied to conventional systems of authority and power. While both mainstream novelists such as Martin Amis and innovative iconoclasts such as Alisdair Gray drew on postmodern techniques, few British authors went as far into the realms of postmodern experimentation as Barthelme or Pynchon. The careers of Graham Swift and Julian Barnes, who both move between conventional realist forms and complex metafictions from novel to novel, embody this peculiarly British form of pragmatic postmodernism. Angela Carter's all-too-brief career (she died in 1991 at the age of forty-two) points to a British author who consistently explored how postmodernity might reform a conventional narrative, yet the explosion of critical writing on her work since her death only highlights her unique place in British literary history.

Fragmenting Fictions

Graham Swift's *The Sweet-Shop Owner* (1980) is both a traditional and transitional first novel, exploring its everyman protagonist Willy Chapman in a series of fragmented narrative sections. The novel is full of literary ancestors; Chapman's unrewarding job as a shopkeeper and his obsession with the past recalls Arthur Miller's Willy Loman in *Death of a Salesman* (1954), while setting the novel on one day in London with a protagonist grappling with suicide suggests a nod to Virginia Woolf's *Mrs Dalloway* (1925). Yet the novel transcends its obvious literary reference points. Like Mrs Dalloway, Willy Chapman moves continually between the past and the present, and is represented both through his own narration, and third-person perspectives by friends, family, and strangers who pass him in the street, yet the novel's focus is as much on history as identity. History is the subject studied by Willy's estranged daughter's partner, as if it might free her from the constraints of her upbringing; history is the oppressive narrative Willy's wife Irene tries to resist through living in the moment, convinced 'we do not belong to history';[8] history is the evasive euphemism for Willy's planned suicide – 'he would be history' (p. 10).

Despite the fragmented narrative, which travels through Willy's final day while also moving back from the 1930s to the present, Willy's sense of rigorous order and decorum works hard to cohere his own story and perspective. In fact, his rigid sense of protocol and appropriate behaviour, which so alienates his daughter, suggests a man out of step with the contingent and relativist world of 1970s Britain. It seems significant that in a scene from the late 1960s, when students rioted in Paris and Barthes declared the death of the author, Willy's daughter's university education is marked by conformity and regimentation: he describes the 'luxurious barracks' where there were 'fifty other girls like you, each with a room like yours with a number on the door and a slot for a name-card' (p. 162). Posthumous narrations from Willy's wife Irene provide similar disillusionments. She was raped by a family friend, Frank Hancock, early in her life but unable to tell Willy, making his presence on their street an ominous threat that is never voiced in the novel. Waiting hopelessly for his daughter to make her peace with him as he dies, Willy concludes that the suffocating spectres of personal and political history are inseparable. His daughter's return is the only thing that might 'dissolve history' (p. 217), but she never comes home. In *The Sweet-Shop Owner*, Swift constructs a novel where history is both causal and casual in its cruelty. His protagonist's narrative shatters conventional chronology like a mirror, but only to free him from taking responsibility for the past.

Like Swift, Barnes takes London suburbia as the subject for his first novel, *Metroland* (1980), which traces the changing relationships between schoolmates Christopher and Toni. The novel is in three sections: Christopher and Toni's sneering adolescent disdain for the comfortable bourgeois life of their parents opens the narrative, set in 1963; the middle section describes Christopher's stay in Paris while completing postgraduate research in 1968; the final section dissects their relationship in 1977, when anarchic scepticism has given way to Christopher's middle-class complacency. This comic, self-effacing memorial to suburban life is both small scale and intimate, and suggestive more widely of a Welfare State generation who are brought up in prosperity and are ultimately reluctant to sacrifice it for any defiant ideology. The novel's formal realism is apologist as well as conventional. As Christopher bashfully confesses to the readers, despite spending the spring of 1968 in Paris, a hotbed of riots and revolutions, a love affair gets in the way of his radicalisation:

> The point is – well I was there all through May, through the burning of the Bourse, the occupation of the Odéon, the Billancourt lock-in, the rumours of tanks roaring back through the night from Germany. But I didn't actually see anything. I can't, to be honest, remember even a smudge of smoke in the sky … My explanation of the troubles, it seems, was that the students were too stupid to understand their courses, became mentally frustrated, and because of the lack of sports facilities had taken to fighting the riot police.[9]

May 1968, the month referred to as *les événements* in French history, saw the biggest ever strike in a Western industrial nation. Spearheaded by students who were critical of authority and embraced a New Left ideology which questioned the trappings of capitalism and state control, the riots, as Christopher suggests in his shame-faced admission, saw buildings burnt, numerous arrests, and the near-collapse of the then government. A series of related though often disparate issues appeared to unite students across the Western world, from the American-led Vietnam war and the Civil Rights movement to the Campaign for Nuclear Disarmament, leading to a series of similar protests throughout the year. The riots were often invoked by cultural commentators and theorists such as Roland Barthes or Michel Foucault as evidence of the radical scepticism and anarchy of modern intellectual discourse. Here was the political embodiment of postmodern practice. Barnes's onlooker Christopher, tellingly, applies the same scepticism to the radical movement itself, pouring pragmatic cold water on the burning fires of anarchy. The most radical moment of postwar intellectual history goes on around him while he remains oblivious. Barnes's position is both querulous and curiously analogous to the postmodern perspective. Christopher is the unwitting bystander to the machinations of history, who bathetically reduces the grand narrative of protest to a student squabble. Barnes's iconoclastic take on the revolutionary summer in *Metroland* flirts with the radical but, like Christopher himself, who loses his virginity in Paris before returning to a comfortable marriage with Marion, never really considers straying.

While the intrigues of the love triangle prove more tempting for Christopher than the promises of anarchy and rebellion, Angela Carter's early novel *Love* undermines the structural principles of the love triangle narrative itself, creating a work that is at once crueller and more ambivalent than Swift's or Barnes's. Much of the novel, which centres on the shifting sexual dynamics between Annabel, her partner Lee, and his brother Buzz, uses intertextual allusions to point its reader towards a traditional realist work. The brothers bicker about Annabel as if she were 'a Victorian heroine' (p. 66) while Lee and Annabel are compared to Paul and Virginie, recalling the innocent protagonists of Jacques-Henri Bernardin de Saint-Pierre's 1787 novel.* Yet the continual reference to the characters as textual creations shatters their affinities with a literary tradition, as in Lee's comparison to 'a boy in a book by Jack London' (p. 7), referring to one of America's first commercial fiction writers. The dizzying contradictions implied in these series of allusions makes the characters literary composites, moving from the mythical or symbolic to the realist or archetypal within one scene. Carter deliberately blurs the boundaries between a character's strategies for self-representation and a novelist's, as in the description of Lee's bedroom which is painted

---

* *Paul et Virginie* (1787) tells the story of two lovers who die in a shipwreck. They are presented as characters who live in harmony with nature, in line with the Enlightenment ideal.

with 'all the dreary paraphernalia of romanticism, landscapes of forests, jungles and ruins inhabited by gorillas, trees with breasts, winged men with pig faces and women whose heads were skulls' (p. 7). The narrative voice hovers half way between disdain for the 'dreary' trapping of a romanticist setting, and a surrealist fascination with its contents. At the same time, it also undermines its verisimilitude and draws attention to its own novelistic techniques. The dichotomy is captured in the opening description of Annabel, who is accused by the narrator of having the capacity for 'changing the real world which is the price paid for those who take too subjective a view of it' (p. 3). Such disjunctive narrative shifts mean that the sexual cruelties inflicted on the characters by each other, including a mutual rape, are both shocking in their violence and morally inscrutable.

This refusal to play out the love triangle narrative in conventional realist form is echoed in setting as well as characterisation, as in the opening storm in a park which seems to hang in mid-air 'above a vast, misty model of a city' (p. 2). Such is the ferocity of the storm, the opening scene suggests, that categories of selfhood and geography themselves collapse, the heavens shattering into 'two contrary states at once', and Annabel dissolving as if 'she might herself have been no more than an emanation of the place or time of year' (p. 3). Viewed through the context of sexual politics, this magic realist* opening ensures that the novel resists polemic; by deliberately destroying realist convention in its opening scenes, Carter is permitted to explore gender relations that similarly subvert binary expectations. As Annabel fears in the opening scene, *Love* presents us with a 'dreadful rebellion of the familiar' (p. 3).

Stories about Stories

Yet, despite the foreboding sense of the uncanny in *Love*, familiarity proves a key concern in the postmodern novel. Recycling, whether through allusion, parody, intertextuality, or inversion, becomes part of the collage of voices that make up the postmodern narrative. For Carter,

---

* Magic realism describes literature that combines a realist framework with fantastical elements.

the cultural assumptions of fairy tale provide one of her most fertile literary stomping grounds. Her first short story collection, *The Bloody Chamber and Other Stories* (1979) recreates Alice in Wonderland, Red Riding Hood, Puss-in-Boots, and Bluebeard but subverts the fantastical Gothic landscapes of the Grimm Brothers to feminist ends. The female subject of incarceration in Bluebeard's Castle is now given voice in 'The Bloody Chamber', and escapes death at the hands of her husband when her mother puts 'a single, irreproachable bullet through [his] head';[10] the Big Bad Wolf becomes an object of sexual desire rather than a fatal intruder in 'The Company of Wolves'; the whimsical girlishness of Alice in Wonderland is reimagined as a wolf-cub hybrid in 'Wolf-Alice', where the girl-animal comes eventually to recognise herself in a mirror, learning the 'invisible cage' (p. 123) of a mirror can also be a site for transformation, self-realisation, and manipulation. Yet these stories subvert our cultural expectations not only through plot and female agency, but through the recreation of the Gothic fairy tale landscape as a space that is as much psychic as folkloric:

> The words enclose and then enclose again, like a system
> of Chinese boxes opening one into another; the intimate
> perspectives of the wood changed endlessly around the interloper,
> the imaginary traveller walking towards an invented distance that
> perpetually receded before me. It is easy to lose yourself in these
> woods. (p. 85)

Carter's inhabiting of this symbolic space at once plays on the clichés of darkness, repression, and enclosure associated with the woods, and reassesses those same clichés; the wood is perpetually receding and yet its perspectives are 'intimate'; they are alienating and yet immediately recognisable as a cultural symbol, every journey through the woods accompanied by an 'imaginary traveller' and an 'invented distance'. The real, the fictive, and the symbolic become endlessly entwined here, like the Chinese boxes used to describe the woods. Carter, by drawing on a series of fairy tales and myths embedded into our cultural consciousness, creates a short story collection that similarly encloses itself within itself. By repositioning these stories from female perspectives, Carter at once opens them out and hints at further textual layering beyond the surface of her narrative.

Graham Swift's conservative tendencies come to the fore in his short stories, his collection *Learning to Swim and Other Stories* (1982) noticeably lacking in self-reflexive narrative. However, escaping from the strictures of the novel seems to liberate Barnes; *A History of the World in 10 ½ Chapters* (1989) is one of his most experimental works, balancing between a short story cycle, an essay collection, and a work of fragmented fiction. Here Barnes replaces Carter's interest in rewriting our literary and folkloric heritage with a focus on the cultural, liturgical, and historical stories we use to understand ourselves. The connecting thread for the majority of stories included in the collection is the ship. The biblical story of the Ark is told from the perspective of a stowaway woodworm in the opening story, setting up a series of images that show history not just being rewritten, but quite literally devoured. The parasitic woodworm demolishes the thing that offers it survival, even if its story offers another kind of longevity. In the same way, as the woodworm rationally points out, the majority of the animals taken on board were there to provide food for the humans rather than to propagate their species. A terrorist takeover of a cruise liner provides the focus for 'The Visitors', an example of a story that is both fictional and heavily influenced by history, gesturing towards the hijacking of the *Achille Lauro* in 1985 by the Palestine Liberation Front.

Yet other stories are more sceptical about the transition from fact into fiction, or disaster into art. 'Shipwreck' is an essayistic response to Gericault's painting *The Raft of the Medusa* (1818–19), questioning the process by which a 'moment of supreme agony' is 'taken up, transformed, justified by art, turned into a sprung and weighted image, then varnished, framed, glazed, hung in a famous art gallery to illuminate our human condition, fixed, final, always there'.[11] As Barnes suggests, art is one of the ways society copes with catastrophe, yet the process is never straightforward: questions of structure, representation, and symbol become political, theological, and moral when real life becomes a framed portrait. In this way, Barnes's work questions its own procedures, aware that the act of making the real-life hijacking of the *Achille Lauro* into a fictive short story carries with it its own moral responsibilities and questions. Story is a problematic process in much of the text, but for the protagonist of 'The Survivor' it becomes a refuge. Here, a survivor of a nuclear explosion escapes on a handmade raft, using narrative to hold onto her own mental stability. Yet the doctors' repeated questioning suggests that her version of events may be no more reliable than the authorities'. They accuse her of fabulation – 'you keep a few true facts and spin a new story around them' (p. 111) – and Barnes leaves the reader deliberately unsure whose version of events to believe.

While the woodworm devours religious authority as well as text itself, other stories in the collection suggest a more problematic attitude towards atheism. The final story, 'The Dream', imagines an after-life. Its world of instant and complete gratification soon becomes meaningless for the protagonist, suggesting hedonism and capitalism make poor substitutes for theology. Once again, the sceptical, ironic mode of postmodernism is itself ironised, as rationalist and moral arguments begin to test the limits of playful pastiche. The half chapter of the title, entitled 'Parenthesis' and unnumbered, raises these questions more directly. Unlike the other stories, it is written as a direct address to the reader from a figure claiming to be Julian Barnes himself, although the narrative admits that they may not be his opinions on the page. Much of his digression supports the postmodern view of history as a patchwork of 'voices echoing in the dark; images that burn for a few centuries and then fade; stories, old stories that sometimes seem to overlap; strange links, impertinent connections' (p. 242). Yet for all this reading of history as a collage, the narrator is reluctant to reduce our human emotions to the learned, the parodied, and the performed. A discussion of Philip Larkin and W. H. Auden prompts a dissection of the language we use to describe love. More specifically, the narrator focuses on Auden's line 'we must love one another or die' from 'September 1, 1939', which Auden later amended to 'we must love another and die', before deleting it altogether (p. 233). The narrator seems less wary than Auden. Human relations at their most intimate resist the onslaught of history, the burden of cultural appropriation, and the spectre of perpetual performance. Even though the work's humanist conclusion comes in a whispered parenthesis, its insistence on love as 'anti-mechanical' and 'anti-materialist' suggests human experience that lies outside narratives of consumerism and capitalist indoctrination (p. 244).

History Lessons

Barnes, Carter, and Swift use rewriting and rereading as deliberate authorial strategies, creating texts that have a complex and ambivalent relationship with their sources. However, their conflicting need for control, order, and linear progress is hinted at in a series of novels which cast their protagonists as teachers, rationalists, or academics. Although the role of the author is questioned in a fiction that thrives on hiding the original or reshaping it, this uncertainty is balanced by figures of authority within their texts that attempt to make these fragmented fictions coherent. In the chaotic and dystopian world of Angela Carter's *The Infernal Desire Machines of Doctor Hoffman* (1972), the power-crazed despot of the title wants to create a world not bound by conventional laws of time and space. Forcing the inhabitants of an unnamed city to be enslaved by desire, he builds machines which manufacture and play out people's erotic fantasies, creating a surreal world full of crime and violence where the gap between reality and the imagination has collapsed. The protagonist Desiderio is given the task of killing him, but in doing so must also kill his own lover, Doctor Hoffman's daughter, Albertina. Here the lure of erotic pleasure and hedonistic desire must be sacrificed for a return to rational order and natural law. Julian Barnes's *Before She Met Me* (1982) uses a similar cocktail of suppressed desire and sexual jealousy to create its bleakly humorous tone. Barnes's protagonist Graham Hendrick is a history teacher who falls in love with an actress. However, their relationship is threatened by his obsessive jealousy, which stems from erotic scenes from her past films. Haunted by these moving images of feigned infidelity, they come to stalk his dreams as well as his waking world, blurring the distinction between the filmic, the subconscious, and the real world. His rationalist and empiricist approach to history is threatened by the power of his own libido, mirroring Desiderio's internal conflict.

Graham Swift's *Waterland* (1983) offers us another history teacher as a protagonist, and remains one of the quintessential examples of what we might call historiographic fiction (i.e., relating to the writing of history), combining local history, personal narrative, and geological history in a messy chronology that questions the relationship between cause and effect while simultaneously underlining the importance of history for understanding the present. As we touched on earlier, the novel's epigraph offers a quasi-dictionary definition of a neologism: 'historia', which is glossed here as '1. inquiry, investigation, learning. 2. a) a narrative of past events, history. b) any kind of narrative: account, tale, story.'[12] The novel traces the tensions between these competing definitions for, as its narrator-protagonist Tom Crick informs us, the truth remains a good deal stranger than fiction.

Tom is a history teacher in the Fens, a marshy area of Cambridgeshire reclaimed and maintained by artificial drainage. As such, its people must navigate an environment always shifting between land and water, solid and liquid, truth and evasion. For Tom, whose ancestors, the Atkinsons, helped to drain the land, this is a burden of familial inheritance as well as of historical fact. The narrative pivots on two historical axes: the present day, where Tom is threatened with losing his job after his mentally unstable wife steals a baby; and the summer of 1943, when Tom and his future wife Mary suffer a series of cataclysmic events which will continue to haunt them throughout their married lives. Tom relates the events of the past through discussions with his A-level history class, so the narrative moves backwards in time even as it propels itself forwards. Underlining the blurring boundaries between history, fiction, and personal testimony, Tom narrates the story of his life to the class in the neutral third-person, as if stating documentary fact: '[h]e made a living – a life's work – out of the past, for which his justification was the children to whom he offered daily the lessons that the past affords' (p. 129). The 'equivocal' gift that is history comes under fire throughout the narrative. The school's authoritarian headmaster is keen to axe history from the syllabus. Tom, meanwhile, begins to question the efficacy of learning about the French Revolution rather than local regional history. His lessons move from the syllabus to take in his own relationship to his native Cambridgeshire, the natural history of the local region, and the lifecycle of the eel native to the Fens. The eel's cyclical journey becomes an analogy for the ever-recurring historical patterns that dominate the lives of the people in the narrative. Alongside this preference for the personal and the regional comes the imperative of history in a world still dealing with the fallout of two World Wars. One of Tom's students, Price, forms the Holocaust Club, and argues that in an era threatened by nuclear holocaust, the lessons of history are meaningless. Tom's narrative then becomes a passionate form of advocacy both for history itself, and the human need to learn from the past. Swift's innovative use of historiography and metafiction draws on postmodern devices but resists the tendency towards amoral playfulness. Here, the techniques of collage, disrupted linearity, and a sceptical attitude towards historical narratives are employed only to reassert the urgency of historical understanding.

Female Frontiers

Postmodern fiction, as we have seen, often generates competing readings of traditionally monolithic narratives, whether Biblical, mythical, or cultural. At times, these are deliberately conscious of gender; writers often use the female perspective to undermine linear 'male' accounts of history. Julian Barnes's *Staring at the Sun* (1986) constructs a war novel that spans one hundred years, the majority of which is narrated by Jean Serjeant. Jean rejects the political feminism of her son's girlfriend, Rachael, convinced that 'war, of course, was men's business. Men conducted it, and men – tapping out their pipes like headmasters – explained it'.[13] She holds back from passing narrative comment on the war she witnesses, but the centrality of her narrative belies the liminal space she apparently occupies. The final section of the novel, which takes place in 2020, finds her son in dialogue with a high-tech computer designed to 'put the whole of human knowledge on to an easily accessible record' (p. 144). But this pointedly male search for empirical knowledge fractures when the speculative or the subjective enters the equation. When Gregory searches for anything nonempirical, the computer's error message reads: 'NOT REAL QUESTION' (p. 179).

Graham Swift's *Out of This World* (1988) shows a similar gesture towards female experience. Like *Waterland*, the novel excavates national history through a family narrative, here dividing itself between Harry, the aerial photographer, and his estranged daughter Sophie, whose interweaving chapters track her conversations with a New York analyst as she struggles to come to terms with her own history. Sophie and Harry are divided by an event which is both personal and political: the death of Harry's father in a terrorist bombing by the IRA. Sophie's childhood memory of it centres around Harry photographing his father's burning car, ensuring there is little distance between the horrific event itself and its subsequent representation. Transformed into an image too soon, the burning car is reimagined in Sophie's conversation with her analyst. These competing representations by Harry and Sophie suggest an implicit contest; Harry's controlled style and his quite literally aerial perspectives seem to dwarf Sophie's angered ramblings, yet what her narrative lacks in authority it makes up for in authenticity. By the novel's conclusion, it is Sophie's description of a flight home which generates hope. Harry, meanwhile, is left to reflect on a simpler world when 'everything was black and white'.[14] The female voice here remains at the mercy of her male audience through the analyst who structures her chapters, yet her perspective offers a challenge to Swift's more usual narrative structure of successive patrilineal concerns.

Angela Carter's *The Magic Toyshop* (1967), meanwhile, offers a much more self-aware presentation of the female subject. As in other early works such as *Love*, Carter's protagonist Melanie enters the narrative with a keen sense of femaleness as a performed role. On the cusp of adolescence, she spends a long hot summer making erotic poses in front of her bedroom mirror, aping the portraiture styles of a Toulouse-Lautrec prostitute or a Pre-Raphaelite muse. These male perspectives on the female body become reimagined as a site of fantasy for the female subject who is now able to choose from a range of competing archetypes. As the narrative wryly notes, after Melanie reads D. H. Lawrence's *Lady Chatterley's Lover* (finally published in 1960), she 'secretly picked forget-me-nots and stuck them in her pubic hair',[15] mirroring the behaviour of Lawrence's titular heroine whose sexual awakening comes at the hands of her husband's game-keeper Mellors. Yet this sense of the female being in control of these projections is undermined by an equally powerful thread of the novel which suggests our sexual behaviour and sense of gender politics are rigidly enforced by the cultural orthodoxies we appear to be parodying.

The novel's first scene ends with Melanie trying on her mother's wedding dress and being forced to abandon it when she climbs an apple tree in the moonlight and tears the dress beyond repair. The apples are heavy with the symbolism of the Garden of Eden, unsettling the more playful and performative aspects of the scene. This double inversion is reinforced when a family death prompts her move from rural comfort to London to live with her Uncle Philip, who runs a toyshop. Philip's ominous obsession with his life-size puppets calls into question Melanie's control over her own identity; she is initially attracted to his son Finn, but her romantic notions are cruelly cut short when his father orders Finn to rehearse the story of Leda and the swan with her.* Here, Carter examines how rape is culturally mediated through story and fable to evade its violence and horror. Uncle Philip's mastery of the other characters suggests a puppetry that goes beyond the workshop, subsuming the autonomous wills of Finn and Melanie to ventriloquism. It is only when they flee the toyshop that Melanie and Finn finally return to the rural garden and are able to face each other in a 'wild surmise' (p. 200). Having begun with a protagonist engaged in postmodern pastiche, then moving her through a series of enforced cultural performances of femininity, Carter finally returns Melanie to the garden, apparently purged of postmodern cultural appropriation. This is a novel which moves from the Fall back to a pre-Fall Garden of Eden, charting a coming-of-age story that replaces shame and subjugation with unchecked desire and individual will.

---

* In Greek mythology, the god Zeus takes the form of a swan and rapes Leda, who is married to the King of Sparta. The story has inspired various artistic recreations, from paintings by Michelangelo to the poem 'Leda and the Swan' (1928) by W. B. Yeats.

Inhabiting History

Graham Swift's *Shuttlecock* (1981) further suggests the difficult navigations between personal and political history, centring on the police clerk Prentis who comes to realise that his father's war memoir, which gives the book its name, is partly fabricated. The novel becomes a process of rejecting his father's narrative and then relinquishing the power its lies have over him. The obsessive haunting of history creates a world where, as Prentis remarks, 'everything goes in circles, or in irreversible regressions'.[16] Only by giving up any personal claims to ancestral history can the subsequent generation move on. Prentis works as an archivist for the police department, collating the files of long-forgotten crimes. His opening admission – that we recall what is pleasant and forget only what we choose not to remember – sets up his job as a necessary corrective to human nature. Yet his father's mental breakdown, which Prentis comes to relate directly to the deceptive stories of military combat in his war memoir, shows an individual undone by the need to archive and recall the past.

His father's betrayal of his country, which is rewritten in his memoir as a heroic escape, becomes a form of textual escape in its deviations from the truth. As Prentis's colleague Quinn points out, the fabricated section of his father's memoir is the most authentic because 'it *is* an escape, a quite real escape' written by a man 'torn between the desire to construct this saving lie and an instinct not to falsify himself completely' (p. 188). Prentis's final comfort comes in reading this fictive memoir as a code which deliberately unscrambles itself before his eyes. His father's attempts to authenticate the story are equally hints to his son that he is not the heroic figure his memoir suggests. His mendacity and evasions come to say as much about Prentis's inability to read his text truthfully as his father's inability to write it. The shuttlecock which gives the memoir its title functions initially as his codename, but it becomes analogous with the competing versions of textual truth at work throughout the narrative. The narrative continually reverses to meet its readers, offering them confirmation of what they already think they know. Both our personal and our political histories become things, as Prentis notes, we 'take swipes at' (p. 49).

Swift continued to take these swipes in his later fictions which, although outside the remit of this study, similarly explore the tensions between historical and personal narratives. *Ever After* (1992) sets two personal stories alongside each other: that of the protagonist Bill Unwin, a struggling academic in contemporary Britain, and his discovery of notebooks belonging to his Victorian ancestor, Matthew Pearce. Here his novel invites comparison with A. S. Byatt's *Possession* (1990), another reimagining of the Victorian period which pits contemporary academia alongside the intrigues of nineteenth-century romance. As in earlier fictions, Swift's techniques are at once metafictional and self-aware while simultaneously harking back to a traditional humanism. The similarities between Pearce and Unwin suggest a permeable gap between past and present, but Unwin's own work as a English literature tutor finds him entirely out of step with the world of theory and pluralism. As he protests, 'I have been doing little more than urging my students to acknowledge that literature is beautiful'.[17] In *Last Orders* (1996), Swift's literary influences are again both experimental and traditional. His story of four South Londoners complying with their friend Jack Dodds's dying request that they make a pilgrimage to the coast and scatter his ashes out at sea looks both to William Faulkner's *As I Lay Dying* (1930) and Chaucer's *Canterbury Tales* (*c.* 1400). Fittingly, the coast, when they finally reach it, smells 'like memory itself',[18] the characters here shuffling quietly in between personal histories and the literary histories that have created them.

While Unwin remains haunted by his Victorian ancestor in Swift's *Ever After*, textual haunting of another kind underpins Julian Barnes's *Flaubert's Parrot* (1984). The narrator, the retired doctor Geoffrey Braithwaite, is a self-styled Flaubert obsessive, and the novel finds him travelling France in search of the famous stuffed parrot which sat on Flaubert's writing desk. As in the playful intrusions of *A History of the World in 10 ½ Chapters*, Barnes uses the mock-biography form with wry flexibility. Braithwaite's digressions on animal imagery in Flaubert, his strained relationships with other Flaubert obsessives, and his increasingly guilty musings on his own wife's suicide make Flaubert a cipher as well as the focal point of the novel. As Braithwaite makes clear at the outset, a life can be told a thousand ways: he offers three competing chronologies of Flaubert's career in the opening chapters, each an apparently bald statement of year and event yet all offering mutually incompatible readings of his life.

The textual traces of Flaubert's life, symbolised by the missing letters between him and Juliet Herbert which are unceremoniously burnt by a misguided academic, always keep him tantalisingly out of reach, like the ever-proliferating number of parrots that may or may not have been Flaubert's original pet. Yet through this constructed biographical pilgrimage, Barnes crafts a novel of human incident and comedy rather than teasing abstraction. Finding fault with a pedantic attack on Flaubert's characterisation in his novels, Braithwaite asserts that 'if you don't know what's true, or what's meant to be true, then the value of what isn't true, or isn't meant to be true, becomes diminished'.[19] Here he gives a sigh for absolutism in a world rendered painfully relativist and meaningless. When his wife kills herself, seemingly without reason, he can only conclude that 'books are where things are explained to you; life is where things aren't' (p. 201). Barnes makes bathetic and poignant comedy out of the gap between Flaubert's solid fictional world and the mindless cruelty of contemporary life. Sometimes, Barnes suggests, literature should provide a refuge rather than a mirror.

A humanist literature re-emerges in Carter's final novel, *Wise Children* (1991), which turns from the Grimm Brothers to Shakespeare for its literary ancestry. This is a Shakespeare rooted in performance, as the farcical recreations of *A Midsummer Night's Dream* suggest, but also rerouted in working-class South London. Vaudeville, ragtime, music hall, and pantomime equally frame the stage here, as twin sisters Dora and Nora Chance spin a tale of rival theatrical dynasties and illegitimacy. The weaving of Shakespeare into the narrative then comes not as a signal of canonical adherence but rather a gesture towards hybridity. Their performances of Shakespeare, like the tottering narratives of their own lives, disguise tragedy as comedy and vice versa. The work suggests that the rebirth of the British postwar novel comes not from a rigorous rejection of moral orthodoxy or working-class realism but rather an embrace of permeable generic categories. Unlike Barnes's Geoffrey Braithwaite, who mourns the passing of the master narrative, the Chance sisters abandon the burden of veracity and integrity for the celebration of carnival. As their narrative concludes, 'what a joy it is to dance and sing!'[20] Following the Russian critic Mikhail Bakhtin, who developed his notion of the carnivalesque in *Rabelais and His World* (1965), Carter sees the novel as space for individual voices to challenge officialdom and hierarchy, subverting convention through anarchy and chaos. In this sense, the novels of Barnes, Swift, and Carter deliberately hold back from enforcing a new orthodoxy. In place of traditional approaches to the realist novel we find a vigorous mixture of apparently opposing binaries: the high and the low, the whimsical and the rationalist, the chronological and the chaotic. The British novel's largely conservative response to postmodernism in fact sets up one more apparent binary to be vigorously challenged, commingled, and explored.

Extended Commentary: Carter, *Nights at the Circus* (1984)

The reporter who comes to interview Carter's protagonist in the opening scene of *Nights at the Circus* is described as a 'kaleidoscope equipped with consciousness'.[21] This might go some way to describing the novel itself, which moves between the dizzy fantasies of magic realism, the Cockney yarn, the newspaper report, and the travelogue with disorientating speed. Although the novel plays fast and loose with anachronism and chronology, it is set in 1899; the turn-of-the-century pivot suggests a world in transformation, and, in a variety of ways, Carter dispenses with the Victorian certainties of the nineteenth-century novel for a work that is provocatively far-fetched and playfully resistant to questioning. Yet even as the novel's setting looks forward to experiments of modernism and postmodernism, it mourns:

> [t]he last, bewildering days before history, that is history as we know it, that is, white history, that is, European history, that is, Yanqui history – in that final little breathing space before history as such extended its tentacles to grasp the entire globe. (p. 314)

What we gain in nonconformity, Carter suggests, we lose in consensus.

The catalyst for the story is American reporter Walser's interview with Fevvers, the aerialiste who claims to have been hatched from an egg and to have two huge bird wings growing from her back. The sceptical journalist is determined to dispel the fantastical rumour of her ancestry yet becomes enthralled by her words and her physical presence. The narrative shares Walser's eye-popping fixation with Fevvers's femininity. Even when Fevvers shows fatigue it is captivating; she yawns mid-way through recounting her life-story with:

> [a] prodigious energy, opening up a crimson maw the size of that of a basking shark, taking in enough air to lift a Montgolfier, and then she stretched herself suddenly and hugely, extending every muscle as a cat does, until it seemed she intended to fill up all the mirror, all the room with her bulk. (p. 57)

Carter's hyperbolic similes ensure that the novel combines the magical with the realist not just through fantastic plot devices, as in Fevvers's baffling escape from danger via a Fabergé egg, but at the level of language. The yawn, that most physical sign of ennui, inspires the narrator to dizzying heights of descriptive prose.

Yet while the carnival setting suggests the anarchy of misrule and the work of Bakhtin, Carter draws in a wider canvas of cultural critiques than in the later *Wise Children*. Burlesque, striptease, and the tight-rope walker offer a performative spectacle, but the figure of the clown punctures the mood of roguish dissent. When the circus travels on to St Petersburg, now with Walser in tow as a trainee clown, the meal at Clown Alley prompts a terrifying spectacle of painted white faces around the table with 'the formal lifelessness of death masks, as if, in some essential sense, they themselves were absent from the repast and left untenanted replicas behind' (p. 134). The clown's doom is to be unchanged and unchanging, and to offer misery as a comic spectacle for the audience's consumption. Fevvers herself must walk a difficult tight-rope between the spectacle she can control and the threat of voyeurism, the notion that she will be objectified by the onlooker and so lose her own identity.

Before joining the circus, she tells Walser, she posed as a living statue of 'Winged Victory' in an upper-class drawing room but then was also reduced to a freakish spectacle in Madame Schreck's display case, which combined a brothel with a freakshow. She triumphs in adversity (the loss of her wings, the lure of the Grand Duke, the freezing temperatures of the Siberian desert) but always at the last minute and beyond the realms of credibility. Perhaps the only way she resists voyeurism for the reader is by refusing to choose between the real and the fantastic. Walser begins by doubting her story, while the reader is finally left to question the notion of narrative altogether. The winged protagonist is both a novelistic gimmick, and a self-created construction the characters themselves draws attention to, blurring the distinctions between the fabricated and the integral.

Carter's novel deliberately mixes modes and genres; its successive shifts of locale further undermine a static, linear reading of the novel. The circus moves from St Petersburg to Siberia on the tour but, when its train is attacked, is forced to disband. This narrative device allows the characters to be exposed to a variety of cultural influences and ideologies. Walser, for example, is introduced to shamanism; having entered the narrative as the empirical, rational reporter, his journey forces him to consider alternative epistemologies. The icy forests of Transbaikalia also house an all-female prison for convicted murderers. This is run by the Countess P., who murders her own husband, then projects her guilt onto her assembly of criminals, only setting them free when she believes they are penitent. Here, Carter again turns away from the carnivalesque to theories of control and punishment. In particular, she draws on the writings of Michel Foucault, whose influential work *Discipline and Punish* (1977) focused on a prison designed in the eighteenth century by Jeremy Bentham called the panopticon. This prison worked on the principle of voyeurism rather than incarceration. Prisoners were arranged in a circle in open cells that were perpetually visible to their jailers. Denied the secrecy of darkness or the privacy of solitary confinement, these prisoners became a spectacle. As Carter's narrative explains: 'during the hours of darkness, the cells were lit up like so many small theatres in which each actor sat by herself in the trap of her visibility' (p. 248). The rigorous policing here offers compelling perspectives on Carter's feminism, and the way in which the female individual is goaded into mass conformity not through punitive measures, but by being perpetually on view as an object. Carter's deliberate choice of a female jailer questions whether it is the male gaze or female complicity which plays the largest part in her incarceration.

The range of influences, settings, and perspectives in the novel are, like Fevvers herself, reluctant to apologise for their hybridity or internal contradictions. A further tension in the text emerges between the theoretically informed novelistic world and the earthy, pragmatic common sense of its characters. Carter's London reeks with period detail and tactile impressions yet combines Bakhtin with social realism. Her Siberia is part Russian fairy tale, and part Foucauldian horror. The novel's conclusion offers a conventional love story between Fevvers and Walser, and even indulges in the winking cartoon cliché of Fevvers laughing 'to think I really fooled you!' (p. 350), yet Carter's enthusiastic embrace of critical theory makes the work a less sceptical, less partial postmodern novel than those of Barnes or Swift. Yet perhaps, tellingly, the one weight the protagonist struggles to contend with is the physical fact of her own wings. Carter permits her the use of wings to escape, to dazzle her clientele, or to embellish her life story. But once her wings are dishevelled and moulting, as in the Siberian section of the novel, they become the dirtiest, wettest, and heaviest of practical burdens. Even in Carter's most fantastic conceit, the wings that allow her protagonist to charge between high and low, between the drawing room and the brothel, between the real and the fantastical, we find a postmodern narrative device condemned to the lens of practical pragmatism.

Notes

1   Angela Carter, *Love* (London: Vintage, 1997), p. 1.
2   John Fowles, *The French Lieutenant's Woman* (London: Jonathan Cape, 1969), p. 97.
3   See Jean-François Lyotard, *The Postmodern Condition: A Report on Knowledge* (Manchester: Manchester University Press, 1979), p. 34.

4   David Lodge, 'Postmodern Fiction', in Bran Nicol (ed.), *Postmodernism and the Contemporary Novel* (Edinburgh: Edinburgh University Press, 2002), p. 34.

5   Mikhail Bakhtin, 'Discourse in the Novel', *The Dialogic Imagination*, trans. Caryl Emerson and Michael Holquist (Austin: University of Texas Press, 1991), p. 54.

6   Roland Barthes, 'The Death of the Author', *Image-Music-Text* (New York: Hill and Wang, 1977), pp. 142–8.

7   Linda Hutcheon, 'Historigraphic Metafiction', in Marjorie Perloff (ed.), *Postmodern Genres* (London: University of Oklahoma Press, 1988).

8   Graham Swift, *The Sweet-Shop Owner* (Harmondsworth: Penguin, 1983), p. 60.

9   Julian Barnes, *Metroland* (London: Picador, 1990), pp. 86–7.

10   Angela Carter, *The Bloody Chamber and Other Stories* (Harmondsworth: Penguin, 1981), p. 10.

11   Julian Barnes, *A History of the World in 10 ½ Chapters* (London: Picador, 1989), p. 136.

12   Graham Swift, *Waterland* (London: Picador, 1992), p. ix.

13   Julian Barnes, *Staring at the Sun* (London: Picador, 1987), p. 17.

14   Graham Swift, *Out of This World* (London: Viking, 1988), p. 203.

15   Angela Carter, *The Magic Toyshop* (London: Virago, 1993), p. 2.

16   Graham Swift, *Shuttlecock* (Harmondsworth: Penguin, 1982), p. 123.

17   Graham Swift, *Ever After* (London: Pan Books, 2002), p. 70.

18   Graham Swift, *Last Orders* (London: Picador, 1996), p. 287.

19   Julian Barnes, *Flaubert's Parrot* (Basingstoke: Macmillan, 1985), p. 84.

20   Angela Carter, *Wise Children* (London: Chatto & Windus, 1991), p. 232.

21   Angela Carter, *Nights at the Circus* (London: Vintage, 2003), p. 7.

The Modern Lyric: Larkin, Plath and Smith

Sylvia Plath's description of her poetic process in her 1962 essay, 'A Comparison',[1] offers a range of ways of thinking about poetry in the postwar period. Her dismissal of epic – '[w]e all know how long they can take' – and, by implication, narrative modes of poetry reflects wider trends in modern verse which, for the most part, have left the long poem behind. She compares the lyrical moment of the 'smaller unofficial garden-variety poem' to a shaken Victorian snow-globe, which seems particularly apt, both in its desperate bid to recapture the certainties of the Victorian world and its consequent disdain for the 'plastic mass-productions' of the modern era, both traits shared by a series of poets writing in the 1950s and 1960s. It is notable, too, that this vision behind glass offers an intimate scene that is 'self-complete', but one where the individual is always contextualised by the 'village or family group'. Poetry as an act of shaking a snow-globe is at once a nostalgic image and one of terrible violence, as Plath's description makes clear – 'everything is changed in a minute'. These series of contests – between violence and nostalgia, mass-production and the individual, and the poet as isolationist and integral member of society – outline the shape of the postwar poetry debate.

While the postwar novel was figured at a crossroads, commentators on poetry suggested that two opposing ways forward had already been taken. The first of these might be represented by Robert Conquest's 1956 collection *New Lines*. This was the anthology of The Movement, as it was termed by J. D. Scott, literary editor of *The Spectator*, in 1954 (see Part Two: 'A Cultural Overview'). The Movement set itself up against both modernist obscurity and the neo-Romantic excess of 1940s poets such as Dylan Thomas. Grouping Philip Larkin together with poets such as Donald Davie and Elizabeth Jennings in the anthology, Conquest describes the organising principle as 'little more than a negative determination to avoid bad principles'.[2] Later commentators were more specific, however, with John Press describing The Movement as 'a general retreat from direct comment or involvement in any political or social doctrine'.[3] To Press's description we might add Philip Larkin's provocative assertion of intellectual philistinism; as he wrote in 1956, 'I make a point of not knowing what poetry is or how to read a page'.[4] Larkin's remark is consciously iconoclastic and glib, but this was a poetry suspicious both of allusion and complexity on the one hand, and the sentimental trend of immediate postwar verse on the other. Its world was inward-looking, local, and everyday.

Al Alvarez's seminal collection *The New Poetry* (1962) makes an anthology into a manifesto through its attack on Movement poetry, dismissing it as 'academic-administrative verse, polite, knowledgeable, efficient, polished, and, in its quiet way, even intelligent' although 'what it had to offer positively was more difficult to describe'.[5] To prove his point, Alvarez offers an indicative poem from *New Lines*, only to reveal the 'poem' is a synthesis of lines from eight of the poets included in it. His attack on what he calls the British gentility principle, like Murdoch's assault on the social-realist novel (see Part Three: 'The Moral Novel'), looks to recent historical events to justify its aesthetic argument. While poets should not feel limited to the concentration camps, the hydrogen bomb, or psychoanalysis as their subjects, he argues, poetry needs to 'drop the pretence that life, give or take a few social distinctions, is the same as ever, that gentility, decency, and all the other social totems will eventually muddle through'. Calling for a 'new seriousness' that echoes Murdoch's request for a 'vocabulary of attention', he demands that a poet 'face the full range of his experience with his full intelligence; not to take the easy exits of either the conventional response or choking incoherence'.[6] Gentility becomes the 'disease' of English culture that only a few contemporaries, such as Ted Hughes, Thom Gunn, or Peter

Porter, might escape. This is less an anthology trumpeting a new voice in British poetry, than one desperately calling for the emergence of one. For Alvarez, this can only be achieved by looking towards America; pointedly, the anthology begins with the work of American poets John Berryman and Robert Lowell. By the time of the 1966 reissue of *The New Poetry*, the work of Sylvia Plath, too, had been posthumously included. Plath's use of disjointed forms, Holocaust imagery, and free verse offers clear oppositions to Larkin's tendency to iambic pentameters and local subjects. Yet it is predominantly the choice of the anthologists, rather than the poets' own formal differences, which put them at opposite ends of the poetic landscape.

The work of the poet, illustrator, and novelist Stevie Smith complicates this binary response. Championed by Larkin during her lifetime,[7] and also a major influence on Plath's work,[8] the variety, humour, and often baffling tonal shifts of her poetry question the efficacy of dividing poetry into self-contained categories. Her career, which messily straddles the 1930s to the 1970s, confuses the shift from pre- to postwar. Her poems are similarly dismissive of poetic groups: in 'To School!' she satirises the poets who are 'gathered together in classes,'[9] while the titular plea of 'No Categories!'[10] makes a similar entreaty. Her vitriol for critical schools and her own intransigent verse not only make her difficult to subsume into a linear 'narrative' about lyric poetry, but also undermine the boundary between Larkin and Plath. Might Larkin's work be less inward, conservative, and static than Alvarez's attack suggests? Was Plath's prescient and fierce confessional poetry more influenced by the poetry of her adopted England than the American avant-garde? By focusing on the poetry of these three writers, we will consider what defined the lyrical impulse of this period, and how far, as Plath's opening image of the snow-globe suggests, the poem might unsettle the ordered glass frame of the world around it.

Reforming the Lyric

The lyric genre, like Robert Conquest's reading of The Movement, is perhaps most easily defined negatively. John Lennard's *Poetry Handbook* traces the term from its bardic origins through the notion of the 'singable' poem in the Renaissance period to its more diffuse modern connotation:

> the term now covers most shorter poems, typically expressing (or thought to express) personal emotion, and is defined mostly by a process of exclusion (not any of the other genres, not narrative, nor martial …).[11]

Despite the ambivalence of the term, the continued relationship between 'lyric' as a musical utterance and a personal one, as opposed to the public quality of the epic, is telling. Through much of the work of Smith, Larkin, and Plath, these characteristics are further dissected and exposed. While the biographical imperative is particularly relevant to poets whose lives are so often used as a corollary for their work and vice versa, many of these poems work by deconstructing the musicality, as well as the personality, of the lyric.

In curious ways, Smith's performance practice offers the nearest approximation to the traditional lyric. She refound her fame during the British Poetry Revival of the 1960s, singing her poems to off-key hymn tunes while an audience who had come to watch male poets half her age listened on, enraptured. Her early poem 'The Songster' suggests a self-awareness about her own eccentric appearance during these readings, with its depiction of an aging female bard who continues her performance although 'nobody knew what she sang about'.[12] Her printed poems often offer the tune in question as their subtitle, as in 'Le Singe Qui Swing' which is set to Greensleeves,[13] and the draft of her 1949 novel *The Holiday* finds her autobiographical protagonist worrying about writing her tunes down, and no-one else knowing how they should be sung.[14] Yet alongside this commitment to the sung poem comes Smith's highly idiosyncratic use of line, rhythm, and metre. Although the wide category of lyric poetry doesn't impose particular metrical structures, conventionally the lyric has looked to regular forms and rhythmic patterns. However, Smith's poems lollop along via a series of contorted, flippant, or disabling rhymes: magenta / might have lent a ('I love …'),[15] dishonesty / everybody ('How do you see?'),[16] or writing

/ dispiriting ('My Muse').[17] Her disruptive use of line also undermines the fluency of her chosen form – her work is full of otherwise perfect three-line stanzas, or tercets, that leave one half-rhyme out in the cold ('The Photograph', 'Gnädiges Fräulein', 'The Weak Monk'). In the 'The Best Beast of the Fat-Stock Show in Earls Court' she creates an entirely monosyllabic poem, which nevertheless shifts from the five-syllable-a line-couplet to the most unsteady of stanzas:

> Not yet to the lift
> Goes the Best Beast,
> He has to walk on the floor to make a show
> First.[18]

Like the lumbering beast described here, her poems draw proud attention to their various rhythmic disfigurements and inequalities. While Smith offers gestures towards the musical in her performances, the lyrical qualities of her verse are consciously bumpy and truncated. Her use of multiple languages, competing speakers, and distracted idiolects (i.e., language use particular to an individual) in her poetry further complicates the purity of the lyrical utterance.

Plath similarly constructs a deliberately disjunctive rhythmic pattern throughout her work. While many of her poems arrange themselves around the tercet ('Ariel', 'Purdah', 'Poppies in October'), her use of free verse frequently forestalls any sense of fluid movement. Such is the collapse of the iambic stress in her line that a beleaguered Sandra M. Gilbert has to edit phrases out of her poem 'Lady Lazarus' altogether to argue it has a prosodic coherence.[19] Graphically, her stanzas are clipped and spiky, leaving spools of white space on her page. Her poem 'Cut', which describes an accidental or perhaps serendipitous cut while chopping an onion in the kitchen, fans out into a sea of related connotative images.[20] The stumps of images Plath offers through this poem, from the scalped pilgrim to the Kamikaze fighter, mirror the fragmented stubs of rhythm and rhyme in her oeuvre, which alternately flinch from and lash out at each other, repelling and attracting like magnets.

While Plath and Smith undermine the lyricism of the lyric, Larkin disavows any pervading tradition in his work. As he famously averred in 1956: 'I believe that every poem must be its own sole freshly created universe, and therefore have no belief in "tradition" or a common myth-kitty or casual allusions in poems to other poems or poets' ('Statement', p. 151). His rejection of genre here is two-fold: even as he asserts his atheist position on tradition, he cocks a particular snook at modernism. Myth and allusion make up its common building blocks, and are explicitly rejected here. As the statement suggests, with its apparent indifference to tradition yet its very particular rejection of one tradition over another, Larkin's poetry evokes as many poetic predecessors as it professes disdain for. In fact, many of his poems, at least formally, use traditional models. Employing an iambic pentameter that is only partly concealed by his use of enjambment, Larkin specialises in opaque forms which modulate perfect rhyme against colloquial fluency. This is made clear in the opening lines of 'Essential Beauty'.[21] The rhyme and metre in the opening sentence of this poem, like the images themselves, which balance the mundane with the surreal, dovetail themselves into near invisibility. Avoiding the end-stopped line throughout, the poem offers the idiolects of speech rather than the certainty of the line break to guide the reader through the poem. Yet this is the work of a perfect technician – still seeking the rhyme word for 'ways', which we will meet later in the stanza, the reader strains for an 'a' sound which half-modulates 'groves' into 'graves'. Larkin seems cautious about revealing the musicality of his lines, and his diction takes further steps to avoid the trap of sentimentality. In 'Sad Steps', we are offered the equivalent of Plath's lyrical snow-globe, as an aged speaker woken late at night considers the symbolism of the moon. The central stanza in the poem apostrophises the moon in mock-Romantic rapture as a 'Lozenge of love! Medallion of art!'[22] while the poem's first lines keep us on our guard: 'Groping back to bed after a piss, / I part thick curtains'. Only by qualifying the would-be Romantic tercet with the banal toilet can Larkin allow himself the possibility of lyrical reflection.

Selfhood and Self-immolation

Larkin, Smith, and Plath were not alone in questioning the efficacy of the lyric. Theodor Adorno asked whether the horrors of Auschwitz meant that poetry could never again have faith in redemptive perception.[23] Martin Heidegger followed Adorno in calling on a new seriousness of vocation and purpose for poetry, arguing that 'the poet in the time of the world's night must utter the holy'.[24] Yet perhaps the most immediate context for British and American poets was not, after all, the cultural impact of the Holocaust, but the critical orthodoxies about ways of reading poetry. The modernist verse of T. S. Eliot and Ezra Pound, with its emphasis on impersonality, had helped create a critical school known as New Criticism. Based around the works of American critics such as Cleanth Brooks and W. K. Wimsatt, New Criticism equated literary interpretation with algebra or simultaneous equations; for Cleanth Brooks, poetic analysis must focus on a poem's structure, for 'the nature of material sets the problem to be solved, and the solution is the ordering of the material'.[25] The language of problem, empirical evaluation, and solution dominates the key critical works of this period, as in Wimsatt's famous assertion that judging a poem is like 'judging a pudding or a machine. One demands that it work'.[26] Rejecting the notion that authors themselves had control over the meaning of their works, or that their own biographies might help us 'close' a poem, the New Critics saw poems as discrete objects entirely separate from their makers. The school sought to systematise interpretation, so that criticism might be as objective as New Critics wanted the poems themselves to become. The two crucial terms New Criticism has given us tell us much about its preoccupations: 1) intentional fallacy, the apparently false belief that an author's own intentions are significant when considering a work of art; and 2) affective fallacy, the similarly questionable idea that a reader's emotional response to a work might tell us something useful about it as critics.[27]

Plath's immediate American context saw a series of writers explicitly breaking with this new orthodoxy of impersonality. Robert Lowell, Plath's former teacher and poetic contemporary, complained of a writing that was now 'divorced from culture', something specialised that was immune to personal experience.[28] In its place, he offered what would be derisively branded as 'confessional poetry'. Reviewing Lowell's 1959 collection *Life Studies*, M. L. Rosenthal describes it as 'a series of personal confidences, rather shameful, that one is honor-bound not to reveal'.[29] This American debate about the relationship between the speaker, the author, and the latter's own biography relates to British concerns too. Throughout their work, Plath, Smith, and Larkin reposition or codify the speaking 'I' in their poems, teasing us with or removing the possibility of authorial identification. This is a lyrical mode where the self is a performance, a mask, or a process of public subterfuge.

Historically, this has been most apparent in the critical response to Plath's work. Her contested position and her relationship to husband Ted Hughes is echoed in the defacement of her grave by Plath 'fans', furious that she is buried under the surname of the man who, they claim, prompted her suicide. Yet this very literal 'rewriting' of the text of her work via the text of her life is reductive. Plath's own poetry shows the self as a canny and cunning performer, and complicates a static, causal relationship between life and work. In 'Daddy', this allows her to perform silence and suppressed speech, as the speaker imagines her Germanic father as a Nazi general.[30] Elsewhere, as in 'Lady Lazarus', the speaker offers suicide as another gripping performance to be devoured by the audience around her.[31] Self-immolation here is also resurrection, a way of ensuring longevity and cyclical renewal (see *CP*, p. 244, l. 21).

While Plath stages her death in ritualised frenzy – see especially the cries of the febrile speaker in 'Fever 103°'[32] – Smith's speakers glimpse their final moments second hand, as in her poem 'Not Waving But Drowning'. Rather than situate the speaker in the submarine world of the poem's seaside suicide, Smith approaches it from the shoreline.

> Oh, no no no, it was much too cold always
> (still the dead one lay moaning)
> I was much too far out all my life
> And not waving but drowning.[33]

The ambiguous parentheses here make it unclear whether the final lines are spoken from beyond the grave by the drowned man or whether the speaker has now taken on the subject's position. As in her poem 'Harold's

Leap' (*CP*, p. 233), where the speaker narrates a man's plunge from a cliff-top with stoical admiration, death becomes the only certainty. These deliberate ambiguities permeate Smith's 'I' voice, whether the speaker's words are tempered by whimsy and escapism ('My Hat', *CP*, p. 315), or make use of allusion and traditional ballad form to complicate our assumptions that there is a correlation between the speaker and the poet ('A Dream of Nourishment', *CP*, p. 344).

Larkin's speakers attempt the opposite, and construct a coherent poetic persona. Their authority comes, in part, from the use of rhetorical devices to play down their power. Larkin's speakers are equivocal, self-deprecating, and use conversational diction to underwrite the efficacy of their pronouncements. In 'Mr Bleaney', the speaker imagines his bedsit's former occupant, concluding that his repetitive, banal, and lonely life would 'make him pretty sure / He warranted no better, I don't know'.[34] The balancing of the 'sure' with the qualifying 'pretty', and the final, shoulder-shrugging dismissal of 'I don't know' situate the speaker alongside his assumed audience, gesturing to a conclusion he is reluctant to make. Yet in the later 'High Windows', it is this ability to imaginatively enter another life, even if the process results in envy, jealousy, or bafflement, that keeps us human. The droll speaker sees two teenagers and surmises 'he's fucking her and she's / Taking pills'. This, he wryly announces, is 'paradise'.[35] He imagines himself as a youngster, and considers whether someone of an older generation might have seen him with similar envy and disdain. Through this wider perception of the self comes at last 'the thought of high windows' (l. 13), the moment of redemptive lyricism that rescues the poem from its nihilistic response to casual sex. Larkin's speakers often seem crabbed, self-preoccupied, and spiteful, but the full force of their idealism is reflected in their unshakeable belief that the self is better not performed, constructed, or qualified, but released from self-reflection via the possibility of the world around it.

It is no small irony that much recent criticism of these poets' work has forgone the investigation of the lyrical moment – the inexplicable change of atmosphere that closes Larkin's 'The Whitsun Weddings'[36] – for the overarching narrative. Larkin and Plath, in particular, have been overwhelmed by biographical details, from Larkin's appalling racism and bigotry to Plath's compelling suicide story, although Smith too came back to critical attention through a 1980 biopic starring Glenda Jackson. As Plath noted presciently in February 1956: 'the dialogue between my Writing and my Life is always in danger of becoming a shifting sliding of responsibility, of evasive rationalizing'.[37] Larkin's late poem 'Posterity' effects a similar clairvoyance, imagining himself as a dreary literary biography that an ambitious American scholar must get out of the way before moving on to research Protest Theatre.[38] This tension between the lyrical impulse in all three writers' works and the sense that they are, as Neil Roberts writes of Plath, being 'beset by narratives',[39] articulates our own current desire to read our writers through stories rather than schools. Larkin has been punished for his posthumously published diaries and letters not living up to the poetic persona readers themselves helped propagate, but perhaps this only shows how effective his colloquial strategies are in building up a coherent speaking voice.[40] These writers question the lyric 'I' both through these knowing strategies for creating personae and masks and in the way we have come to read them: their often compelling biographies both invite and resist easy readings between text and life.

The Lyrical Landscape

The wider world offers Larkin's speaker in 'High Windows' one possible escape route from the staged dramas of the self. Yet throughout the work of these three poets, the lyrical landscape signals cruelty more often than comfort. Smith's work, with a vocabulary drenched in Romantic, Victorian, and Edwardian diction, seems to share the sensibilities of its inheritance. The natural world is often enchanted ('Fairy Wood', *CP*, p. 412; 'The Frozen Lake', *CP*, p. 393) or literally offers an escape for the speaker who is whisked away to a magical landscape from their suburban boredom ('Deeply Morbid', *CP*, p. 297). Yet elsewhere, the literary precursors to her work only highlight the failure of the natural world to perform its poetic function. In 'Childe Rolandine', Smith reworks Robert Browning's 'Childe Rolande to the Dark Tower Came' (1855), recasting the knight who meets his death in an allegorical wilderness as a frustrated secretary, condemned to waste her life for the 'privilege of the rich'.[41]

Two late poems distil this sense of transmuted unease at the landscape. 'Pretty' begins as an observational, even kitsch, poem, noting that the word pretty is 'underrated', before applying it to a series of woodland animals: the pike, the otter, the beaver, and the owl. Yet the glib evasions of the word, as the poem later reveals, hide terror and cruelty under its surface:

> And it is careless, and that is always pretty
> This field, this owl, this pike, this pool are careless,
> As Nature is always careless and indifferent
> Who sees, who steps, means nothing, and this is pretty.[42]

As the gulf between the speaker's assessment of the natural world and the connotations of 'pretty' becomes ever wider, the charge of 'careless' might be directed not only at nature itself, but the unthinking poet, who naively sees in the animal kingdom only goodness and natural law. The Romantic project has failed; the poet's powers of perception are now void, and what they see 'means nothing'. Similarly, the poem 'Cock-a-doo' opens with almost monosyllabic observations on a natural world apparently without guile:

> I love to hear the cock crow in
> The middle of the day[43]

Yet as the scene develops, with its burnt yellow grass and grey flint path, it offers the speaker less a moment of transcendence than a presentiment of death:

> this
> Seeing, because of tiredness, becomes
> A transfixion of seeing, more sharp
> Than mirages are. (p. 536, ll. 19–22)

These sharp images threaten, rather than transform, the perception of the speaker, moving us away from the Romantic sublime to an eerie sort of uncanny.

This bewildering psychic landscape is echoed in Plath's work, which returns to the full-throated promise of the transcendental only to offer a relationship with nature which is paranoid, accusatory, and morbid. In 'Blackberrying', Plath unravels the notion of the poet as an elevated figure with a privileged relationship with the natural world. Here, the solitary mind is turbulent rather than tranquil, finding itself alone on a lane of blackberry bushes.[44] The absences here become nihilistic, and the full-fruited promise of the blackberries becomes an ugly glut of berries like eyes that seem to stare at her (l. 5). The speaker constructs a series of increasingly unnatural relationships with the landscape around her, from the menstrual ritual (l. 8) she identifies with the squashed berries to the ominous flocks of birds that dive like towards her (l. 11). Rather than prove a catalyst for the poem itself, the birds appear as a brutal parody of a written text, here destroyed and charred. The poem navigates itself via a row of blackberry hooks, and by the time the speaker finally reaches the hilltop, where the sea wind beats like a silversmith (l. 27), we find that harvest has become a processional torture; nature has plundered the subject itself.

These twisted, sterile landscapes, drawing on the visual prompts of German Expressionist painters such as George Grosz and Edvard Munch, offer competition, rather than consolation, to Plath's startled subjects. In 'Winter Trees', the split branches mock human notions of fecundity and plenitude, when even in barren months, as the speaker sarcastically notes, 'they seed so effortlessly!'.[45] Like Smith's enchanted exteriors, Plath's landscapes are full of guile and threat, offering respite more through the malignance of oblivion than the magic of escape. In 'Sheep in Fog', the speaker's bones themselves give in to the glower of the morning on the hills.[46] Heaven here is without cosmic compass or paternity, and merely replaces Lady Lazarus's repeated descent into hell with an unknown darkness.

While Larkin's perceived conservatism suggests his place in the 'English line', a poetic tradition critics have traced through Wordsworth, Hardy, and Edward Thomas, we find that the 'unfulfilled desires and longings' that characterise this tradition begin to unravel in Larkin's work.[47] Desire itself is now found wanting. In 'Talking in Bed', Larkin summons an intimate scene with a lover, but whereas a John Donne or Andrew Marvell poem might have argued that the passage of time necessitated the lovers' union, now the external world acts as a barrier rather than a catalyst to their love:

> Outside, the wind's incomplete unrest
> Builds and disperses clouds about the sky,
>
> And dark towns heap up on the horizon.
> None of this cares for us.[48]

Momentarily erasing those uncaring towns for the intensity of love becomes increasingly impossible for the speaker. Like Smith's indifferent woodland scene which renders its onlooker meaningless, or the intractable wind that buffets Plath's speaker in 'Blackberrying', here the natural world with its 'incomplete unrest' is as obstinate as the monotonous grey landscapes of postwar suburbia.

Larkin's poem 'First Sight' offers a fleeting glimpse of hope through rebirth, imagining winter-born lambs that will soon come to learn through the surprising wonders of spring.[49] It seems to place Larkin nearer to the pastoral mode of nineteenth-century poets like John Clare than the menacing world of Plath's 'Sheep in Fog'. Yet for all the promise of open-ended possibility, Larkin's speaker offers a fine balance between reawakening himself to the wonder of innocence, and suggesting that the lambs' capacity for wonder is closer to ignorance than naivety. More usually, Larkin's landscapes shift, reform, and heap themselves up around the sides of his subjects, blocking their view or offering them only a dim awareness of the smallness of their lives. Many of Larkin's poems are in continual motion, from the curving railway lines of 'Here' to the train-window observations of 'The Whitsun Weddings', as if to attempt to play the landscape at its own game, and catch it in the process of changing. In the poem 'To the Sea', Larkin's speaker returns to the site of his childhood beach holidays but finds everything altered; the hazy sunshine only further obscures his memories.[50] The English lyric has traditionally represented the isolated rural scene as a respite from human conflict that welcomes the poet's meditations on the surroundings, from Thomas Gray's 'Elegy in a Country Church-Yard' (1750) to Wordsworth's 'Tintern Abbey' (1798). Yet Plath re-envisioned the lyric poem as a shaken snow-globe, and it would seem that the glass more often than not separates and contains its subjects rather than giving them a meaningful frame. Like Smith's speaker in 'Every Lovely Limb's a Desolation', these poets turn obsessively to view the natural world, but see it only as blurred and obsured, as from the fleeting perspective of a prisoner on a train.[51]

Faith and Fallacy

The consolation of Christianity follows the knowledge of the natural world in finding itself wanting in these poets' works. Plath's poetic landscape uncovers a heaven without stars ('Sheep in Fog', l. 15) and a hell that is dulled and cannot absolve human sin ('Fever 103°', ll. 5–6), and faith, too, falters in its efforts to comfort, terrify, or resolve. Raised a Unitarian but later turning to a sceptical atheism, Plath offers through her work a hostile dissection of the icons and images of her abandoned creed. 'Dull' is a word often used in Plath's theological poems, and in 'Magi' the dull hell of 'Fever 103°' finds its reflection in heaven too.[52] Here, art has colluded with religious orthodoxy, as Plath describes a nativity scene rendered in crude card and paper. Yet the focus of the poem is not the model's inauthentic representation but its revelatory image up close, the image of the wholly good and divine is bland and sterile (ll. 6–7). These faces, devoid of characters or distinguishing features, come to signify the whitewash that is the biblical story. This is humankind sanitised. Only the divine child, here reimagined as female, is conscious of evil (l. 12), but finds it no more pressing than a belly ache.

Although the blank-faced abstracts of 'Magi' suggest an objective distance from religious iconography, Plath's poem 'Medusa' aligns Mariolatry (worship of the Virgin Mary) and matricide, the speaker desperate to exorcise her mother. This is a process that, for Plath, must first take place at the symbolic, rather than the personal, level. In a poem whose central figure of the gorgon Medusa is linked to religious sacrifice, from the recurring suggestion of stigmata to the surreal image of jellyfish with hair like Jesus,[53] the mother herself finds little escape from religious identification (ll. 27–31). Notions of femininity here collide with the symbolic practice of Christian ritual, as the speaker turns to the oppressive trappings of Catholic hierarchy to suggest the violent guilt and self-paralysis caused by the mother figure. The pointed rejection of maternal influence is expressed both as a refusal to take communion, but also a displacing of the Garden of Eden story, as the snake-like mother proffers an apple the subject will no longer accept.

Like Plath, who dissects the notion of the mother as Mary and the daughter as Eve, Smith takes a similar interest in the divided nature of religious female iconography. These differences express themselves in Smith's work through the jilting phonic of a half-rhyme rather than the submarine horror of the Medusa. In 'A Dream of Comparison', she imagines a dialogue between Mary and Eve as they walk by an estuary:

> And they talked until nightfall,
> But the difference between them was radical.[54]

Although the poem includes the 'radical' here, it is partly subsumed into the phonic patterns of the rhyming couplets. Much of Smith's religious poetry attempts to contain similar iconoclasms. Her poems are full of indignant ire for the Church of England and Christian theology. Like Plath, she rails against the use of the 'fairy story' of Creation told as fact.[55] Her poems are at their most frustrated when making religious entreaties. After an extended apostrophe to Christianity she fumes:

> Oh what do you mean, what do you mean?
> You never answer our questions.[56]

Yet this is the frustration of a modulating agnostic rather than a sceptic. The text that causes her most anxiety is also her clearest literary influence. Her verse is haunted by biblical cadences, and several poems salute the wonder of liturgy directly, whether through a tribute to Thomas

Cranmer, a leader of the English Reformation and the first to publish the service in the English vernacular ('Admire Cranmer!'),[57] or the subeditor who decides to print biblical quotations in the *Daily Telegraph* ('Magnificent Words').[58] Poems such as 'God the Eater' shift Smith closer to seventeenth-century religious poets such as George Herbert than to Plath's secular appropriations of religious iconography. Yet if her work suggests anger towards the human institutions shoring up her cautious Christianity, it also takes fascinated delight in the creaky workings of postwar Anglicanism, as in her late narrative poem 'The House of Over-Dew', where a proselytising husband moves his suburban family to a missionary retreat. The mother watches their savings plummet:

> But her husband
> Spoke of faith.[59]

Here, with a zeal that recalls Jocelin in William Golding's novel *The Spire* (1964),* the husband devotes himself to religious reclamation only to discover he has pushed himself and his family to the edges of their own lives.

Of the three poets, it is Larkin who has provided British literature with its most famous image of anxious agnosticism. In 'Church-going', the speaker enters an empty church, removing his bicycle clips self-consciously.[60] As he shuffles uncomfortably around the tatty pews, he asks whether the country's deserted parish churches are more museums than places of worship, and suggests the continued need for a public building full of solemnity and respect for the dead. It is where we convince ourselves that our personal desires are our destinies (*CP*, p. 59, l. 57). His colloquial language of equivocation has made Larkin's the archetypal poetic voice of the postwar years; it is one whose hesitant pronouncements are particularly suited to the British evasions of religious debate. It comes as a surprise then that, despite the cynical perspectives of poems such as Larkin's 'Faith Healing', which details an American evangelical preacher at work, some of Larkin's most open-ended idealism is found not in the remnants of the English past, but in

---

* See Part Three: 'The Moral Novel' for discussion of *The Spire*.

the possibilities of religious renewal. In 'Water', Larkin imagines himself 'called in' (l. 1) to construct a new religion, a phrase which already suggests the weary routines of the provincial bank manager. Yet here the suggestions of bureaucratic postwar Britain end; the poem imagines a religion founded on the natural properties of water, with its ritualistic symbolism and its physical characteristics providing its doctrine:

> And I should raise in the east
> A glass of water
> Where any-angled light
> Would congregate endlessly.[61]

This provides the poem's closing image. It is a moment of heightened lyricism. Here, fleetingly, Larkin looks to the unified form and expression of religious lyrics such as George Herbert's 'Easter Wings' (1633), which finds religious devotion providing solace, method, and motivation for its own composition. Its promise of the perpetual via the encounter between glass, water, and light also suggests affinities with Plath's description of the childhood snow-globe. Yet if her analogy for the lyrical impulse defines it in terms of an arresting shock which changes things irrevocably, here we find the linear narrative turned to lyric not because it is forever altered, but because it is infinite.

Extended Commentary: Smith, 'Thoughts about the Person from Porlock' (1962)

Smith's work is idiosyncratic rather than archetypal, and stubbornly resists categorisation. Yet, for all this hostility to generic trends, her best poems offer more than awkward intransigence and ambivalent responses to tradition. 'Thoughts about the Person from Porlock' (1962), first published by Longman in her collection *Selected Poems*, is a useful example of this. The title announces a post-Romantic lyric, taking as its starting point Coleridge's poetic fragment 'Kubla Kahn' (1816). Coleridge's fragment was allegedly composed in Somerset after an opium-induced dream vision but, as his own note records, was cut painfully short when a visitor from nearby Porlock disturbed his writing. He returned an hour later to find the memory of the vision had vanished.[62] The fragment, along with Coleridge's authorial justification for leaving it incomplete, has become subsumed into literary argot; the phrase 'person from Porlock' is used to describe any figure that interrupts the artistic process. Smith's treatment of this apocryphal story initially mines it for pragmatic scepticism. As the poem notes, Coleridge was under no obligation to let the person in. Smith's first explanation suggests this person was an expedient rather than a distraction:

> As the truth is I think he was already stuck
> With Kubla Khan.
>
> He was weeping and wailing: I am finished, finished,
> I shall never write another word of it,
> When along comes the Person from Porlock
> And takes the blame for it.[63]

The reduction of the visionary seer to the petulant author is typically Smithian in its bathos, rewriting the intruder as a welcome relief and dismissing the Romantic visionary with an English briskness. Yet Smith's writing career, which stretched from 1936 to 1971, suggests darker intruders. References to the person from Porlock creep into a series of works from this period, including Louis MacNeice's radio play *Persons from Porlock* (1969), suggesting that poets writing during the Second World War found here, too, was a necessary distraction which made poetry impossible to continue. In this way the poem deflates the notion of the poet as an elevated figure, while also suggesting an unspeakable scar across the twentieth-century landscape, an interruption that has caused an irreparable fissure.

As if eager to fend off political readings, the poem's second section descends from bathos to whimsy, as the lumbering tetrameter gives way to cadences of the nursery rhyme:

> May we inquire the name of the Person from Porlock?
> Why, Porson, don't you know?
> He lived at the bottom of Porlock Hill
> So had a long way to go, (ll. 15–18)

The voice has also moved from the pragmatic speaker of the first section to the split-subject pantomime call-and-response we see here. While the first section attacked Coleridge for his partial vision, the poem has now in effect interrupted itself, moving from empirical humour to a self-conscious kind of light verse. All visions and epiphanies must be partial for the postwar poet, whether expressed through Larkin's colloquial qualifiers, or Smith's bewildering shifts in tone. Like Coleridge's fragment, the poem pre-empts charges of a gradually eroding lyricism by defiantly marking with an asterisk its own disjunctive segments. We have moved from Coleridge's glimpsed vision to Smith's messily impressionistic 'thoughts'.

Yet the poem affects its most extreme about-turn by moving from the fanciful speculations about the person from Porlock to a sombre request that he visit Smith, too. Now he is invoked in reverential tones, as the speaker pleads with him to come and 'bring my thoughts to an end' (p. 386, l. 37). The request to have the speaker's thoughts brought to an end suggests both an invocation to death, and a plea for the formal close of the poem itself. The speaker's 'thoughts' are a synecdoche* both for Smith's consciousness and for her poem, 'Thoughts about the Person from Porlock'. The cruellest irony of the poem is not the puncturing of Coleridge's Romantic self-delusion but the way in which the speaker's request to bring the poem to an end is never complied with. Instead, the speaker is forced to continue enviously speculating on those who are permitted to 'finish', remaining baffled as to why they grumble so much when 'they might have had to go on' (l. 45). Here, Smith's work shares with Plath's the welcome embrace of death, and with Larkin's the morbidly comic use of colloquial phrases like 'go on' to denote both everyday endurance and the escape from suicide. Here quietism seems close to nihilism. The speaker's desperate plea for

---

* A synecdoche describes the substitution of a part for the whole, or vice versa, i.e. 'the government rejected the bill' means 'the ministers who sit in the government building rejected the bill'.

an ending is further undermined by the lopsided rhymes of 'benison / to go on'; there is little comfort offered by these jangling phonics. By the poem's final section, the speaker has still not been able to finish, but can only 'go on' by abandoning the pretence of lyricism altogether, irregular trimeters breaking down into the conversational idiolects of free verse:

> we should smile as well as submitting
> To the purpose of One Above who is experimenting
> With various mixtures of human character which goes best,
> All is interesting for him it is exciting, but not for us.
> There I go again. (ll. 48–52)

Here the speaker looks to the consolation of an Almighty to alleviate the gloom of human existence and explain its terrible cruelties, but more with a resigned stoicism than a presentiment of eternity. As the colloquial corrective intervenes, 'there I go again'. Now 'to go' is purged of its temporary connotations of dying or taking a leave of absence, but refers to the speaker's inability to avoid rambling observations. 'Going' is both the death that will provide release from the banalities of existence and also the lyrical impulse that will make, however momentarily, that same existence bearable again.

Notes

1   Sylvia Plath, 'A Comparison', in W. N. Herbert and Matthew Hollis (eds), *Strong Words: Modern Poets on Modern Poetry* (Newcastle: Bloodaxe, 2000), pp. 145–7.

2   Robert Conquest, *New Lines: An Anthology* (London: Macmillan, 1956), p. 5.

3   As quoted in Neil Roberts, *A Companion to Twentieth-Century Poetry* (Oxford: Blackwell, 2001), p. 214.

4   Philip Larkin, 'Statement', in *Strong Words*, pp. 150–1.

5   Al Alvarez, *The New Poetry*, 2nd edn (Harmondsworth: Penguin. 1970), p. 23.

6   Alvarez, *The New Poetry*, p. 28.

7   See Philip Larkin's influential *New Statesman* review, 'Frivolous and Vulnerable', reprinted in *Required Writing: Miscellaneous Pieces 1955–1982* (London: Faber, 1983), pp. 153–8.

8   One of Plath's final letters is to Stevie Smith, confessing she is a 'desperate Smith-addict', 19 November 1962, in Jack Barbera and William McBrien (eds), *Me Again: the uncollected writings of Stevie Smith* (London: Virago, 1982), p. 6.

9   Stevie Smith, 'To School!', *Collected Poems* (hereafter *CP*) (Harmondsworth: Penguin, 1978), p. 269, l. 1.

10 Stevie Smith, 'No Categories', *CP*, p. 258.

11 John Lennard, *The Poetry Handbook*, 2nd edn (Oxford; Oxford University Press, 2005), p. 66.

12 Stevie Smith, 'The Songster', *CP*, p. 30, l. 3.

13 Stevie Smith, 'Le Singe Qui Swing', *CP*, p. 252.

14 *The Holiday*, manuscript copy, Stevie Smith Collection, McFarlin Library, University of Tulsa. See also her letter to Sally Chilver detailing how carefully she notated the transcribed tunes for her poems, 2 January 1948, McFarlin Library.

15 Stevie Smith, 'I love ...', *CP*, p. 498, ll. 5, 6.

16 Stevie Smith, 'How do you see?', *CP*, p. 523, ll. 46, 47.

17 Stevie Smith, 'My Muse', *CP*, p. 405, ll. 3, 4.

18 Stevie Smith, 'The Best Beast of the Fat-Stock Show in Earls Court', *CP*, p. 412, ll. 9–12.

19 See Sandra M. Gilbert, 'Glass Joints: A Meditation of the Line', in Robert Frank and Henry Sayre (eds), *The Line in Postmodern Poetry* (Urbana: University of Illinois Press, 1988), which finds 'Lady Lazarus' 'haunted by iambic pentameter', p. 46.

20 Sylvia Plath, 'Cut', *Collected Poems* (London: Faber, 1981), p. 236, ll. 37–40.

21 Philip Larkin, 'Essential Beauty', *Collected Poems* (London: Faber, 2003), p. 113, ll. 1–6.

22 Philip Larkin, 'Sad Steps', *CP*, p. 144, l. 11.

23 Theodor Adorno, 'Kulturkritik und Gesellschaft', in Nigel Gibson and Andrew Rubin (eds), *Adorno: A Critical Reader* (Oxford: Blackwell, 2002), p. 2.

24 Martin Heidegger, 'What are Poets For?', in *Poetry, Language, Thought* (New York: HarperCollins, 1971), p. 92.

25 Cleanth Brooks, *The Well-Wrought Urn*, 2nd edn (London: Methuen, 1971), p. 159.

26 W. K. Wimsatt, *The Verbal Icon* (London: Methuen, 1954), p. 4.

27 See Wimsatt's *The Verbal Icon* for an extended discussion of these terms.

28   Robert Lowell, 'The Art of Poetry', *A Collection of Critical Essays* (Englewood Cliffs, NJ: Prentice-Hall, 1968), p. 19.

29   M. L. Rosenthal, 'Poetry and Confession', *The Nation*, 19 September 1959, p. 56.

30   Sylvia Plath, 'Daddy', *CP*, p. 223, ll. 27–8.

31   Sylvia Plath, 'Lady Lazarus', *CP*, p. 245, l. 26.

32   Sylvia Plath, 'Fever 103°', *CP*, p. 232, l. 21.

33   Stevie Smith, 'Not Waving But Drowning', *CP*, p. 303, ll. 9–12.

34   Philip Larkin, 'Mr Bleaney', *CP*, p. 81, ll. 27–8.

35   Philip Larkin, 'High Windows', *CP*, p. 129, ll. 2–3, 4.

36   Philip Larkin, 'The Whitsun Weddings', *CP*, p. 94, l. 4.

37   Sylvia Plath, *The Journal of Sylvia Plath 1950–1962* (London: Faber, 2000), p. 208.

38   Philip Larkin, 'Posterity', *CP*, p. 139.

39   Neil Roberts, *Narrative and Voice in Postwar Poetry* (London: Longman, 1994), p. 19.

40   See John Osborne's *Larkin, Ideology and Critical Violence: A Case of Wrongful Conviction* (Basingstoke: Macmillan, 2008) for a lively, iconoclastic defence of Larkin's supposed bigotry and conservative quietism.

41   Stevie Smith, 'Childe Rolandine', *CP*, p. 331, l. 5.

42   Stevie Smith, 'Pretty', *CP*, p. 469, ll. 25–8.

43   Stevie Smith, 'Cock-a-doo', *CP*, p. 536, ll. 1–2.

44   Sylvia Plath, 'Blackberrying', *CP*, p. 168, l. 1.

45   Sylvia Plath, 'Winter Trees', *CP*, p. 258, l. 8.

46   Sylvia Plath, 'Sheep in Fog', *CP*, p. 262, ll. 13–15.

47   John Powell Ward, *The English Line* (Basingstoke: Macmillan, 1991), p. 176.

48   Philip Larkin, 'Talking in Bed', *CP*, p. 100, ll. 5–8.

49   Philip Larkin, 'First Sight', *CP*, p. 107, l. 11.

50   Philip Larkin, 'To the Sea', *CP*, p. 121, l. 30.

51   Stevie Smith, 'Every Lovely Limb's a Desolation', *CP*, p. 342, l. 6–8.

52   Sylvia Plath, 'Magi', *CP*, p. 148, ll. 1–3.

53   Sylvia Plath, 'Medusa', *CP*, p. 225, l. 11.

54   Stevie Smith, 'A Dream of Comparison', *CP*, p. 314, ll. 19–20.

55   Stevie Smith, 'How do you see?', *CP*, p. 517.

56   Stevie Smith, 'Oh Christianity, Christianity', *CP*, p. 417, ll. 39–40.

57   Stevie Smith, 'Admire Cranmer!', *CP*, p. 398.

58   Stevie Smith, 'Magnificent Words', *CP*, p. 493.

59   Stevie Smith, 'The House of Over-Dew', *CP*, p. 560, ll. 144–5.

60   Philip Larkin, 'Church-going', *CP*, p. 58, l. 9.

61   Philip Larkin, 'Water', *CP*, p. 91, ll. 10–13.

62   S. T. Coleridge, 'Kubla Kahn, Or, A Vision in a Dream. A Fragment', *Selected Poems*, ed. Richard Holmes (London: Penguin, 2000), p. 229.

63   Stevie Smith, 'Thoughts about the Person from Porlock', *CP*, p. 385, ll. 7–12.

The Bardic Line: Harrison, Heaney and Hughes

In W. H. Auden's poetic tribute to the Irish poet W. B. Yeats, he famously averred that 'poetry makes nothing happen'.[1] Reading Yeats's life through the lens of his political struggles and his poetic representations of events such as the Easter Uprising of 1916, Auden concludes that 'Mad Ireland hurt you into poetry' (l. 34). This version of events, which finds domestic politics to be both incitement and barrier to the work of the bard, is reconsidered by Seamus Heaney in his 1987 essay 'The Government of the Tongue'.[2]

Given as part of Heaney's T. S. Eliot Memorial Lectures, his public pronouncement challenges Auden's notion of poetry as socially moribund. In its place is an art form which is not 'instrumental or effective' but which nevertheless offers a 'pure concentration' found in no other discursive space. While it isn't a political catalyst, it is far from an exclusive world of sealed aesthetics. Instead, it operates as a mediating language between the public and the private, between the political 'solution' and the self-reflexive sound of a voice in isolation.

This apparent conversation with Auden is deliberate on Heaney's part. Auden's attempt to memorialise Yeats is rendered problematic by Heaney; Auden, reading Yeats through Irish politics, sees him from the perspective of the British establishment rather than as a fellow poet. Heaney's poetic career has been full of similarly deliberate gestures, most famously in 1983, when he wrote the poem 'An Open Letter' in response to being included in a British poetry anthology. The poem rails against his 'green' (i.e. Irish) passport being raised to 'toast *The Queen*'.[3] Yet his public polemical aversion to being elided with a British tradition was not simply prompted by personal anger. As Heaney wrote of the event nearly a decade later:

> My sense of being Irish was simply a given of my life, something that was with me from the start, something reinforced rather than eroded by the experience of living in a Northern Ireland that insisted that it – and I – was British … in the early eighties, we were in the bitter aftermath of dirty protests and hunger strikes, in the middle of the IRA's campaign, and at that polarized moment, the Morrison and Motion book was published. I had the feeling that if my British audience were not kept appraised of my stand-off with the 'British' nomenclature, and indeed if my Unionist readers were not kept reminded of it, I would be guilty of more than evasiveness.[4]

Heaney's inclusion in this very book, which is concerned primarily with British rather than Irish literature is, by extension, equally problematic. Yet what is striking about the reasons he gives for writing the poem is that they are prompted as much by the needs and feelings of his supposed audience as any individual desire. Both his 'British audience' and his 'Unionist readers' expected him to take offence, and to voice his disapproval publicly; he willingly complies with this unspoken request. Not to speak would have been to acquiesce, or to be actively silenced. This acute sense of poets as public figures with responsibilities not just to their poetic practice or their personal ambition but to their audience raises a number of difficulties. As Heaney suggests, the audience is comprised of different, often overlapping, groups of readers with sometimes contradictory ideas about a poet's civic function. Heaney's poetic career, which has seen him complete five years as Professor of Poetry at Oxford University as well as lecture as a Nobel Prize winner, has afforded many opportunities to publicly situate his work, both politically and artistically. Yet, as he suggests here, these are also opportunities for competing expectations to meet, coalesce, or conflict. They are expectations, as he writes in 'Crediting Poetry', 'not of poetry as such but of political positions variously approvable by mutually disapproving groups'.[5]

Heaney's relationship with the British poet Ted Hughes is instructive here. Hughes's work first inspired Heaney to write poetry, and through a series of coedited poetry anthologies, essays on each other's work, and artistic collaborations, they have prompted numerous critical comparisons. Yet while Seamus Heaney's most famous reference to the Queen is to point out he is not one her subjects, Ted Hughes, during his time as Poet Laureate (1984–98), composed verses to celebrate the birthday of the Queen Mother. Poetic practice provides them with parallels, but public personae make them polarised. Might these political and cultural differences offer ways of reading their work, or, as Dillon Johnson suggests, do these divides tell us more about the expediencies of selling poetry to a reading public than 'the apparently antithetical positions of the English Monarchist and the Irish Republican'?[6] The vicissitudes of Hughes's career provide further caveats and qualifications on the efficacy of speaking as a bard. His own controversial part in Sylvia Plath's literary career, and his posthumous editorial control over her work, meant that the 1980s saw him vilified by large sections of the poetry-reading public. Ironically, just as he assumed the country's only national poetry position in 1984, his work was silenced under personal attacks about his treatment of Plath, whose own public persona was shaped by the dramas of self rather than the demands of public service. Hughes's early verse 'Famous Poet' is oddly prophetic here, finding the lionised poet transformed into a caged animal, his work given up to glorious spectacle as he is left to 'blink behind bars at the zoo'.[7]

Although modern readers use the word 'bard' more generally to denote an epic or nationally prized author, such as Shakespeare, the word has its origins in medieval Gaelic and Celtic culture, where it referred to a poet paid by a king to publicly praise him. The competing honour and servitude suggested by the role creates interesting tensions which are echoed in Hughes's and Heaney's careers. While Leeds-born poet Tony Harrison has received less critical attention than Hughes or Heaney, his own sense of a poet's civic vocation provides useful parallels.

He has described all of his varied poetic output for books, readings, theatre, opera houses, and television programmes as 'part of the same quest for a public poetry, though in that word "public" I would never want to exclude inwardness'.[8] Yet the contest between the public and the inward response often provides the catalyst for Harrison's work. When newspaper reports suggested that Harrison was widely tipped for the Laureateship after Hughes's death in 1998, his vitriolic response was a volume entitled *Laureate's Block* (2000). The collection's eponymous poem is dedicated to Queen Elizabeth, but it is a dedication that seeks abdication rather than patronage:

> There should be no successor to Ted Hughes.
> 'The saponaceous qualities of sack'
> are purest poison if paid poets lose
> their freedom as PM's or monarch's hack.[9]

His republican attack on the British monarchy critiques the current system not because poetry should be partisan or apolitical, but because it should never be subservient to the institutions it critiques. The poem also refers to those who have turned down the laureateship, quoting nineteenth-century poet Thomas Gray's refusal of the position and its 'sack' (the sweet wine given as annual payment). While poetry is always a speaking *for* as well as a speaking *to*, Harrison rallies for a poetry more engaged with working people than the engines of power. In an earlier poem, 'An Old Score', Harrison writes of filial conflict as he grows both away from and towards his father. Yet the source of their antagonism focuses particularly on Harrison's chosen career:

> I walk along the street where he dropped dead,
> my hair cut his length now, although I'm called
> *poet*, in my passport.[10]

While here Harrison writes of personal discord rather than political systems, his link of the poet's role to the international symbol of individual identity, the passport, situates him as a civic bard. Like

Heaney's provocatively green passport, which challenged his inclusion in a British poetry anthology, Harrison's passport offers an official badge of public affiliation.

Biographical incident, critical reception, and civic position all provide anecdotal links between these three poets; their choice of genres and media underscore their sense of themselves in a public, bardic tradition. All three poets have translated classical and contemporary European poetry, allowing them to explore the narrative and the epic over and above the lyric. All three have been involved in theatrical collaborations, voicing their work in public in a very literal sense. The traditions of poetic drama and narrative verse have been important in all their oeuvres. For these very reasons, Harrison, Hughes, and Heaney have often looked outside the predominant British movements of the period, excavating Anglo-Saxon elegies, Greek epigrams, or contemporary Eastern European verse to inform their writing. As if mindful of the need to root themselves in a sense of place, all three have turned to the geology of their native landscapes, mining them for antecedent traditions which will allow them to speak back to their predecessors as well as out to their audiences. These complementary formal choices suggest three poets whose decisions about the public role of poetry make their aesthetic decisions for them. However, that same public forum offers scrutiny as well as a listening audience. As Heaney notes, the dangers of a 'professing poet' are manifest; what begin as personal and urgent clarion calls soon become 'familiar points of reference, and may even attain the force of prescriptions'.[11] Their own work dramatises these very dilemmas.

The Necessities of Translation

For all three poets, translation offers a way forwards as well as a gesture to the past. Heaney reads the British interest in translated verse as an admission that our nuclear security and apparent immunity from many of the terrors of the twentieth century have lessened the efficacy of our collective experience: '[c]onsequently, we are all the more susceptible to translations which arrive like messages from those holding their own much, much further down the road not taken by us – because, happily, it was a road not open to us.'[12] Heaney's explanation hints at a fetishisation of the tattered poetic remains of countries in crisis, where to publish at all is a politically significant act. The already secure alleviate their own guilt about their silent part in these bloody histories by celebrating a poetry whose very existence is a testament to that struggle. The work of the Romanian poet Paul Célan or Russian poet Marina Tsvetaeva spring to mind here, both of whom were translated and republished in volumes such as *The Penguin Book of German Verse* (1957) and *The Penguin Book of Russian Verse* (1965). British appropriation of Irish verse offers a similar parallel. The recently decolonised are invited to speak to an audience ready to be exonerated for their part in the process. In this context, the appointment of both Seamus Heaney and Paul Muldoon to the post of Oxford Professor of Poetry is recent years is telling.

Hughes offers similar paper trails of his literary tastes through his early translation works. While later collections such as *Tales from Ovid* (1997) found Hughes drawing attention to translation itself as an act of poetic engagement, he offers up translations of the Hungarian poet János Pilinszky's work in 1976 as mere gestures which 'will have served their purpose if they serve as pointers, to help a reader re-imagine what those originals must be'.[13] Harrison, too, valorises works from Eastern Europe, with translation acting as a spur for revitalising English poetry. In a communist country where 'the normal aspirations of a writer's work are blocked by censorship',[14] translation is given a renewed political urgency. As with Heaney, translation is also an opportunity to explore a history and heritage. As the prefatory note to the Faber edition of Harrison's *Mysteries* play cycle has it, his involvement in the 1985 Royal National Theatre production was as 'a Yorkshire poet who came to read the meter and to monitor the preservation of the plays' Northern character'.[15] Here the poet-translator – self-effacingly aligned with the meter-reader – makes no claims for the centrality of his role, but rather acts as a barometer of fidelity. Just as translated poetry with its record of terrifying experience might rejuvenate and shake up the suburban comforts of British poetry, so here might the reliably 'Northern' poet offer a marker of the authentic for the Mystery play, the medieval form kept alive through local tradition rather than academic canonicity. Medieval Mystery plays were usually based on Biblical and liturgical texts, and were performed by town guilds or local tradespeople (the name 'mystery' comes from the Medieval Latin *misterium*, which denotes a trade guild or company). Harrison retained the importance of an indigenous working-class community drama in his 1977 adaptation, which opened with modern traders – shopkeepers and plumbers – explaining their parts in the cycle. Performed as processional plays, with the audience standing in for the crowd in the crucifixion scenes, *The Mysteries* returned a civic theatre to its roots. Yet ironically, Harrison's popular reimagining of the plays proved instrumental in returning them to the British theatre repertoire.

The concept of 'fidelity' for Heaney, Hughes, and Harrison is problematic in other ways too. Harrison is the only one with a university training in classics and linguistics, a scholarship boy still reaping the conflicting benefits of the postwar expansion of education. Yet despite, or perhaps because of, his abilities as a linguist, his 'translations' often take the greatest liberties with the original, faithful in spirit rather than in the particulars. As he remarks, tellingly, of the act of translation: '[t]ranslations are not built to survive though their original survives through translation's many flowerings and decays… The translation is fixed but reinvigorates its original by its decay.'[16] This notion of decay informs his own translating practice. His *Palladas: Poems* (1975) re-envisions conception itself, unpicking layers of past facsimiles to reappropriate the notion of origin:

> Think of your conception, you'll soon forget
> what Plato puffs you up with, all that
> 'immortality' and 'divine life' stuff.
>
> *Man, why dost thou think of Heaven? Nay*
> *Consider thine origins in common clay*
>
> 's one way of putting it but not blunt enough.
>
> Think of your father, sweating, drooling, drunk,
> you, his spark of lust, his spurt of spunk.[17]

His translations offer an alternative to the 'one way of putting it'; in a rhythm often as blunt as the diction, Harrison creates a deliberately iconoclastic and anachronistic voice. In the original Greek poem, Palladas instructs the reader to leave off Platonic musing to consider the scatological physicality of copulation. Harrison cleverly represents Palladas's own mockery by juxtaposing modern colloquial diction with a feigned Shakespearean idiom: '*Man, why dost thou think of Heaven?*'. In Harrison's version, language can be evasive and abstract or brawny and blunt, and his poem works by emphasising the disparity between the two.

The neoclassical phrasings of the seventeenth century here are quoted and parodied through their juxtaposition with the glottal-stopped demotic (everyday speech) of urban Leeds. Lofty abstractions on the idea of conception – a literal conceptualising of the act of creation – are reduced to the Anglo-Saxon brute fact of 'spunk'. A similar tactic is at work in his collection *US Martial* (1981), where the epigrammatic Greek poet Martial is reimagined in modern-day New York, as in 'The Joys of Separation':

> *She* wants more and more and more new men in her.
> *He* finally finishes *Anna Karenina*.[18]

Again, the deictic (or direct) language of the poem points to the contrast between the opening depiction of a modern-day woman with a rapacious sexual appetite and the subsequent undermining context, which finds she is in fact a famous literary heroine being rediscovered by a contemporary reader. Harrison's work forces its readers to reassess its notions of taste and decorum, and the collective whitewashing of classical heritage by a post-Enlightenment world of gentility and privilege. As he recalls in his poem 'Classics Society', translation enters his life as an opportunity to impose class boundaries and reinstate the legitimacy of Received Pronunciation:

> We boys can take old Hansards and translate
> the British Empire into SPQR
> but nothing demotic or too up-to-date,
> and *not* the English that I speak at home,

not Hansard standards, and if Antonius
spoke like a delinquent Latin back in Rome
he'd probably get gamma double minus.[19]

Translation has offered British audiences only half of its insights, suggests Harrison; the hegemonies of the upper class seek to make the classics available only to the small proportion of the population who recognise their demotic in the rigid rules of Standard English.

Heaney's translations similarly reshape the orthodoxies of the British literary canon, excavating a specifically Celtic literary heritage in *Sweeney Astray* (1983). The poem is based on the ancient Celtic poem *Buile Shuibhne*, which tells the story of Shuibhne (Sweeney), an Irish King who is cursed with madness when he mocks Christian ritual in battle. In the poem, his madness is represented by his transformation into a bird. Efforts to curb his insanity by his kinsmen are then also efforts to clip his wings. His plight becomes a metaphor for translation itself, destined to encircle a world to which it can never return.[20] As the speaker's quatrains suggest, translation becomes a kind of haunting, a return which is also an act of spectral renewal. While Harrison's works use deliberately anachronistic disjuncture to suggest social inequalities and literary hierarchies in modern-day Britain, Heaney's translations have the fidelity of a nonlinguist; a celebrity poet working from a crib who cannot afford to take liberties.

The laudable thematic concern of Heaney's translated works is freedom, although they may yet be too free. While they never stray far from the original, they are usually mediated by a previous translation. Paul Turner reads Seamus Heaney's verse translation of Sophocles, *The Cure at Troy* (1990), as a disturbing precedent, suggesting a future where 'literal, or even faithful, translation becomes almost a term of contempt, and no work of classical literature is ever read'.[21] Yet despite Turner's anxiety, the work barely announces itself as a translation. Much of its relevance to the contemporary political situation in Ireland suggests that Heaney, like Harrison, is mining the past for precedents. It depicts an ancient Greece where victims are devoted to showing their wounds, and perpetrators of injustice always find expedient ways to defend their decisions. In its opening discussion of poetry and its power to comment on contemporary events, *The Cure at Troy* also questions the efficacy of politicised art. Yet Heaney's own production notes are reluctant to offer the work up as a modern political allegory, maintaining that whilst 'there are parallels, and wonderfully suggestive ones' between 'certain characters in the play and certain parties and conditions in Northern Ireland', the 'parallels are richly incidental rather than essential to the version.'[22] While all three poets highlight contemporary allusion through their translation work, they balance precariously between self-promotion and self-effacement, from Harrison's image of the meter-reader to Heaney's profession of 'incidental' analogy. Rather, as we will see below, translation becomes a way of mapping the geologies of language itself.

Geologies of Language

For writers seeking a poetic language that turns away from the dominant British canon or from the binaries of political and social debate, the earth itself becomes the treasure-house of language. It is no coincidence that Seamus Heaney's collected poems are entitled *Opened Ground*: much of the work of these writers attempts to exhume the very soil from national boundaries or feudal ownership, as if to clear a space for a new dialogue. For Hughes, this comes primarily through a deliberate return to the Anglo-Saxon. His poetic diction eschews the Latinate or the Norman to carry the reader back to an elemental Englishness, as in his poem 'Wind' from his first collection *The Hawk in the Rain* (1957).[23] Here, Hughes depersonalises the personifying simile, so the wind becomes more alien, rather than more human, through its comparison with a 'mad eye'. While this is a poem of the elements, its archaisms – as in the Anglo-Saxon kenning 'blade-light' * – reinvigorate the process of description. These are Old English formations recharged for battle.

The hills are transformed into 'new places' through the excavations into the rich seams of an older language. Hughes's 1967 essay 'Poetry

---

* A kenning is a compound phrase which replaces a common noun, and formed the basis of much Anglo-Saxon poetry. A 'people-carrier' as a synonym for a car is a Modern English example.

in the Making' tellingly insists on the use of 'living' words in poetry; words that are immediately tactile, intensely visual, or onomatopoeic, challenging the turn towards the abstract.[24] Although Hughes rarely uses blank verse, his poetry is often alliterative, as in the above passage, a phonic link back to an earlier, oral tradition. When a human 'I' makes a rare incursion into Hughes's early work, as in the poem 'Wodwo', it is a primitive Neanderthal speaker that is invoked.[25] As the speaker attempts to situate himself in relation to the natural world around him, it is language and the act of naming that prompts the realisation of difference. Despite his primitive perception, the speaker also articulates the modern human dilemma: how is the desire for freedom reconcilable with the need to be rooted and grounded? Even as the speaker asserts there are no threads 'fastening' him, the Old English provenance of the word 'fasten' anchors his querulous interjections.

Heaney is able to reclaim Hughes from his monarchism through his use of language; for Heaney, Hughes's work traces: 'the stark outline and vitality of the Anglo-Saxon that paid into the Middle English alliterative tradition and then went underground to sustain the folk poetry, the ballads, and the ebullience of Shakespeare and the Elizabethans'. He describes it as 'an England as King Lear's heath which now becomes a Yorkshire moor.'[26] Yet the sense of the Northern dialect as offering an alternative vernacular tradition to English verse applies to Harrison's work too. At its most surreal, this takes the form of Harrison reimagining the Northeast into unthinkable foreignness in 'Newcastle is Peru'. The poem takes a conceit from the metaphysical poet John Cleveland* at face value, and constructs an alternative understanding of the city as the speaker traces the body of the city 'like an endless maze'.[27] Hughes's diction summons up Yorkshire rather than London; Harrison makes those competing dialect (and so dialectical) traditions a subject of his poetry itself. As in the Cornish epigram which completes his poem 'National Trust', 'the tongueless man gets his land took';[28] the ability

---

* The poet John Cleveland (1613–58) spent time in the Northeast after the English Civil War when it is believed he wrote 'News from Newcastle' (1651), which uses the metaphor 'Newcastle is Peru' to argue that the city is as advanced as the ancient Aztec civilisations.

to speak and the social cache of how you speak not only defines man's relationship with society, but also permits his right to the land itself. Like Hughes, Harrison argues for a living language, but looks for its vitality less through a return to the Anglo-Saxon word-hoard than a greater attention to the regional varieties of modern vernacular English. Self-styled 'preservers' of the English language receive short shrift in Harrison's work, as in 'Art & Extinction':

> The struggle to preserve once spoken words
> from already too well-stuffed taxonomies
> is a bit like Audubon's when painting birds,
> whose method an admirer said was this:
> *Kill 'em, wire'em, paint 'em, kill a fresh 'un!*[29]

Recalling the fastidious taxonomies of the American painter John James Audubon (1785–1851) whose animals had to be stuffed before they could be captured in art, Harrison imagines a conservative approach to the language which is cyclical and fatal. Like Hughes, Harrison sees language everywhere, but more often as a form of social branding than a sign of natural splendour. In 'Marked with D.', the poet speaker recalls his baker father and their subsequent estrangement. While his father's daily language rituals involved marking loaves according to their weight and ingredients, his own poetic practice divides them irrevocably:

> I get it all from Earth my daily bread
> But he hungered for release from mortal speech
> that kept him down, the tongue that weighed like lead.[30]

Frequently, the older generation in Harrison's poems lack the confidence in their living vernacular to articulate their desires. Language becomes a barrier rather than a bridge; it is a passport they do not possess. The new generation can learn a set of phrases that will assure their passage to the middle class, but it will render communication with the past impossible.

Like Harrison, Heaney's work draws on childhood memories, and struggles to situate the poet in relation to his reticent ancestors yet, as

Sandie Byrne has noted, in Heaney's poetry 'the inarticulate are silent rather than silenced, grudging of speech, and their economy makes the poet feel garrulous in his eloquence'.[31] Heaney's poem 'Clearances' marries Hughes's need to return to elemental beginnings with Harrison's consciousness of language as a social determinant in its depiction of a prodigal son's uneasy relationship with his own vocabulary.[32] His title 'Clearances' also refers to the land clearances in the Highlands in the eighteenth and nineteenth centuries, which saw Gaelic clans evicted from their homes by the landowners. A violent part of our cultural history echoes the painful rupture between father and son.

Yet more often in Heaney's poetry, the language is handed on without division. In 'Anahorish', Heaney recalls Hughes's preoccupation with naming and the living process of language, recreating rural Irish villages from the phonics of their names alone.[33] Here language interacts with its landscape as an open exchange, a 'vowel-meadow', rather than an elemental primitivism. Only later in the 'after-image' come the traces of human habitation, with the gentle sway of the evening lanterns. This 'after-image' might have more ominous historical undercurrents – the nineteenth century saw the English government enforcing the teaching of English in schools, and Anglicising Gaelic towns and place names – but this subtext is never made explicit in the poem. The phonic quality of 'Anahorish' hovers somewhere between the land itself and the community that agreed on its name.

Heaney returns to the Neanderthal utterances of Hughes's 'Wodwo' in his brilliant series of 'Bog' poems. Like his early poem 'Digging', which finds an analogy between the community of peat-diggers he grew up with and writing as a form of excavation, these works voice the subterranean possibilities of a land in conflict. In 'Bog Queen', the underground speaker situates herself as part and process of the land itself.[34] Her body, both decaying and preserved, recalling Harrison's definition of translation, becomes a sort of palimpsest, a page that has been scraped clean and used again. The geological shifts and ruptures in the earth's history are mapped on her body, a human form of trunk rings leaving a tangible text for the reader to discern. Here, the body itself is broken down into the debris of the soil, and resurfaces as a prehistoric language of its own. Heaney's 'Bog' poems return to the rich secrets of the past to discover a language without region, dialect, or social demarcation. Her words suggest the regal – as in the French loan word 'demesne' – and the Anglo-Saxon – with the kenning 'turf-face' – yet the notion of her body as 'braille' allows her to absorb and combine these various influences. However, elsewhere, his work is as acutely aware as Harrison's of the political boundaries and frontiers our modern tongue rails against and reaffirms. In his prose poem 'England's Difficulty', Heaney tracks his progress from country to country not as a geological explorer but as a marked man.[35] Language becomes a series of secret codes and passwords. Even in the speaker's canny defiance of the policed state in this poem, the act of excavating a language has broken down into personal invasion. Consequently, the act of poetic communication must tread a difficult line between renewing and reneging on its own traditional vocabularies.

The Bardic Voice

The centrality of the bardic voice in the three poets' work is closely related to this notion of a buried, subterranean language. Much of their poetry defines its relation to the reader in terms of orality, in other words the sound the words produce when read aloud. The most successful poetry anthology of the postwar period, *The Mersey Sound* (1967), collected together the work of three Liverpool poets whose performances became synonymous with the Beatles and Mod culture. Yet orality for Hughes, Heaney, and Harrison is less a determination to return to a performed poetry than to recall the oral tradition their printed work looks back towards. Hughes's 'The Thought-Fox' suggests an analogy between the quick movements of the fox, the working of the conscious mind, and the production of a poem. Tellingly, the poem concludes with a reference to the printed page,[36] this is a mechanical process seemingly abstracted from its author, with no sense of an audible voice. Yet elsewhere, the work of these writers seems more anxious about the gap between the printed and the performed poem.

For Hughes, the vernacular oral tradition can be read in two opposing ways: '[o]n the one hand, [the British ballad] is the indigenous form of narrative song, emerging from pure melody as no other poetic form does, and tending ... to archetypal themes opening backwards into religious myth', but '[o]n the other hand, it is the indigenous popular humdrum form of poetic narration, simply a way of telling ordinary though striking tales.'[37] His own work sits between these two categories, contesting the claims of both definitions. The notion of 'pure melody' is anaesthetised and scrutinised with particular incision in Hughes's poetry, sceptical of the term's Romantic evasion. John Keats's 'Ode to a Nightingale' finds the bird's song is as beautiful as death, but the speaker holds himself back from complete immersion in it. In 'Skylarks', Hughes returns to an avine subject that denotes fluid and full-throated song, yet the poem finds the subject nearer to the malevolent than the sublime.[38] Here, the skylark's song is more of a punishment than a gift, and its subsequent swoop back down to the hill is full of sharp streams (*CP*, p. 175, l. 86). The choice between death and further ascent is a mandatory imposition rather than a willed desire here; this is a natural song with a gun to its head. Other individual poems by Hughes juggle with similar contradictions: 'Singers' celebrates communal singing in working-class culture but ends with a barbed comment on the loss of this culture;[39] 'Thrushes' finds another avine specimen that is more mechanical than real;[40] 'Ballad from a Fairy Tale' tells the story of an angelic visitation, yet its celebration of the proclamation and the spoken word is undermined by the meaning of the divine message, which remains unwritten.[41]

Yet it is in Hughes's narrative work that the tensions he outlines between the ballad as 'archetypal myth' and 'humdrum form of poetic narration' are writ large. His prose poem sequence *Gaudete* (1977) is built around the narrator Lumb, a speaker full of sexual compulsions and morbid desire. Hughes navigates the world of suppressed emotion and conflicting impulses through Lumb's relationship with his twin. This pivoting is reflected in the movement between poetry and prose: the work opens with a prose introduction before moving into a narrative of poems; another prose insertion leads to a final poetic epilogue. This construction of the prose poem as both poetry and prose, rather than a fusion of the two, suggests a refusal to cohere. A similar tension operates throughout the work in the contest between spoken and written dialogue. As Lumb suggests in the closing epilogue: speech is now an impossible passageway (a 'fistula') between thinking and communication, as the gnarly primacy of the spoken word is subsumed into the irrelevance of 'chat'.[42] Words themselves are constrictive, a means of closing down the possibility of the voice. Grammar becomes a science of cryogenics, as the cry of the bird refuses to 'chill' into syntax. Hughes's obsession with a primeval nature suggests an easy affinity with the oral tradition, but in his poetry the primitive frequently offers barriers to direct speech.

By contrast, Heaney's interest in the Celtic tradition finds a culture still alive to the musical possibilities of speech and the fundamental role poetry plays in Irish communities. His poem 'The Singer's House' recalls the Irish poet Louis MacNeice in its reference to Carrickfergus, but replaces his displaced ambivalence with a rousing assurance. The poem is unequivocal in its final, guileless assertion that we still believe what we hear.[43] Political propaganda cannot dull the ear's enraptured response to melody. 'A New Song' finds the Irish vernacular similarly in the ascendant.[44] The politically sensitised language becomes only more vocal in its need for self-preservation here. The poem itself performs the rousing and resounding song that its own stanzas call for. Heaney's birds, like Hughes's, sometimes deviate from the script, but here their idiosyncrasies are recorded with an anecdotal generosity rather than an eerie sense of presentiment, as in Heaney's recollection of the nightingale in 'Serenades', whose rackety warbling is unexpectedly discordant for an Irish bird.[45]

While Heaney's celebration of the speaking voice combines political and lyrical agency, the efficacy of that voice is often threatened by social institutions or larger governmental systems. 'The Canton of Expectation' in his collection *The Haw Lantern* (1987) records with some ambivalence the effects of encroaching literacy on his rural upbringing.[46] While the turn from the agrarian to the prescriptive is marked with a reassuring vocabulary of 'paving' and 'causeways', suggesting a continuity of rural experience, the reader is left to wonder at the ethics of sacrificing the milkmaid's dream, never transcribed, for the schematic annotations of the literary canon. Elsewhere, as in Heaney's autobiographical poetic sequence *Singing School*, the young poet maintains a winking irreverence for the dictates of Standard English. The title of one of these poems, 'The Ministry of Fear',[47] alludes to Graham Greene's 1944 spy novel, but here the expectation of oppression and malevolent control is confounded. Although there is an implied conflict between personal expression and the law(n)s of Received Pronunciation in this poem, the speaker treats the contradiction with a shoulder-shrugging impudence. The tension propagates his poetry, rather than stymies it, as suggested by the neologism of 'innovated' to describe his use of rhyme.

Yet the even-handed dissolution of this conflict is never possible in the work of Tony Harrison. His poem 'Them & [Uz]', taken from the sonnet sequence *The School of Eloquence* (1976), is as full of innovation as Heaney's 'The Ministry of Fear', and also full of invective, as the following extract suggests:

> I chewed up Littererchewer and spat the bones
> into the lap of dozing Daniel Jones,
> dropped the initials I'd been harried as
> and used my *name* and my own voice: [uz] [uz] [uz],
> ended sentences with by, with, from,
> and spoke the language that I spoke at home.
> …
> You can tell the Receivers where to go
> (and not aspirate it) once you know
> Wordsworth's *matter/water* are full rhymes,
> [uz] can be loving as well as funny.
>
> My one mention in the *Times*
> automatically made Tony Anthony.[48]

Like the 'buckling' words of the speaker in Ted Hughes's *Gaudete*, Harrison forgoes prescribed speech for mastication and expulsion. While his poem adheres rigidly to the sonnet form rather than a vernacular ballad, it deconstructs the phonic assumptions of the language. Wordsworth's poetry is revitalised with the knowledge that it was conceived of in Yorkshire dialect, where 'water' and 'matter' are full rhymes. Literary history with its institutional prejudices has transformed the phonics of Wordsworth's verse in the interests of conformity. Harrison's use of dialect shows more self-awareness than Wordsworth, but must mark his '[Uz]' with the phonetic clue of the linguist, knowing his reader will default to Standard English. Grammar and dialect, as with Heaney, return to their roots here, but with an angry iconoclasm rather than a furtive transgression. Literature itself becomes an exercise in distracted chewing – 'Littererchewer' – for the unthinking bodies that rigidly enforce the hegemonies of written English. As Harrison notes acerbically, even the poet's name – Tony – will be transformed into the upper-class Anthony in the interests of formal journalism. The poetic return to the bardic voice – whether through the elemental cries of the medieval, the musical traditions of a national culture, or the socialist necessities of political diatribe – offer all three poets inclusion in a longer tradition, yet often replace continuity with a tense incongruence.

In part, these tensions are resolved when their verse moves from the page to the theatre. All three poets have worked collaboratively with musicians, directors, and dramatists during their career. Much of Harrison's early work is for the stage, from his version of Molière's *The Misanthrope* (1973) to his rhyming iambic adaptation of Racine in *Phaedra Britannica* (1975). The latter is particularly effective in altering the stresses of its metre to the meaning, as in Thomas's prophetic foretelling of chaos: 'Reason's unseated. / Nobody can rein runaway passions into line again.'[49] Harrison never compromises clarity here, but shows chaos itself eating away at the regular iambics. Much of his work has also looked to contemporary music – he provided libretti for Harrison Birtwistle's *The Bartered Bride* (1978) and *Bow Down* (1977). His new version of Aeschylus's *Oresteia* for the National Theatre in 1981, meanwhile, prompted a revealing comment on the lure of poetic drama: '[a]s a Northerner I am drawn to the physicality of Aeschylus' language. I relish its cragginess and momentum.' He recalls that at school he was 'never allowed to read verse out loud because of [his] Yorkshire accent'. While his 'translation of Aeschylus isn't what you'd call deliberate revenge, it is most emphatically a rediscovery of the dignity of the accent.'[50] Aeschylus not only dignifies the demotic, the language of the common man, as in Harrison's recreation of the Northern Mystery plays in 1985, but offers a classical tradition built on the tensions between anarchy and civilisation.

Harrison's project of 'revenge' rebrands his 'barbarian' tongue as lyrical, classical, eloquent. It is on the stage, rather than on the page, that the shackles of an inarticulate heredity are removed.

Ted Hughes's work with Peter Brook during the 1960s and 1970s provides useful parallels with Harrison, from his adaptation of Seneca's *Oedipus* (1968) to the large-scale performance of *Orghast* (1971), which was produced for the International Centre for Theatre Research. Yet in these works, Hughes found a language that could not be rendered in conventional prose. In contrast to Harrison, who created a direct and concise version of classical tragedy with his use of the demotic, Hughes turned away from a comprehensible dialect altogether, using the theatre to explore a language of gesture and symbol. This led, in *Orghast*, to Hughes creating his own signifying system. The Promethean myth* that underpins the narrative is represented in a demarcated, controlled vocabulary:

> CHORUS: AMEM
> MAN: GAVE
> CHORUS: NEMEM
> MOA: GAVE[51]

In this reading of the theatre as a semiotic space, the actors themselves become another signifying system. For Hughes, the challenges of poetry in the theatre are not finding the metre and diction that makes dramatic verse possible, but rather sensitising the actor to 'the poetic reality of a situation',[52] attempting to return him or her to the selfless world of an innocent signifier. Here, Lumb's fistula speech in *Gaudete* becomes analogous to all poetic pronouncement. Language, representation, and the efficacy of the speaking voice continue to define the work itself. In this sense, the dramatic works of Heaney, Hughes, and Harrison are distillations of their own poetic practice. As in Heaney's *The Cure at Troy* (1990), the poet's public arena is not the lecture hall or the Sunday broadsheet, but rather the stage. All three poets

---

* In Ancient Greek mythology, Prometheus is a wily figure who stole fire from Zeus to give to the mortals. He was punished by being chained to a rock where an eagle would come and eat his liver, only to return the next day when his liver had grown back to eat it again.

116

are then equally provoked, inspired, and shaped by the demands of a public poetry, whether through their interest in translation, their acute sense of the responsibilities of the artist in society, or the centrality of dramatic spoken verse to their work. Their notion of the poet is informed as much by their civic role as their individual preoccupations. Though, at moments in each of their careers, this has introduced a tension in their work, or a conflict between their critical reception and their public persona, as Harrison notes, 'silence and poetry have their own reserves'.[53]

Extended Commentary: Harrison, *v.* (1985)

Harrison's poem *v.*, which found its first audience on Channel 4 rather than in a volume of poetry, defines the changing parameters of the modern poet. Both its critical reception and its own generic exploration of the narrative poem refract the changing perceptions of poetry as a public medium. It opens in a cemetery, recalling Thomas Gray's 'Elegy in a Country Church-Yard', but soon departs from the stoicism of Gray's 1751 poem. The 'v.' of some football graffiti by his father's grave begins the speaker's dissection of class conflict and binary opposition. The poem's title suggests a pun on the words verses and versus, suggesting a poetry that is iconoclastic and oppositional. Versus offers both division and a necessary form of dissent:

> These Vs are all the versus of life
> from LEEDS v. DERBY, Black/White
> and (as I've known to my cost) man v. wife,
> Communist v. Fascist, Left v. Right,[54]

While the poem's first stanza gestures to the inward, with Harrison noting his own grave won't be with 'the family dead', it moves immediately to consider Harrison as a public entity, situating himself within a bardic tradition of Byron and Wordsworth. Appropriately, the initial reaction to the poem was sensational public hysteria. When tabloid papers published expletive-filled lines with disgusted headlines prior to the broadcast of the filmed poem, transmission was held back until 11pm; it was finally aired on Channel 4 on 25 January 1985. As Byrne notes, 'it seemed as though every journalist in Britain was taking a stance, *v.* or v *v.*',[55] pointing out that the programme was only cleared for transmission because it would have been impossible to bleep or cut. The furore provoked much media interest in Harrison, but also suggested the contradictions and limitations inherent in the role of the public poet. Hughes's occasional verses of royal patronage provoked indifference or embarrassed evasions by literary critics, while Harrison's direct dialogue with the mass media of television suggested that this poem would be remembered more for its four-letter words than its political force.

Yet the poem not only finds the figure of the poet 'going public', but considers the way in which language itself is appropriated, managed, or vandalised by society, as in Harrison's description of the depleted West Yorkshire mines:

> Some, where kids use aerosols, use giant signs
> to let the people know who's forged their letters
> like PRI CE O WALES above West Yorkshire mines
> (no prizes for who nicked the missing letters!) (p. 264, ll. 132–5)

Here, the vandalism isn't the mindless work of hooligans, or the defamatory gestures of a republican, but, as Harrison wryly notes, the National Front (the NF). The physical manifestation of language here suggests both the decaying industry of Harrison's native Yorkshire and the politicisation of language itself. It becomes a contested ground in a way that mirrors the poem's own vexed reception. Similarly, the 'fucks' and 'cunts' Harrison finds littering the tombstone in the graveyard are not paraded for sensational appeal but dissected within the poem itself:

> What is it that these crude words are revealing?
> What is it that this aggro act implies?
> Giving the dead their xenophobic feeling
> Or just a *cri-de-coeur* because man dies?

So what's a cri-de-coeur, *cunt? Can't you speak*
the language that yer mam spoke. Think of 'er!
Can yer only get yer tongue round fucking Greek?
Go and fuck yerself with cri-de-coeur! (p. 265, ll. 160–7)

Here the poet's reasoned empathy with the apparently mindless graffiti is disrupted by the internal voice or ventriloquised response from his imagined addressee, a racist skinhead. The poem's direct language and parallel syntax is designed for immediate impact on its television audience, any deviation from colloquial diction becomes another form of language transgression, as in the *cri-de-coeur*. For Harrison's projected addressee, the imported French phrase, with its connotations of impassioned plea, is a bourgeois affectation, and so another form of cultural graffiti, desecrating the 'purity' of Anglo-Saxon. At both these points, the poem anticipates its audience, the philistinism and disgust of the addressee here mimicking the outrage of the tabloid newspapers at the poem's expletives. Racist and sexist language can be aerosolled through a public cemetery, but its use in the sanitised world of television offends a very different notion of audience. Yet as the dialogue between poet and skinhead graffiti artist continues, their argument is absorbed into self-division. When the skinhead argues he doesn't need a working-class poet to represent him with his *'poufy words'* and that he can *'write mi own'* (p. 267, l. 270), Harrison challenges him to sign his name under the graffiti he is apparently so proud of. In that act, the skinhead is revealed as Harrison himself.

The poem's reception and interrogation of language already situates the work as a political gesture; Harrison's reference to the National Front, the government programme of mining closures, and the muddled postwar policy to 'educate' the working class similarly locate the poem at the intersection of the meritocracy and the suffocating control of the state. While sceptical of the benefits of conformity, the speaker can only justify an art that attempts to heal division. He returns to the domestic comforts of his wife, but the turn to the interior finds no solace in self-sufficiency. Instead, the television news reports the couple watch only highlight the political divisions their comfortable marriage belies:

As the coal with reddish dust cools in the grate
on the late-night national news we see
police v. pickets at a coke-plant gate,
old violence and old disunity.

The map that's colour-coded Ulster/Eire's
flashed on again as almost every night.
Behind a tiny coffin with two bearers
men in masks with arms show off their might. (p. 268, ll. 389–96)

Irish terrorism claims the life of a child as fights rage on between trade union leaders and the Tory government on miners' rights. Even as the television exploits the terrible pathos of the infanticide with the 'tiny coffin', an unwanted image of dominance emerges from the 'men in masks' in the background, a further sort of ambivalent division. Although the poet loses his argument with the skinhead, and seeks the comfort of home life only to be reminded of the perpetual conflicts in the world outside, perhaps the only solace for the public poet is that the same television that offers nightly bulletins of disunity to its brain-dead audiences is the one that will be broadcasting the poem itself.

Notes

1   W. H. Auden, 'In Memory of W.B. Yeats', *Collected Poems* (London: Faber, 1994), p. 237, l. 36.

2   Seamus Heaney, 'The Government of the Tongue', *Government of the Tongue* (London: Faber, 1998), p. 108.

3   Seamus Heaney, 'An Open Letter', *Ireland's Field Day* (Notre Dame, IN: University of Notre Dame Press, 1986), p. 25, l. 8.

4   Seamus Heaney, 'Through-other places, through-other times: the Irish poet and Britain', *Finders Keepers: Selected Prose: 1971–2001* (London: Faber, 2002), p. 368.

5   Seamus Heaney, 'Crediting Poetry', *Opened Ground: Poems 1966–1996* (hereafter *OG*) (London: Faber, 1998), p. 451.

6   Dillon Johnson, *The Poetic Economies of England and Ireland, 1912–2000* (Basingstoke: Palgrave, 2001), p. 195.

7 Ted Hughes, 'Famous Poet', *Collected Poems* (hereafter *CP*) (London: Faber, 2003), p. 23, l. 40.
8 Tony Harrison, quoted in Neil Astley (ed.), *Bloodaxe Critical Anthologies 1: Tony Harrison* (Newcastle: Bloodaxe, 1991), p. 10.
9 Tony Harrison, 'Laureate's Block', *Collected Poems* (hereafter *CP*), (London: Viking, 2007) p. 329, ll. 43–6.
10 Tony Harrison, 'An Old Score', *CP*, p. 150, ll. 3–5.
11 Seamus Heaney, 'On poetry and professing', *Finders Keepers*, p. 70.
12 Seamus Heaney, 'The Impact of Translation', *Finders Keepers*, pp. 43–4.
13 Ted Hughes, 'János Pilinszky', *Winter Pollen: Occasional Prose* (London: Faber, 2005), p. 236.
14 Tony Harrison, 'Interview', *Bloodaxe I*, p. 236.
15 As quoted in Joe Kelleher, *Tony Harrison* (Plymouth: Northcote House, 1996), p. 33.
16 As quoted in Tony Harrison, 'Preface to *The Misanthrope*', in *Bloodaxe I*, p. 146.
17 Tony Harrison, *Palladas: Poems*, *CP*, p. 79, ll. 1–8.
18 Tony Harrison, *US Martial*, *CP*, p. 103, ll. 1–2.
19 Tony Harrison, 'Classics Society', *CP*, p. 130, ll. 6–12.
20 Seamus Heaney, *Sweeney Astray* (Derry: Field Day, 1983), p. 65, section 67.
21 Paul Turner, '*The Cure at Troy*: Sophocles or Heaney?', in Ashby Bland Crowder and Jason David Hall (eds), *Seamus Heaney: Poet, Critic, Translator*, pp. 121–36, p. 135.
22 Seamus Heaney, '*The Cure at Troy*: production notes in no particular order', in M. McDonald and J. M. Walton (eds), *Amidst Our Troubles: Irish Versions of Greek Tragedy* (London: Methuen, 2002), p. 175.
23 Ted Hughes, 'Wind', *CP*, p. 36, ll. 5–8.
24 Ted Hughes 'Poetry in the Making', *Winter Pollen*, p. 12.
25 Ted Hughes, 'Wodwo', *CP*, p. 183, ll. 8–15.
26 Seamus Heaney, 'Englands of the mind', *Finders Keepers*, p. 79.
27 Tony Harrison, 'Newcastle is Peru', *CP*, p. 64, l. 34.
28 Tony Harrison, 'National Trust', *CP*, p. 131, l. 16.
29 Tony Harrison, 'Art & Extinction', *CP*, p. 204, ll. 1–5.
30 Tony Harrison, 'Marked with D.', *CP*, p. 168, ll. 10–12.
31 Sandie Byrne, H, *v*. & O: The Poetry of *Tony Harrison* (Manchester: Manchester University Press, 1998), p. 38, ll. 56–7.
32 Seamus Heaney, 'Clearances', *OG*, p. 310.
33 Seamus Heaney, 'Anahorish', *OG*, p. 46, ll. 7–11.
34 Seamus Heaney, 'Bog Queen', *OG*, p. 108, ll. 1–6.
35 Seamus Heaney, 'England's Difficulty', *OG*, p. 185, ll. 20–3.
36 Ted Hughes, 'The Thought-Fox', *CP*, p. 21, l. 24.

37   Ted Hughes, 'Myths, Metres, Rhythms', *Winter Pollen*, p. 332.
38   Ted Hughes, 'Skylarks', *CP*, p. 173, ll. 19–25.
39   Ted Hughes, 'Singers', *CP*, p. 83, l. 12.
40   Ted Hughes, 'Thrushes', *CP*, p. 82, l. 2.
41   Ted Hughes, 'Ballad from a Fairy Tale', *CP*, p. 172, l. 28.
42   Ted Hughes, '[The Epilogue Poems]', *Gaudete*, *CP*, p. 357, ll. 13–23.
43   Seamus Heaney, 'The Singer's House', *OG*, p. 153, ll. 30, 31.
44   Seamus Heaney, 'A New Song', *OG*, p. 58, ll. 11, 15.
45   Seamus Heaney, 'Serenades', *OG*, p. 72, ll. 30–1.
46   Seamus Heaney, 'The Canton of Expectation', *OG*, p. 319, ll. 18–23.
47   Seamus Heaney, 'The Ministry of Fear' from *Singing School*, *OG*, p. 135, ll. 25–30.
48   Tony Harrison, 'Them & [Uz]', *CP*, p. 122, ll. 19–24, 27–32.
49   Tony Harrison, *Phaedra Britannica*, in *Plays: Two* (London: Faber, 2002), p. 164.
50   Tony Harrison, quoted in Stephen Fay and Philip Oakes, 'Mystery behind the mask', in *Bloodaxe I*, pp. 290–1.
51   Ted Hughes, 'Orghast', *Selected Translations* (London: Faber, 2006), p. 195, ll. 7–10.
52   Ted Hughes, '*Orghast*: talking without words', *Winter Pollen*, p. 126.
53   Tony Harrison, 'Art & Extinction', *CP*, p. 189, l. 16.
54   Tony Harrison, *v.*, *CP*, p. 263, ll. 64–7.
55   Sandie Byrne, H, *v. and* O, p. 67.

Social Dramas: Bond, Osborne and Churchill

> There can be no modern art which is not socialist. Art in the society which had … good government would be socialist art which had inherited its kingdom. Till then socialist art is a weapon in the struggle to create good government.
>
> Edward Bond, 'The Rational Theatre' (1974)[1]

Edward Bond's statement on the socialist leanings of modern drama at first appears to mimic Iris Murdoch's cry for a morally attentive fiction. Here is a call to arms and a proclamation, declaring theatre as an art form to be integrally related to the workings of society. Yet while Murdoch's manifesto was prescriptive, Bond's seems dogmatic. It insists not only on a socially engaged art form, but on its political persuasion. Bond's perspective is heavily influenced by the German playwright and director Bertolt Brecht (1898–1956), who sought to replace the comforting theatre of catharsis with an epic theatre that would effect social change and discomfort its audience. Most famously, in *Mother Courage* (1939), Brecht wrote against the rise of Nazism, in a play which depicts its eponymous protagonist hoping to profit from the Thirty Years War but losing her three children in succession. Brecht's practice hovered between theatre as didacticism and theatre as entertainment, ever mindful of the 'socially practical significance' of the modern stage.[2] His methods for epic theatre, however, were largely consistent: alienation effects, such as actors holding placards, breaking off into song, or acknowledging the artifice of the stage, would help draw audiences' attention to the stage as a spectacle. Brecht reasoned that an unsettled audience would engage more actively with the play itself. Yet if Brecht bequeathed Bond a theatre with a social agenda, he also saw the modern stage as a process rather than a practice. Tellingly, theatre director Peter Brook's exploration of modern drama was called *The Empty Space* (1968); this was stage that had often been encumbered with historical precedent or the deadly theatre of convention, in Brook's words. Now, it was in the business of clearance and reconfiguration.

John Osborne's position is in apparent contrast to Bond's rigid definition of drama's socialist imperative. For Osborne, the common enemy of art is neither communism nor capitalism, but the bewildering world of pluralism. In 1967, he protested that: [w]e live in a society of such lurching flexibility that it is no longer possible to construct a dramatic method based on a shared social or ethical system.' He believed that a 'theatre audience is no longer linked by anything but the climate of disassociation in which it tries to live out its baffled lives.'[3] Here, we find frustration with a liberal relativism that offers no common consensus but only tolerant acceptance of other positions. Osborne's notion of 'lurching flexibility' seems far from the political hegemony implied by Bond. Yet perhaps these statements by Osborne and Bond are two ways of expressing a similar anxiety. In a country newly distracted by television, convinced of the merits of comfortable conformity, and complacent in its outlook, what role might theatre have to play? Might its middle-class audiences and its tendency towards the establishment not situate theatre as part of this cultural malaise rather than working against it? Both Bond's intractable absolutes and Osborne's resigned relativism suggest playwrights unsure of what they should be writing or whom they are writing for.

Bond's and Osborne's careers in British theatre are an awkward testament to this double-edged response. Both began their careers with plays that transcended the limits of the theatre to become cultural events. Modern drama is often dated from the first performance of Osborne's *Look Back in Anger* (1956). The early puzzlement of critics quickly turned to praise. Soon, Osborne and his creation Jimmy Porter spearheaded the Angry Young Man movement, and the playwright had become an internationally recognised figure.* This was a play that revolutionised British theatre less through its gestures to Brecht or its belated response to modernist European playwrights such as Antonin Artaud but through its use of a working-class vernacular. This was a social, rather than formal, innovation. Edward Bond's *Saved* (1965) became another cause célèbre, when its controversial onstage infanticide fell foul of the Lord Chamberlain, the member of the Royal Household at that time responsible for licensing all new plays prior to performance. Rather than rewrite his work, Bond offered up the play as a test case. Its semi-public performance risked prosecution, but ultimately led to the parliamentary committee that would overturn the Lord Chamberlain's role in theatre censorship. Yet these auspicious and high-profile catalysts for their careers also unravelled their subsequent work. Osborne, increasingly frustrated by the poor reviews for his plays in the early 1960s and what he saw as the tyranny of the establishment, effectively exiled himself to France, printing an open letter to his 'fellow countrymen' in the *Tribune*: 'damn you, England. You're rotting now, and quite soon you'll disappear. My hate will outrun you yet, if only for a few seconds. I wish it could be eternal.'[4] Although he returned in the 1980s, Osborne's vituperative attacks on his critics throughout his career suggest that the 'lurching flexibility' he saw in British society was a red herring, an expedient for him to explain away the often hostile responses of theatre-goers. Bond, too, took an enforced artistic exile; after strained relationships with the National Theatre and the Royal Court Theatre, he moved to France in the mid-1970s, and the majority of his work since then has been produced with French and German companies.

Caryl Churchill, like Osborne and Bond, articulates a clear commitment to undermining capitalist orthodoxy in her work; her imagined ideal society is 'decentralized, non-authoritarian, communist, non-sexist' yet she worries that 'it always sounds both ridiculous and unattainable when you put it into words'.[5] As if mindful of this caveat, and anxious to avoid the dangers of idealism and self-righteousness, her own drama often self-consciously probes these predilections. Her work has moved from the realist polemic of the 1970s to provocatively postmodern

---

* See Part Two: 'A Cultural Overview' for a discussion of the Angry Young Man movement.

tactics, including the use of double characters, gender-blind casting, or anti-linear, metatheatrical narratives. Yet her formal innovations come in direct response to the social questions her plays pose, rather than through a desire to innovate. Like Bond, the influence of Brecht runs throughout her work, both in its social commitment and its use of defamiliarising effects which deliberately draw attention to the play as an artificial entity. Her use of improvised dialogue, or developing a play through workshops with actors, similarly suggests a need for the participants in her dramas, whether they are actors or audience, to explore their own social codes and assumptions. This improvisational theatre called for new working methods and performance venues. Like Bond and Osborne, Churchill is symbolic of a move away from the Royal Court to other theatrical spaces. In 1968 both the Arts Lab and the Open Space were founded in London, and while Churchill spent a year as resident dramatist with the Royal Court in 1974, it was her work with the Joint Stock Theatre Company and Monstrous Regiment that would prove key in establishing her voice. Taken together, the work of these three playwrights highlights a trend in British postwar theatre that unites dramatists as disparate as Howard Barker, David Hare, Dennis Potter, and Arnold Wesker. While this was a drama that was slow to pick up on the innovative work of European practitioners, it remained committed to transforming British theatre from a social activity to an act that engaged directly with society. Tellingly, theatre director Peter Brook's exploration of modern drama was called *The Empty Space* (1968); this was a stage that had often been encumbered with historical precedent, but was now in the business of clearance and reconfiguration.

Violent Spectators

Such was the eventual impact of John Osborne's *Look Back in Anger* that it has often been seen as a synecdoche* for postwar theatre itself. The titles of various studies of recent British drama – *1956 and All That*,

---

* A synecdoche describes the substitution of a part for the whole, or vice versa, i.e. 'the government rejected the bill' means 'the ministers who sit in the government building rejected the bill'.

Anger and After, *Look Back in Gender* [6] – all place it as year zero, its iconic first performance in 1956 the date from which all subsequent theatre is measured. Its reception defined the play as revolutionary, forcing the somewhat bewildered Osborne to provocatively describe it as a 'formal, old-fashioned play', [7] as if the only way to offer the unorthodox view was to see it as conservative and reactionary. It is important to realise that critics still use the play as a synecdoche, calling up a number of related developments in British drama: the rise of a new breed of working-class and Left Wing playwrights and directors, from Shelagh Delaney to Joan Littlewood, who challenged the dominance of drawing room dramas by Noel Coward or Terence Rattigan; the use of workshops and repertory theatres to showcase innovative new work; the new dialogue between stage and screen, which meant the 'New Wave' of Osborne would be guaranteed a cinema audience. This new realism also placed importance on the playwright's own background. As Stephen Lacey notes, critics of the New Wave tended to see the works as 'an unreconstructed "reflection" of social reality, which relied on the personal situation of the writers to guarantee the "truth" of the text, its sociological validity'. [8] Yet, as Osborne notes, the play itself challenges its audience's expectations not through narrative – the play sticks doggedly to the formal constraints of the well-made play – but through language.

The infamous protagonist of *Look Back in Anger*, Jimmy Porter, is a frustrated intellectual – damning of his friend Cliff and wife Alison for their philistinism and passivity, yet equally scornful of the Sunday broadsheet papers with their untranslated French and their attempts to instil a sense of inadequacy in their readers. He is half Hamlet, with his vituperative, tainted idealism, and half a wayward onstage director, furious that his own tirades and monologues find Cliff and Alison merely listening rather than engaging. Their flat is a constrictive space which the play never leaves – the second act finds Alison being replaced at the ironing board by her friend Helena, who temporarily becomes Jimmy's lover; Alison resumes her place by the play's conclusion. Jimmy's fury, which gave birth, however inadvertently, to the critics' 'Angry Young Man' tag, ranges from class war to colonial anxiety. Alison becomes a trophy not of status, but of his desecration of conventional class hierarchies – he 'steals' her from the upper class. His impotent rage comes partly from the conformity of postwar culture, and partly from the knowledge that the heroic wars of his father's generation or the political incitements of the Spanish Civil War will never rouse him or his peers to action. This is the age to work up suffocating contentment, rather than start a revolution. In this way, Osborne's apparently realist drama looks forward to the ahistoric anachronisms of Caryl Churchill. While she combines characters from different periods of history to offer contemporary comments on society, Osborne gives us an iconoclastic hero in an age that has no need for heroism. Alison calls him an 'Eminent Victorian', while Helena sees him 'in the middle of the French revolution'.[9] His tearing up of the theatrical precedent is then curiously nostalgic as well as forward looking. In the effort to note his anger, critics have been slow to explore why and how far Jimmy looks back.

Jimmy's tirades seemingly inflict only verbal cruelty, yet one of the play's most brutal acts finds his violent language becoming a curse. Enraged by his wife's indifference, he taunts her by saying that if she lost a baby it would wake her out of her stupor. Although he is not aware of her pregnancy at this stage, her eventual miscarriage makes his words prophecy rather than petulant point-scoring. The barriers Alison erects against his words also seem mental, rather than physical. Edward Bond's *Saved* (1965) similarly centres its violence around the death of a baby, but what in Osborne is the cruel absence of concern at a wife's miscarriage becomes in Bond the senseless stoning of a baby by its father and his friends and a mother seemingly indifferent to its murder. The characters in Bond's play are ravaged by poverty, both material and imaginative; the shocking onstage murder is only a metaphor for their day-to-day existence, which takes little pleasure in life and its possibilities. Although Osborne's vernacular language went some way to removing theatrical dialogue from its upper-class shackles, Bond strips its vocabulary down still further, reducing the onstage dialogue to a series of inarticulate grunts and emissions, as in this exchange between Len and Mary as they watch television:

> MARY (*watching TV*). I ain't goin' up for yer. (*Still watching TV.*) High time it 'ad a father. (*To* LEN). There's plenty a tea in the pot.

LEN (*watching TV*). Yeh.
MARY (*watching TV*). That's what it needs. No wonder it cries.
(*Pause. To* LEN.) Busy?
LEN. Murder.[10]

In their often monosyllabic exchanges, these characters achieve a morbid sort of poetry. Len's colloquial 'murder' inadvertently offers the audience a hint of the infanticide to come, while the grammatical precision with which Bond outlines their exchange draws our attention to the fact that the tea is given more agency through its accompanying article than Pam's baby (Mary's grandchild), who remains a stubborn object, a constant distraction from the television.

Like Osborne, Bond found himself subjected to a barrage of critical opinion in response to the play. Osborne's knowing description of *Look Back in Anger* as an old-fashioned play is called to mind by Bond's insistence that *Saved* is 'irresponsibly optimistic'.[11] Yet through the character of Len, who lives through the baby's murder yet refuses to condemn or reject the perpetrators, the play offers the nearest thing to goodness. Although not the baby's father, Len's monosyllabic agreement with Mary in the exchange quoted above suggests a growing sense of paternal responsibility. Many of us believe violence and its spectatorship are morally corrupting, yet *Saved* presents us with a central character so good that even the utterly depraved cannot endanger his steady reliability. The final scene finds Len mending a chair. As a symbolic gesture of hope, it struggles to balance a baby being stoned in a park, but Bond's own comments call for a subversive rereading of the central act of violence:

> Clearly the stoning to death of a baby in a London park is typical English understatement. Compared to the 'strategic' bombing of German towns it is a negligible atrocity, compared to the cultural and emotional deprivation of most of our children its consequences are insignificant. ('Introduction', p. 6)

Bond's graphic representation of violence on stage, looking forward to the work of later playwrights such as Sarah Kane or Mark Ravenhill, enacts a further violent transformation when explained by the playwright. Like Pam, the indifferent mother who loses the baby, it is read here glibly as an 'understatement'. Yet the forced confrontation with this world, like the cruelty Jimmy inflicts on his wife, belies the notion of the theatrically complacent audience. Even as they look away, the watching audience remain complicit, charged with the responsibility of navigating their goodness around the terror of the events depicted onstage.

In *Softcops* (1975), Caryl Churchill similarly makes use of onstage violence, but in a way that prompts a consideration of the audience's role rather than the ethical purpose of the playwright. Like Angela Carter's *Nights At The Circus* (1984) the play turns to Foucault, and his explication of Jeremy Bentham's Panopticon jail.* As one of the characters remarks, 'the darkness of the dungeon is some protection, so to be always in the light is pitiless'.[12] The play is stewarded by the character Pierre, who is presenting a series of scenes depicting a nineteenth-century French prison for a visiting school party. His dialogue with the headmaster gives Churchill the opportunity to explore the ethics of staging violence and conflict. Pierre begins half as moral didact, half ambitious theatre director:

> PIERRE: There is a balance if I can get it. Terror, but also information. Information, but also terror. But I dream of something covering several acres and completely transforming – as you know. I won't bore you. But if the minister is impressed today I hope for a park. (p. 7)

He is caught between the need to communicate a moral message, and to expand his own theatrical empire. Pierre can't resist highlighting his own crude symbolism in his staging, drawing the children's attention to his use of red ribbons to represent 'the blood shed by passion and the blood shed by Reason in justice and grief' (p. 6). Are these asides designed to reinforce the effect of the theatre or to celebrate the skill of his direction? As the play progresses, the actors refuse to co-operate with his staging

* See the Extended Commentary on Angela Carter's *Nights At The Circus* (1984) in Part Three: 'The Postmodern Novel' for a fuller consideration of the Panopticon. Although Foucault's work was not published in English in full until 1977, it seems likely that Churchill was drawing on his ideas here.

of prison riots and hangings. The grisly spectacle the audience have been led to expect is continually deferred, forcing them to interrogate their own positions as voyeurs. By the play's conclusion, when the innocent schoolchildren have become embroiled in the restaging of prison-room torture, Pierre reveals himself as an expedient entertainer rather than a serious moralist. Assured that his play has had a profound effect on the ministry, Pierre is more concerned with the cachet of being asked to make a speech than the content of it:

> The unemployed are educated. The ignorant are punished. No. I'll need to rehearse this a little. The ignorant are normalised. Right. The sick are punished. The insane are educated. The workers are cured. The criminals are cured. The unemployed are punished. The criminals are normalised. Something along those lines. (p. 49)

While Osborne's claustrophobic front room shows the middle-brow malaise that fills the vacuum of protest and revolution, and Bond's graphic onstage violence points the finger at the audience themselves as the complacent spectators, Churchill's play questions the motives and methods of representing destruction on stage.

Anarchy and Power

The theatrical New Wave is often defined as 'the automatic rejection of "official" attitudes'.[13] However, the word 'automatic' conceals the deep engagement these works have with the state they are trying to overhaul. Their depiction of 'postwar youth as [they] really [were]' (*Look Back in Anger*, p. 177) was balanced with a committed interest in government, monarchy, and systems of control and governance. It was through these plays that postwar theatre sought to examine its own relationship with the Establishment. Churchill's *Light Shining in Buckinghamshire* (1976) returns to the Republican moment of the English Civil War and removes hindsight from its history. As her prefatory note points out: 'we are 'told of a step forward to today's democracy but not of a revolution that didn't happen; we are told of Charles and Cromwell but not of the thousands of men and women who tried to change their lives.'[14] In a studied ventriloquising of seventeenth-century diction, Churchill charts the ebbing belief of the revolutionaries. This realist, quasi-documentary approach mimics the failure of the Republican revolution. Seismic change is subsumed into the return towards inherited privilege and the restitution of order. While the use of metanarration and newspaper reportage adds a sense of Brechtian alienation, the characters' tendency to monologue rather than dialogue deliberately inhibits their revolutionary project. The play takes the form of a series of related scenes rather than a narrative, but each subsequent vignette is charged with the increasing inevitability of the Restoration. Radical change cannot come about without the destruction of property, and the Ranters' final debate on sexual and economic freedom is undermined by its increasing abstraction. As Sexby admits, 'though liberty was our end, there is a degeneration from it' (p. 215).

Meanwhile, Osborne's *The Blood of the Bambergs* (1962), caused a furore on its first performance, not only for its satirical portrait of a royal wedding, but its inclusion alongside Osborne's exploration of sado-masochism in *Under Plain Covers* (1962), both performed under the title *Plays for England* (premiered 1962). The analogy between the Royal Family and a sado-masochistic relationship suggested that the monarchy had little to offer the people other than the perverse pleasure its subjects took in being subjugated. The play follows Russell as he prepares to marry into the Royal Family. As he testily enquires about his land rights and financial incentives to marry a woman he has never met, journalists and servants flutter around him. Osborne's strongest satire comes not at the expense of the mercenary bridegroom but the media who offer their evasive commentary on the occasion, as in the concluding words of the fifth journalist:

> It may be mysterious, incomprehensible, but it's moving, certainly most important of all, it's moving. And a vindication of the Western Way of Life, against the threat of the Communist world. In all of this, my friends, our bastion lies.[15]

In a political system so unsure of its ideology that monarchism is the only alternative to communism, royalty becomes uneasy compromise rather than national monument. As the journalist's obsequious summary suggests, the wedding becomes iconic for its fantastical and quasi-religious mystery rather than its romantic or political significance. Royalty becomes a familiar punching bag for Osborne not only because of the Lord Chamberlain and the association of censorship with the Royal Household, but because of the unthinking elision between myth and reality. It is no accident that the play is subtitled 'a fairy story'; in a theatre attempting to strip away its language to direct vernacular, the pomp and ceremony of royalty threatens the stage with exactly the grandeur it is hoping to abandon. While the preoccupation of postwar dramatists with the Royal Family might seem archaic to the contemporary reader, its significance is two-fold. It becomes both a practical barrier to free expression in the theatre and a synecdoche for institutional conservatism and inherited privilege.

This same barrier incites the farce and iconoclasm of Edward Bond's *Early Morning* (1968), written deliberately to provoke the royal censors, and later performed without cuts despite being banned by the Lord Chamberlain. Its mixture of cross-dressing, lampoon, and parody, as in the lesbian relationship between Florence Nightingale and Queen Victoria, seems designed to shock and yet, for all this revolutionary bluster, some of the play's more thoughtful transgressions come not through sapphic experiment but formal innovation: Bond's fluid movement between historical periods and geographical space pre-empts the anti-realist strategies of Churchill, and is as iconic in its turn towards Brechtian alienation as it is to real-life mimicry. Here, the stuffy institutions of monarchy and state prompt a liberating turn towards theatrical anarchy. While Osborne's play reads a royal wedding as an evasive social opiate, Bond sees it as an expedient political opportunity. As Benjamin Disraeli whispers to Prince Albert in the opening scene: 'She knows a royal wedding will pacify the people, so we must strike now'.[16] The remainder of the play offers similar subversions: Florence Nightingale's reputation as an 'expert sanitarian' is read opportunistically by Queen Victoria as 'a branch of eugenics' (p. 15); Albert's death doesn't prompt an outpouring of royal grief, but an excuse for cannibalism; lesbianism is transformed from something the Queen cannot imagine happening to a default sexual appetite. The need to carry on lampooning a statecraft apparently long dismantled suggests an inability to give up the Victorian legacy. Once again, the monarchy become a symbol not just for political oppression and state-sponsored censorship, but, more ambivalently, for the necessary curbs on anarchic artists. Even the revolutionary must have its constraint, and the conservative tendencies of early works by Bond and Churchill, or later works by Osborne, suggest that royalty and censorship are as much a symbolic cipher here as a legitimate political target.

Colonising the Stage

While representations of the monarchy in the work of these playwrights suggest a reticence about revolution, their depictions of larger political systems and colonial relationships suggest a return to Brechtian principles of socially relevant theatre. Churchill, Bond, and Osborne reject catharsis for discomforting works which ask their audience difficult questions. As Osborne suggests of his own *West of Suez* (1971): 'the play is about the decaying of tongues ... not just of colonial empires but of emotional empires, too'.[17] It is set in an imaginary former British colony and its central character, Wyatt Gillman, is an elderly writer-figure grubbily resistant to change and the process of decolonisation. Only the play's titular hint prompts its audience to locate this conservative senility in a contemporary political context, calling up the Suez Crisis of 1956 (see Part Two: 'A Cultural Overview'). Although poorly received in the early 1970s, its insights into colonial complacency make it one of the most effective of Osborne's later works. Even the opening stage directions communicate a weary disdain for the cultural accretions of colonialism, with its setting of '*a subtropical island, neither Africa nor Europe, but some of both, also less than both*'.[18] Even the telling 'subtropical' suggests dilution and desecration. Edward's distracted opening dialogue with his wife Frederica continues the series of parallels and unequal binaries, describing the native workers' mixture of 'lethargy and hysteria' or the island's combination of 'brutality and sentimentality' (p. 151). These uneven combinations set up the language of the play, which finds its theatrical world made up of addition and subsequent diminution. Wyatt's racist rhetoric wanders woozily over terms, barely seeing the distinction between 'ex-colonies' and 'independent states' (p. 183) even as he brands himself effacingly as 'a pontificating old English buffer' (p. 203). Yet in the midst of his newspaper interview at the beginning of Act Two emerges his anxiety about the 'in-between' nature of his surroundings. When asked about his own sense of Englishness, and whether he considers nationality important to his writing, he dismisses the English imagination as a certain form of 'cloud formation' (p. 206). The ineffable and incorporeal sensibility of a national literature is of no more substance than water vapour.

Bond's *Narrow Road to the Deep North* (1968) is more direct in its depiction of state control. The narrative follows the Japanese poet Basho, who witnesses the downfall of the political dictator Shogo, only to see the imperial power of English Christianity rear up in its place, with another restrictive set of cultural assumptions. There are clear parallels between Shogo's despotic rule, which sees him building a whole city in his image, and the proselytising of the Christian missionary Georgina, whose murder ends the play. The dissection of spectatorship that informed Churchill's *Softcops* is present here, too; the innocent onlookers in the play's fight for political supremacy soon become tainted with complicity. Yet Bond's strongest critique is reserved for Georgina's missionary shortsightedness. Dressed in Victorian crinoline and shaking a tambourine throughout, her evangelical zeal only partially conceals her imperial desire. The missionary imperative becomes another weapon in arms trading. As she tells the besieged Prime Minister:

> We will give you soldiers and guns to kill your enemies – and in return you must love Jesus, give up bad language, foreswear cards, refuse spicy foods, abandon women, forsake drink and – and *stop* singing on Sundays –[19]

The comic absurdism of her bartering is closer to farce than despotism but, as she takes control over the running of the city, she moves closer to the fascist leader she opposes. After a week of rule, she describes her changes to the city's infrastructure like an alternative creation myth, but substitutes the creation of day and night for the imposition of a city-wide curfew. Only the onlooking poet, branding her an 'inscrutable' Westerner, warns her that 'people who raise ghosts become haunted' (p. 42). In the final scene, sensing revolt, Georgina imagines her capture and rape with a glee that is closer to sexual delight than terror. Violence becomes a suppressed urge her religion both subsumes and permits her to indulge in. Religious rule comes no closer to fair governance than the power-hungry totalitarianism of the despot.

Music and Movement

Despotic rulers, religious authorities, and the monarchy become frequent subjects for postwar socialist playwrights, yet their most effective works stage these dramas of power, resignation, and subjection not through the recreation of massed political coups or royal suicides but through the lonely monologues of the historical observer. John Osborne's *The Entertainer* (1957) creates, in the actor-protagonist Archie Rice, one of postwar theatre's most iconic figures. Archie's nostalgic look back to the music-hall tradition that has left him politically and socially isolated reveals his self-delusions and evasions through popular culture itself. Through Archie, Osborne constructs his own eulogy for a theatre that was grounded in community and working-class culture, even if it sought to offer them entertainment rather than edification. Archie's crumbling world of sea-side entertainment offers another sort of pathos for the modern theatre, as he drunkenly descants on his performances to empty music halls in Hartlepool, frail and wary of the consolation that 'it's better to be a has-been than a never-was'.[20] The Welfare State which ensures that 'nobody wants, and nobody goes without' (p. 53) proves a crutch no less damaging than Archie's nightly alcohol, and the most poignant part of the play's narrative comes when Archie realises his own marginality to the modern world. Like a forgotten Falstaff, Archie measures his tragedy by its very insignificance: '[we]'re drunks, we're crazy, we're bonkers, the whole flaming bunch of us … we're characters out of something that nobody believes in' (p. 54). The performer has lost his ability to convince his audience; the final scene finds him hanging up his hat and offering to watch us perform tomorrow night, aware that contemporary audiences are more concerned with their own petty dramas than the art of vaudeville. His regular songs which punctuate the narrative tableau are gently off-key with their patriotism and feigned confidence in the supremacy of the Empire. Like Wyatt Gillman, he has become a walking anachronism, drowning his political disaffection and loneliness in alcohol, but there is pathos, rather than perfidy, in his demise here. His increasingly desperate metaphors as we watch his nightly performances subsume anxiety and isolation under the imperative to keep his audience laughing – life is like 'sucking a sweet with the wrapper on' (p. 87). Osborne finds in the language of music hall and vaudeville a new poignancy that belies the railing iconoclasm of Jimmy Porter's monologues. For all of Archie's showmanship and bluster, this is a play that anxiously expects silence, rather than applause, when the music stops playing.

A Mouthful of Birds (1986), coauthored with David Lan, was a deliberate attempt on Churchill's part to expand the range of her theatrical language. Taking its cue from Euripides's *Bacchae* and the Greek god of chaos and madness, Dionysus, the play presents seven characters who become possessed. For the female characters in particular, such as the secretary Doreen and the telephone operator Marcia, these possessions offer the opportunity to explore pent-up, or Penthean,* reserves of violence. Infanticide, murder, and animalistic impulses all overtake their ordered lives. This onstage possession finds its formal reflection in Churchill's onstage language, which abandons text for physical movement. From the scene where Doreen and her masseuse Mrs Blair throw crockery and bang saucepans to the 'fruit ballet' scene, which finds the whole cast in a wordless choreography based on the sensuous properties of fruit, Churchill moves from the ordered world of language to found sound and

---

* In Euripides's *The Bacchae*, Pentheus tries to ban the worship of Dionysus, the god of ecstasy and madness. Dionysus punishes him by luring him to a mountain where the women of Thebes are celebrating a Bacchic ritual. They mistake Pentheus for an animal and tear him limb from limb.

bodily expression. The epic allusions throughout the play call up anarchy rather than tradition, and the words that accompany the cast's dancing and musical performances are often subsumed to physical movement, as in the quoted newspaper headlines which accompany one of the dance set-pieces. By the play's conclusion, which finds the seven characters reflecting on how their possessions have changed them, an impossible gap has opened up between internal experience and the capacity to express it in speech, as in Doreen's final monologue:

> I can find no rest. My head is filled with horrible images. I can't say I actually see them, it's more that I feel them ... I carry on my work as a secretary. [21]

Although these are the final words spoken on stage, the last scene is given over to Dionysus's dance. Anarchy has triumphed over order, and the theatre has escaped from the restrictions of language by finding meaning in the movement of the body rather than the lips.

Staging the Real

The restrictions imposed on Churchill's characters echo those on playwrights working before 1968, not least the suggestion that they should try and avoid depictions of living persons or historical figures.* This was a recommendation designed to prevent heretic depictions of the monarch rather than preserve the memory of particular politicians, yet a series of postwar plays tellingly excavate iconic characters of the past. Osborne's *Luther* (1961) finds in the narrative of the German protestant reformer Martin Luther a model for the Angry Young Man. Luther's insistence on the vernacular, his translations of the Bible, and his attack on the indulgences of the papacy all find their analogies in Jimmy Porter's impotent rage at the complacent middle class. Yet if there is a precedent here, there is also a kind of historical envy for a time where one

---

* Although the Lord Chamberlain was never given explicit guidelines on censorship practice, from 1909 the person in post worked from a list drawn up by a select committee.

man's actions could determine the path of Western civilisation. Luther's conversation with his father hints at an apocalyptic self-awareness: 'I heard the other day they're saying the world's going to end in 1532.'[22] The Cold War context of *Luther*'s composition and performance makes Armageddon itself another historical cycle, a continual process of crisis and renewal. The play seeks a historical model for the Angry Young Man's frustrated belligerence, but it also humanises its historical subject, making Luther's conflict with his father and the burden of his familial inheritance as significant as his religious reforms. Luther's scepticism of Catholic excess and papal corruption offers another analogy for the theatre itself; divorced from the principles of its faith, and reluctant to communicate with the people that support it. At the beginning of Act Three, Luther's public questioning by the Pope finds the stage expanding. The stage directions suggest that Luther should stand on a projected rostrum to achieve '*a sense of physical participation in the theatre, as if everyone watching had their chins resting on the sides of a boxing-ring*' (p. 81). It is no accident that Osborne's analogy is to the ugly drama of boxing. He returns to history less to authenticate and find a tradition for his anchorless suburban anti-heroes than to offer the revolutionary iconoclasm of the past as a way of shattering the complacency of the viewing audience.

In contrast to Osborne's heroic dramatisation of Luther, Edward Bond's *Bingo* (1973) recreates Shakespeare as a senile, jealous feudalist. Drawing on biographical material, Bond focuses on Shakespeare's income from the Welcombe enclosure near Stratford. Landowners wanted to take the fields over from the labourers, and Shakespeare registered no opposition. For Bond, this offers the biographical opportunity to explore Shakespeare's life through a Marxist prism. This portrait of the late Shakespeare finds him unable to write, and more anxious about his land rates than his empty pages. Yet this reading of him as a greedy materialist is not merely iconoclastic. His character comes closer to King Lear than Prospero; the opening scene of *King Lear*, which finds the senile king dividing his land between his daughters, is echoed in Shakespeare's own anxieties about his estate. As he lies near death, he offers an apology to his daughter Judith that mirrors Lear's to Cordelia, but Shakespeare's only reaffirms his antipathy towards her: 'there's no limit to my hate … it can't be satisfied by cruelty'.[23] The analogies between the fictional Shakespeare and Lear suggest an attempt by Bond to question how far artists can write beyond themselves. Lear is one of Shakespeare's cruellest creations, but also his most profound. As Bond's preface suggests:

> if you understand so much about suffering and violence, the partiality of authority, and the final innocence of all defenceless things, *and yet* live in a time when you can do nothing about it – then you feel the suffering you describe, and your writing mimics that suffering.[24]

Bond recreates Shakespeare as a jealous and self-serving old man not to question his literary genius, but to articulate his notion that in an unjust society, the moral may themselves be corrupted just as soon as become dissidents.

While Osborne and Bond look to heroic lives of the past to explore contemporary issues of moral responsibility, Churchill in *Top Girls* (1982) uses a series of iconic female figures to frame a specifically feminist consideration of gender roles. Her play begins with a character, Marlene, who is celebrating her recent promotion, making her the 'top girl' of the title. Yet the friends that join her for dinner are a series of cultural, mythological, or fictive characters from the past: Griselda from Chaucer's *Canterbury Tales*, who accepted the death of her two children as part of a test of loyalty by her future husband; the barbaric mythological figure of Dull Gret, who was pictured at the mouth of hell in paintings by Breughel; Pope Joan, the putative female pope who disguised herself as man only to be stoned to death when childbirth revealed her true sex; the nineteenth-century explorer Isabella Bird, and Lady Nijo, a thirteen-century Japanese concubine. These women provide contrasting perspectives on Marlene's frustrated compromise between success as a businesswoman and personal fulfilment: the incriminating childbirth of Joan's story offering an analogy for contemporary attitudes towards women in the workplace; Gret's babbling anger, an embodiment of the ruthless woman as barbaric.

140

The following scene disrupts the already anachronistic play, depicting Marlene in her workplace before the dinner. The play's final act, which shows her visiting her sister and niece, takes place a year earlier. Only here do we learn that Marlene's niece Angie is in fact her daughter, and that she forced her sister, Joyce to raise her. This knowledge asks the audience to consider whether Marlene's secret surrogacy is in fact the modern equivalent of Patient Griselda's abandonment of her children. If society no longer demands unwavering fidelity from a woman to her husband, does it require a new kind of loyalty to her career? Churchill mixes 1980s office politics with historical antecedents to undermine the cult of the individual. Even the self-determined and self-serving have their historical precedents. For all three playwrights, the opportunity to stage real-life characters offers the chance to effectively dehistoricise their political positions. They are resurrected less to defame their reputation than to reframe the social contests operating within the playwrights' theatrical worlds. Yet despite these gestures, the majority of this theatre remains locked in the period that produced it. As Bryan Appleyard has remarked, it remains 'bizarrely specialized',[25] and did not energise the proletariat audience as it so longed to do. Given that 1956 began with a play apparently showing postwar youth as it really was, many of these works tell us as much about British theatre in the 1960s and 1970s as they do about Britain itself.

Extended Commentary: Churchill, *Cloud Nine* (1979)

Caryl Churchill's *Cloud Nine*[26] presents us with a theatre that is at once socially committed and innovative. It questions the constructs of gender, sexuality, and nationhood less through realist debate and the staging of character conflict than through the use of cross-gender and cross-racial casting. Created with director Max Stafford-Clark and the Joint Stock Theatre company in 1979 after their collaboration on *Light Shining in Buckinghamshire*, its concerns echo several plays by Osborne and Bond – the embers of the British empire, the efficacies of rule and authority, the social imposition of gender, class, and racial categories – but it tunes itself to comedy. The farce of a man playing a woman or a white actor playing a black servant offers slapstick, but finds its darker double in the repressive world of the play itself, where the gay character Harry is forced to marry Ellen, who is a lesbian. Structurally, the play divides itself into two permeable historical points in time. Act One takes place in a British colony in Africa in Victorian times, while Act Two takes place in London in 1979. Yet, as in *Top Girls*, these boundaries are porous; for the characters on stage only twenty-five years passes between the two acts. The Victorian age with its rigid gender hierarchies continues to dominate contemporary Britain, and Churchill chooses to show this through historical rupture rather than through realist representation.

The anti-realist decisions of Churchill's casting and setting suggest a contest between essentialist* and performative notions of gender and race. Part of the play's comedy is generated by the knowing dialogue which upsets the binary oppositions this inscribes. In the opening scene, the black manservant Joshua is played by a white actor, while Edward, son of Clive, the head of the house, is played by a woman, and is encouraged by his father to grow up to be a man.[26] The rhyming iambic pentameter they speak forces the characters into a phonic and metrical pattern that mirrors their own demarcated social position. Tradition shows them how to dress, and orthodoxy dictates how they should speak. The comedy works both by drawing attention to Churchill's cross-gender, cross-racial casting and playing it 'straight', eliding the metatheatrical hints with the assumed prejudices of white supremacy. Clive wishes Joshua white because his goodness challenges Clive's racial assumptions about black men; Clive's assertion that he will 'teach' his son to be a man is a Victorian commonplace, yet also presents the cross-dressed Edward as someone who will 'learn' gender.

This technique balances neatly between the assumptions of the Victorian period and the poststructuralist gender theories of writers such as Judith Butler, who reads gender itself as a social performance and maps a theoretical space where 'the subject of "woman" is nowhere

---

* Essentialism suggests that essence is prior to existence, and would see gender as an intrinsic category rather than a socially determined one.

presumed'.[27] These comic operations of the first act continually draw the audience's attention not just to the prejudices of the Victorian period, but their own inscribed assumptions. Betty, Clive's wife, is played by a man in Act One, and when she tells her husband she has spent the day reading poetry, he praises her for her delicacy (p. 253). The humour of the remark seems to come at Clive's expense – a man dressed up as a woman would not usually be described as 'delicate' – yet it also comes at the audience's. There is no reason why a transvestite should not be as 'delicate' as a woman.

The tightly woven plot of the first act further undermines these doublings, as the subversive coupling between Joshua, the manservant, and Harry, the explorer, or Ellen, Edward's governess, and Betty, Clive's wife, comes to resemble an unhinged version of Oscar Wilde. Throughout the play, Churchill offers a gradated notion of cultural conformity and visibility. While both Harry and Ellen are gay, Harry's homosexuality is visible enough to be confessed to Clive, although the latter is repulsed by it and encourages him to marry and suppress his desire. By contrast, Ellen's homosexuality goes unrecognised, even by herself, as it occupies a submerged societal space that cannot be named. Queen Victoria's famous proclamation that lesbianism was a fiction and therefore needn't be made illegal isolates Ellen further from the hegemonic structure of nineteenth-century society. In the second act, set in modern-day London, Churchill offers a continuity of characters but recasts them to show their changing political status. Betty is played by a woman in Act Two, suggesting the influence of feminism and women's liberation in giving women a voice. Her soliloquy on masturbation enacts a similar process of self-realisation. Worried that she might find nothing there (p. 316), she discovers her own body can be a site of sexual gratification.

Betty's sexual pleasures suggest a gradual empowering of the disenfranchised, while other characters stumble towards a more provisional legitimacy. Her lover Martin asserts feminist leanings and a desire to prioritise female pleasure, yet Betty's refusal to give in immediately to multiple orgasms, prompts angry petulance from him (p. 301). Edward, the awkward Victorian boy of Act One, is now confident in his sexuality, but his desire for an emotional intimacy that goes beyond sexual encounters in a train-carriage or a one-night stands isolates him from the gay community. The shackles of colonialism are also hard to shake off; we hear, obliquely, of a civilian dying in the Northern Irish conflict, suggesting a Britain that has still not come to terms with its position, and the mournful Clive prowls the stage like a dispossessed Wyatt Gillman from John Osborne's *West of Suez*, recalling the high ideals of Empire (p. 320). Clive's reluctant abandonment of his performance as colonial patriarch highlights the vacuum left by prescriptive social ideals. Here is a missing generation that no longer knows how to perform without the script of social hegemony by its side.

Churchill's cross-gender and cross-racial casting along with her deliberate historical discontinuities suggest a radical and political reading of identity. Yet perhaps she is at her most subversive when questioning the efficacy of historicising categories of gender and race. A series of exchanges between Victoria, Betty's daughter, and her misanthropic lover Lin find a conflict between pragmatics and politics. Their attempt at a female orgy is continually transformed by Victoria into a lecture: she insists that sexual politics cannot be divorced from economics (p. 309). Elsewhere, their views of men set up starkly reductive binaries against Victoria's Marxist contexts: Lin hates men, but to Victoria their 'behaviour' dates back to the industrial revolution (p. 292).

By offering up both Lin's and Victoria's views for comment and critique, Churchill allows the audience to question her politicised reading of gender and race. Cross-dressing posits gender as nonessentialist, determined by our clothes rather than our genes; the undermining of Victoria's position here suggests that Marxist approaches to identity can be equally short-sighted and damaging, offering dangerously mitigating circumstances for individual choices and actions. Even though society shapes and contains us, it doesn't excuse us. The title of Churchill's play seems appropriately knowing in this context: the apparent utopia promised by 'Cloud Nine' can only be achieved by glib pronouncements, restrictive hierarchies, or suppressing personal desires. Characters from both time periods are equally guilty of sublimating individuals to an ideology. Churchill's play, meanwhile, resists this strait-jacketing; if her alienating techniques of cross-gender casting show her affinity with Brecht, she answers his dichotomy by creating a work that is both instructive and farcically entertaining.

Notes

1   Edward Bond, 'The Rational Theatre', *Plays: Two* (London: Methuen, 1998), p. xiv.

2   Bertolt Brecht, 'The Street Scene', trans. John Willet, *The Theory of the Modern Stage*, ed. Eric Bentley (Harmondsworth: Penguin, 1968), p. 86.

3   John Osborne, 'All words and no performance', *Damn You, England: Collected Prose* (London: Faber, 1994), p. 20.

4   John Osborne, 'A letter to my fellow countrymen', *Damn You England*, p. 194.

5   Judith Thurman, 'The Playwright who makes you laugh about orgasm, racism, class struggle, homophobia, woman-hating, the British Empire, and the irrepressible strangeness of the human heart', *Ms.*, May 1982, pp. 51–6, p. 54.

6   See Dan Rebellato, *1956 and All That: The Making of Modern British Drama* (London: Routledge, 1999), John Russell Taylor, *Anger and After: a guide to the new British theatre* (Harmondsworth: Pelican, 1968), and Michelene Wandor, *Look Back in Gender: Sexuality and Family in the Postwar British Drama* (London: Methuen, 1987).

7   John Osborne, 'Introduction', *Look Back in Anger and other plays* (London: Faber, 1993), p. xii.

8   Stephen Lacey, *British Realist Theatre: the New Wave in its context* (London: Routledge, 1995), p. 77.

9   John Osborne, *Look Back in Anger* (London: Faber, 1996), p. 96.

10 Edward Bond, *Saved* (London: Methuen, 1969), p. 37.

11 Edward Bond, 'Introduction', *Saved*, p. 6.

12 Caryl Churchill, *Softcops*, in *Plays: Two* (London: Methuen, 1990), p. 39.

13 Kenneth Tynan, 'Look Back in Anger', *A View of the English Stage* (London: Methuen, 1975), p. 178.

14 Caryl Churchill, *Light Shining in Buckinghamshire*, in *Plays: One* (London: Methuen, 1985), p. 183.

15 John Osborne, *The Blood of the Bambergs*, in *Plays for England/Watch it Come Down* (London: Oberon, 1999), p. 69.

16 Edward Bond, *Early Morning* (London: Calder and Boyars, 1968), p. 7.

17 John Osborne, quoted in John Heilpern, *John Osborne: A Patriot for Us* (London: Chatto & Windus, 2006), p. 367.

18 John Osborne, *West of Suez*, in *Plays: Two* (London: Faber, 1998), p. 151.

19 Edward Bond, *Narrow Road to the Deep North* (London: Methuen, 1968), p. 32.

20 John Osborne, *The Entertainer* (London: Faber, 1957), p. 49.

21   Caryl Churchill, *A Mouthful of Birds*, in *Plays: Three* (London: Nick Hern, 1998), p. 53.
22   John Osborne, *Luther* (London: Faber, 1961), p. 97.
23   Edward Bond, *Bingo*, in *Plays: Three* (London: Methuen, 1999), p. 56.
24   Edward Bond, 'Introduction', *Bingo*, p. 4.
25   Bryan Appleyard, *The Pleasures of Peace: art and imagination in post-war Britain* (London: Faber, 1989), p. 285.
26   Caryl Churchill, *Cloud Nine*, in *Plays One* (London: Methuen, 1996), p. 252.
27   Judith Butler, *Gender Trouble* (London: Routledge, 1990), p. 8.

New Stages: Beckett, Pinter and Stoppard

In a prose piece from the 1960s, the playwright Samuel Beckett explicitly rejects God or a teleological reading of the universe (i.e. one defined by outcome): '[t]he creation of the world did not take place once and for all time, but takes place every day.'[1] In its place we have the everyday, and the importance of human habit. Habit is the fundamental way humans create the world around them. For Beckett, this process is repetitive, obsessive, and banal. He embraces the mundane, but this does not create a realist social drama which, like Osborne's or Bond's, might pride itself on the veracity and relevance of its representations. Instead, the decontextualising of our habitual negotiations with the world creates drama that deliberately works against theatrical convention. A Beckett play might be written in two acts, but offer a near repetition of itself in place of development. As the incredulous critic Vivian Mercier said of *Waiting for Godot* (1955), it is a play in which nothing happens twice.[2] Characters might refer to a specific time or place but will inhabit a stage world shorn of realist referents or recognisable props; although they gesture to a world offstage, it is a world they barely know. In this way, Beckett's stage is at once in thrall to dramatic convention and a deliberate attempt to deconstruct it. Through the metatheatrical use of generic conventions, he creates characters condemned to the stage. Though his drama is preoccupied with our daily rituals, its effect on the audience is to make them continually question their habits as theatre-goers and humans.

Beckett's drama seems a radical break from theatrical habit, but it remains influenced by a series of European philosophers and playwrights clustering round France during the 1930s and 1940s, just as it would in turn influence the next two generations of British playwright. The playfully postmodern and absurdist works of Luigi Pirandello or Eugene Ionesco had already used the stage as a site of deconstruction. In Pirandello's *Six Characters in Search of an Author* (1921) we find a company rehearsing one of Pirandello's own works before six strangers interrupt proceedings. The French-Romanian playwright Ionesco, Beckett's contemporary, created a series of absurdist one-act plays in the early 1950s he would refer to as *anti-pièce* (anti-play). Relying on cyclical repetition and nonsequiturs rather than conventional character development, works such as *The Lesson* (1952) subject their bourgeois characters to surreal diversions, power games, and language play. The influential theatrical writings of Antonin Artaud and Bertolt Brecht had similarly called for a deliberate break with realist form, structuring theatre around cruelty, hostility, or the strategic alienation of the audience or actors. The writings of Jean-Paul Sartre and Albert Camus and the philosophical movements of nihilism and existentialism also offer vital contexts for reading Beckett's works. The fallout of the Second World War questioned the efficacy of beliefs and dogmas, and the godless worldview of nihilism and the notion that man created himself first and defined himself later provided important starting points for a new theatre, full of characters without obvious motivation or drive.

The conservative trend in postwar British poetry and fiction strengthened the sense of the avant-garde being centred on the stage. Tellingly, the theatre critic Martin Esslin had to look outside Britain for reference points when defining the revolutionary 'theatre of the absurd':

> The Theatre of the Absurd is thus part of the 'anti-literary' movement of our time, which has found its expression in abstract painting, with its rejection of 'literary' elements in pictures; or in the 'new novel' in France, with its reliance on the description of objects and its rejection of empathy and anthropomorphism.[3]

While few playwrights used Esslin's terminology to define themselves, British playwrights such as Pinter and, later, Tom Stoppard, shared the move towards metatheatrical techniques, a radical deconstruction of language, a rejection of the well-made play, and a reliance on the absurd or deliberately disorientating. Stoppard first came to prominence with *Rosencrantz and Guildenstern Are Dead* (1966), a work that pays knowing homage to Beckett. Osborne and Bond created works that revolutionised the British stage with their use of everyday language; Beckett, Pinter, and Stoppard applied similar scrutiny not just to the verbal language on stage, but to the formal language of theatrical convention itself.

Undermining Body and Self

Beckett's theatre is at once radically alienating and a form stripped to its fundamental essence. As Raymond Williams has suggested of modern drama, it continues the eternal concern with 'man trapped in bourgeois society and unable to escape from it'.[4] Beckett's stage is a place of physical obstacles, disembodied figures, and characters reluctant to remind themselves their life is a performance, but seemingly unable to withstand the temptation. Soliloquies, audience asides, and the standbys of vaudeville, slapstick, and skit become desperate and fleeting answers to the problems of a world without God. By drawing attention to the total artifice of theatre, Beckett deconstructs its realist principles as convention and finds a dark and often bleakly comic world in its place. *Not I* (1972) is both dramatic monologue and a laying bare of the traditional soliloquy. At the centre of its stage is a mouth hovering eight feet above stage level, denied distinguishing context by deep shadow. This speaking vessel is further stripped of autonomy by the presence of an auditor, enveloped throughout in a black djellaba, a loose-fitting robe often worn in North Africa. This forbidding onstage spectator condemns the mouth (played by a female actor) to recitation rather than confession, to surveillance rather than understanding. Only the 'gesture of helpless compassion' signalled by the mouth actor raising her arms offers the possibility of escape, or challenges the mouth's 'vehement refusal to relinquish third person'.[5] Here is a soliloquy that neither goes unnoticed by the onstage characters nor permits the speaker the agency of first person. In its place, Beckett's speaker offers a stuttering collage of phrases, distractedly telling the story of a girl in a godless world. As her closing lines suggest, the need to speak is a perpetual compulsion, but is followed with the self-recrimination of having said too much:

> sudden urge to … tell … then rush out stop the first she saw … nearest lavatory … start pouring it out … steady stream … mad stuff … half the vowels wrong … (p. 383)

Speech is both emetic and destabilised here, struggling to tie itself down either to recognisable phonics or fixed referents. The self is reduced to an apologetic third person, while the occluded body struggles to make itself distinguishable behind covered fabric or stage black-out.

Pinter's *The Birthday Party* (1958) apparently offers a conventional, realist stage, much of the action taking place in *'the living-room of a house in a seaside town'*.[6] Yet the everyday is soon undermined by unspecified threat, and the innocent soon destroyed by what Jeanette R. Malkin has seen as a 'violent verbal assault'.[7] Stanley, allegedly a lodger in Meg and Petey's boarding house, is preparing for the birthday party of the title, yet by the play's conclusion we are neither sure it was his birthday nor that the celebration that has taken place isn't closer to torture. Meg's first exchanges with him are a disturbing mixture of the maternal and the sexual, confusing our understanding of their relationship; throughout the play, Pinter disorientates our generic response by refusing to clearly delineate hierarchies, familial relations, or character histories. The play focuses on Goldberg and McCann, two shadowy figures whose addresses to Stanley combine verbal taunting and threats with obsequious cajoling. While they provide a menacing foil to Meg's comedy, their own relationship casts them as more complex than merely malevolent intruders. The final act finds Goldberg apparently offering a neat assertion of his beliefs, as if promising to reveal the reason for his casual cruelty to the baffled audience:

And you'll find – that what I say is true.
Because I believe that the world … (*Vacant.*) …
Because I believe that the world … (*Desperate.*) …
BECAUSE I BELIEVE THAT THE WORLD … (*Lost.*) …
(p. 108)

This is a play that resists, too, the formulaic revelations of denouement. Goldberg is a brutalised figure without belief, and the passive victims of his anger are no more able to offer up a creed than he is. Nihilism takes the place of dogma. Goldberg and McCann remove Stanley from the house without comment, while Meg is happy to evade subsequent questions, dropping her sexual and maternal response to Stanley in the self-serving interests of returning to her role as indifferent landlady. Her silence becomes more inappropriate and terrifying than the erotic overtures to her lodger which opened the play. *The Birthday Party* undermines our conventional response to theatre, self, and character by continually reminding us that selves are qualified, performed, and often offered as commodities for exchange in the context of social relationships.

While Pinter questions the authenticity or motivation of his characters with menacing ellipsis, Stoppard's *The Real Thing* (1982) mines this same process for comic appeal, exploring notions of love, expression, and integrity in a witty and complex play-within-a-play. Love is the intimate connection between two people that apparently belies our strategic and self-serving presentation of ourselves in public but, as Stoppard points out, the language we speak, even in whispered conversations pledging fidelity to a partner, is full of guile and equivocation. The complex structure of his play centres on a playwright, Max, who is rehearsing a play on love called 'House of Cards'. *The Real Thing* cuts between scenes from Max's play and his own interaction with his actress-wife Charlotte, who is playing an adulterous wife in the play. Along the way, various other dramatic depictions of love form an intertextual net for these two opposing realities, as in John Ford's *'Tis Pity She's A Whore* (1633) and Strindberg's *Miss Julie* (1888).

One of the selves deconstructed in Stoppard's play is the acting self. Charlotte is unconvinced by the character she plays in her husband's work; a real discovery of infidelity, she suggests, would not produce the acid remarks in Max's play: 'You don't in reality think that if Henry caught me out with a lover, he'd sit around being witty about place mats?'[8] Stoppard in part deconstructs his own writing self here, too, presenting us with a first scene which the audience assumes is 'his' play, only to have it dissected in scene two by its onstage author and actress. The opening scene, which finds Max and Charlotte raking over the coals of her infidelity, finds a bitter Max complimenting her on 'those little touches that lift adultery out of the moral arena and make it a matter of style' (p. 13). Style as a substitute for substance, or more particularly language as a obstacle to self-expression, means that these characters, although in a very different theatrical world from Beckett's mouth or Pinter's Meg, find themselves equally unable to convince those on stage of their own presence. Every word they speak carries the artifice of rhetorical flourish or the studied banality of 'real life'. Even the pursuit of love comes less from a selfless desire and more from the nagging need for self-knowledge, 'not of the flesh but through the flesh, knowledge of self, the real him, the real her, *in extremis*, the mask slipped from the face' (p. 63). The more ingeniously these arguments are rehearsed, as Henry comes to learn, the further language travels from the notion of the authentic.

Reproducing the Voice

The distrust of language and the relationship between signifier and signified* comes to define the work of all three playwrights, from Pinter's infamous silences to the muted or enclosed voices of Beckett. More specifically, both Beckett and Stoppard construct works around the mechanical reproduction of a voice, in *Krapp's Last Tape* (1958) and *Artist Descending a Staircase* (1973) respectively. In these works, the tape player ventriloquises characters who are either dead, in Stoppard's case, or effectively dead to the cynical listener on stage, as in Beckett's.

---

* The terms signifier and signified were used by the Swiss linguist Ferdinand de Saussure and later theorists such as Roland Barthes. For Saussure, the signifier is the phonic shape of a word (e.g. b-o-o-k for book), and the signified is the object or idea it represents.

Language is a facsimile of meaning, a shared code that nevertheless remains slippery and subjective, yet here the simple phonic certainty of a voice on stage is undermined by denying it a physical presence. What we hear is not what we see. The interest of all three playwrights, particularly Beckett, in radio drama, suggests not only an engagement with new audiences and modes of communication, but also a preoccupation with disembodied voices or, as in the pauses of Pinter, with voiceless bodies.

Beckett's one-act play *Krapp's Last Tape* presents us with a 'wearish old man'[9] at a gloomy table, recording his annual recollection of the previous year. He interrupts the recording by listening to the corresponding tape he made as a man of thirty-nine, pausing to reflect on 'that stupid bastard I took myself for thirty years ago, hard to believe I was ever as bad as that' (p. 222). However, his ensuing cynicism does not grant him authority; as the incriminating old tape shows, his rejection of his younger self only mimics his earlier rejection of the same at thirty-nine: the younger Krapp comments on a tape from his twenties, laughing off with arrogant dismissal an old relationship as 'well out of that, Jesus yes!' (p. 218). Even within the younger Krapp's recounting of an older tape, he glosses how a much younger Krapp 'sneers at what he calls his youth and thanks to God that it's over' (p. 218). All that has altered then is Krapp's response to the perceived 'change' in himself, from humorous disbelief to bitter incredulity. Here the past self is both a terrible reminder of mortality and the most fragile of companions. The mechanically reproduced sound of the speaking voice must stand in for the absent other that might offer the opportunity for dialogue. What appears to be a rigorous process of documenting a life becomes a crabbed spectacle of self-incrimination. As Krapp ultimately knows, the past tapes he disowns will eventually outlive him. This is a play that keeps returning to the body, from Krapp's bowel movements to his child-like joy in repeating the word 'spool'. However, it is the recording device that runs on in silence at the play's conclusion, by which time Krapp is motionless; the mechanical hiss of the tape has the final word.

While *Krapp's Last Tape* presents the recorded voice as a precursor of death, or the dissection of a life into a series of discrete, disowned selves, Stoppard's radio play *Artist Descending a Staircase* uses a tape recording to reconstruct the final moments of a murdered man. While Stoppard comically exploits the possibilities and limitations of the radio drama to consider the conflict between what we hear and what we feel to be true, the play's bravura energy remains haunted by the mechanised disenchantment of Beckett's Krapp. The play opens with artists and friends Beauchamp and Martello attempting to piece together the death of their mutual friend Donner, when they discover him dead in his home with a tape recorder on. Yet this premise is also an opportunity to stage their ongoing debate about the nature of art and mimesis (the use of imitation to represent characters). For Beauchamp, a sonic artist, his recordings of found sounds and everyday noises are unacknowledged masterpieces. The decoding of Donner's soundtrack to his death only proves, for him, the ambivalence of the everyday and his insistence that 'imagination without skill gives us modern art'.[10] Yet, as a flashback recalls, the traditional portrait painter Donner found in the 'tonal debris' of Beauchamp's work only 'rubbish' (p. 122). Martello's abstract approach is equally hostile to Donner's realism; as Martello argues, if the purpose of art is to emulate nature 'the greater the success, the more false the result' (p. 140). All three artists' positions are perhaps further undermined by the tape recording itself. Sounds they hear as Donner snoring turn out to be a fly buzzing; the recording of his murder turns out to be the swatting of a fly. The recording becomes pregnant with meaning not because of the intentions of its creator – it comes to exist, quite literally, through the death of the artist rather than through deliberate contrivance. However, for that very reason, the competing 'readings' of the recording mean that, far from documenting a specific moment in time, it offers listeners a series of different interpretations. The recording, a mechanical reproduction of an event, seems many-layered as a poem.

Both Beckett and Stoppard end their plays with a tape spooling on into silence, its quiet hiss an aural reminder of the speech that is missing from the dramatic soundscape. For Pinter, this moment of deliberate space and omission defines his early plays and the critical reception to them. What was termed the 'Pinteresque pause' – the awkward gap that interrupts dialogue – gradually comes to threaten his characters as much as the other figure on stage. Max, the patriarch at the centre of *The Homecoming* (1965), boasts that when he used to walk into a bar with his friend MacGregor 'you never heard such silence'.[11] The traditional male swagger is replaced with the ability to render the astounded onlookers mute. Pinter's early plays often had a similar effect on their audience. Throughout *The Homecoming*, which focuses on the return of Max's grown son, Teddy, from America along with his wife Ruth, speech and the ability to speak become symbolically important acts. As Ruth notes, 'the fact that [my lips] move is more significant … than the words which come through them' (p. 53). Yet the verbal male jousting between Max, Teddy, and his two brothers that makes up so much of the play is ultimately subservient to physical dominance. Despite the misogynist rants directed at Ruth and Jessie, Max's dead wife, the play ends, symbolically, with Ruth in the ascendant. The voice has become an instrument of evasion, enacting a literal lip service throughout the work of all three playwrights.

Doubled Acts

Waiting for Godot (1955), first performed in French in 1953 but translated by Beckett the following year, remains the most famous English-language play of the postwar period, or perhaps the twentieth century. Its bare stage, inhabited only by a starkly artificial tree and a road that leads to and from nowhere, is impossible both to escape and to meaningfully inhabit. Attempting this impossible challenge are Vladimir and Estragon, a pair of tramps whose inability either to leave the stage or to commit suicide defines the inertia of the play. The two acts mimic each other in cruel parody, denying the characters a sense of agency or the promise of change. Both find the pair engrossed, distracted, or bored by their phatic conversation,* debating whether to leave or wait for the play's eponymous subject to meet them. A messenger boy breaks their monotony but offers them only a perpetual deferring of their vacant subject, putting them off again at the play's conclusion. Both acts find further parallels in disruptions by Lucky and Pozzo, a wizened and

---

* Trivial verbal contact that establishes social connections rather than exchanging ideas.

shackled man and his master, who pass them by in Act One only to return, blind and aged, in Act Two. Vladimir and Estragon swap roles within their relationship as often as they swap hats, while Lucky and Pozzo are defined by Lucky's servitude. Lucky's name is perhaps only half ironic; with serfdom comes a clear sense of purpose and an escape from freedom with its concomitant responsibilities and anxieties.

Tellingly the play's first spoken lines are 'nothing to be done';[12] the immediate dramatic referent is Estragon's boot, which stubbornly refuses to come off, giving us the sense of nothing to be done *about it*. Yet the phrase is more widely applicable to the characters onstage, both in its passivity and its implied imperative. This is a world without human agency, full of compulsions without convictions. Vladimir and Estragon's discussion of the bible, in particular the parable of the thieves, suggests a religious context, but critics who have read 'Godot' as 'God' miss the play's resigned ambivalence. Logical thought itself is unravelled and revealed as cant; in the first act, Vladimir, Estragon, and Pozzo all urge Lucky to think, yet this imperative is barely sentient. To think in this context is to perform a wicked parody of academic intellect; the previously silent Lucky utters an emetic stream of nonsense and pseudo-academic verbiage as Pozzo goads him on *'with increasing suffering'* (p. 12). The play's theatrical language is halfway between vaudeville, philosophy, and skit, the dialogue, despite the dramatic inertia, running back and forth between the banal and the profound. Pointedly, Vladimir's only extended speech begins with an imperative: 'let us not waste our time in idle discourse' (p. 75). Whatever force his rhetoric has is entirely undermined by the fact he continues with thirty lines of stodgy prose. Even as his words advocate action, they refuse to stop. These open contradictions between thought and action create a work that is both comic and tragic, as its subtitle – 'a tragicomedy' – suggests. The pairings suggest companionship, but are driven by necessity rather than desire.

Stoppard reflects Beckett's interest in pairs not only by structuring *Rosencrantz and Guildenstern Are Dead* (1966) around the offstage deliberations of two unwitting bit-players, but by juggling both Beckett's *Waiting for Godot* and Shakespeare's *Hamlet* throughout the play. Just as the grandly named Vladimir and Estragon rely for their continued existence on the go-between messages of the young boy, Rosencrantz and Guildenstern are equally at the beck and call of offstage forces. These forces are the same ones that take centre stage in *Hamlet*: while in Shakespeare's play the pair are bit players in a tragedy, charged to discover the motivations for Hamlet's increasingly strange behaviour, here they are the central characters. Their inability to understand the implication of Hamlet's actions means that they experience the play as a comedy. Only in their final death, which we never see, do we realise that for them, too, the play must finally be a tragedy. Like Vladimir and Estragon, their distracted, stichomythic* dialogues are a mixture of farcical exchanges and unwitting philosophising, pitched halfway between boredom and anxiety at their eventual fate. Just as the play presents itself as an echo of both Beckett and Shakespeare, Guildenstern finds frustrated companionship in his parroting dialogues with Rosencrantz:

> GUIL: (*Turning on him furiously*) Why don't you say something original! No wonder the whole thing is so stagnant! You don't take me up on anything – you just repeat it in a different order.
> ROS: I can't think of anything original. I'm only good in support.[13]

The dialogues throw up a knowing metatheatrical comment on the play itself, which repeats lines from *Hamlet* with a renewed emphasis. *Hamlet*, too, finds players putting on 'The Mouse-trap', a play-within-a-play specifically staged by Hamlet to assess his stepfather's guilt. Does *Rosencrantz and Guildenstern* offer a similarly intrinsic relationship to its original? For much of the play, both characters have a sense of agency denied either Hamlet or Vladimir and Estragon, even if they choose not to exercise it: 'we are not restricted … spontaneity and whim are the order of the day' (p. 85). Their perverse misreading of *Hamlet* stresses contingency and possibility, suggesting an alternative approach to a play seemingly governed by fate. *Hamlet* the text has condemned them to die by the end of the play, but Hamlet the character still allows them the possibility of survival.

---

* Stichomythic dialogue comprises a series of alternating exchanges, where characters use each other's phrases in order to refute them.

Pinter, too, returns to *Waiting for Godot* in *The Caretaker* (1960). The boots that Estragon cannot take off in the first scene of Beckett's play are recalled here by the mentally unstable Aston, who insists 'you've got to have a good pair of shoes'.[14] Where Stoppard turns Beckett absurdist by making his characters revel in the meaningless of life, Pinter expands on Beckett's sense of unspecified menace. The three characters on stage for much of the play trade details of the past like assertions of power. Mick, the apparent owner of the house, plagues the other characters with darkness and threats of violence. Aston, his housemate, gradually reveals the suppressed terror behind his electric shock treatment for depression. Davies, the tramp whose arrival at the house prompts the play's central action, continually apologises for, erases, and defers the question of his past, repeating like a mantra his desire to fetch his papers from Sidcup. His missing papers make him a vulnerable refugee as well as homeless tramp – 'I can't move without them … they tell you who I am' (p. 18). He waits for the same meaningless absolution that Vladimir and Estragon expect in *Godot*, his papers offering the gesture of agency that Rosencrantz and Guildenstern demand from the text of *Hamlet*. Davies admits to the use of a pseudonym to keep him safe, but his presence as a marginal outsider points to other projections of 'menace' in the play, as in the obsessively repeated references to 'them Blacks' (p. 222) next door, who become both cipher for Mick's hatred of the foreigner and convenient scapegoat for the untoward sounds that haunt their house. By the play's conclusion, Mick's assertion that Davies is 'violent … erratic' and 'just completely unpredictable' (p. 71) disguises self-diagnosis under revelation. In their destructive triangle of power, caretaking is the only possible substitute for belonging. Yet, despite Davies's continual refrain, he can no more leave the stage for Sidcup than Vladimir and Estragon. As with Beckett, Pinter's play ends with stasis and silence.

Memory Plays

The profound ambivalence towards the past suggested in *The Caretaker* highlights a series of works by Pinter, Stoppard, and Beckett that draw on the apparent comforts of memory to reform and unravel the histories of their characters. Once again, words become unstable, frail, and dissembling things that contort the experience they attempt to recreate. In Beckett's words, yesterday is 'irremediably part of us, within us, heavy and dangerous'.[15] Winnie in Beckett's *Happy Days* (1960) is a 'well-preserved'[16] woman whose repeated cry of 'happy days' is both a eulogy to an unlikely past and an increasingly ironic comment on her onstage present: Act One finds her buried up to her waist, while by Act Two the mound has reached her neck, leaving her little beyond facial expressions to dramatise her apparent ebullience. Her 'preservation' suggests less an active middle age than being embalmed. As the set envelops her body, her breezy holiday mood and entreaties to the silent onstage Willie sound increasingly desperate. Her obsessive rituals of brushing her teeth, pinning and replacing her hat, and fixing her hair are revealed as empty gestures, like a method actor preparing for a difficult role. Her incarceration in Act Two makes these evasions, or expressions, of personality, impossible. Even while she still has the use of her arms, her physical and verbal signals to the audience that she is 'remembering' seem unwieldy and distracted:

> I close my eyes – [*she takes off spectacles and does so, hat in one hand, spectacles in another*, WILLIE *turns page*] – and am sitting on his knees again, in the back garden at Borough Green, under the horse-beech. [*Pause. She opens eyes, puts on spectacles, fiddles with hat.*] Oh the happy memories! (p. 142)

Here, the return to the past must be accompanied by elaborate physical gesture, as if it can be recalled only with the present out of focus. The indifferent presence of Willie, who spends much of the play reading the newspaper, sets up the pull of personal memory against the obsessive interest in the now. Little of her reminiscence can distract him from the contemporary and ephemeral seduction of the paper. Winnie's past is recalled as a way of avoiding the present, which finds her head literally being buried in the sand. However, Willie's stubborn evasion of their personal history further undermines the authenticity of her speech.

Pinter's *No Man's Land* (1975) places similar structural pressure on the past. Only the moment lived out on stage carries any degree of authority. The play centres on Spooner and Hirst, two characters who cannot agree on whether they are strangers, adversaries, or old friends. For Spooner, experience is 'a paltry thing', only of interest to the 'psychological interpreters'; he remains determined that 'the present will not be distorted'.[17] Hirst's earnest digressions on his past and upbringing prompt disbelief, indifference, and mimicry from Spooner, who spitefully draws out his stories until there is nothing left but silence:

> Tell me more about the quaint little perversions of your life and times. Tell me more, with the all the authority and brilliance you can muster, about the socio-politico-economic structure of the environment in which you attained to the age of reason. (p. 94)

Once Hirst's memory bank is exhausted, Foster enters the room, another character who attempts to learn from history and past events only for Spooner to insist 'you would be wise to grant the event no integrity whatsoever' (p. 106). Spooner's erasure of the past and its lessons eventually suggest cultural oppression and political subjugation as much as a personal disdain for nostalgia. Despite Spooner's private suspicion that he has 'known this before' (p. 121), suggesting a past that has been suppressed but not forgotten, the play ends with Spooner inflicting the worst of all possible tortures on the assembled characters: the eternal present. The no man's land of the title is finally revealed as a silent room 'which never moves, which never changes, which never grows older, but which remains forever, icy and silent' (p. 157). Like the engulfing sands which paralyse Winnie in *Happy Days*, here the characters must bear the stasis and inertia of the empty stage without the possibility of returning to the past, even in the mind.

Mistaken identities and a vigorously contested past shape the dynamics of *No Man's Land*, representing memory as a subjective and often manipulative force. Stoppard's *Travesties* (1974), as its name suggests, goes one step further, and centres on the documentary recreation of three iconic figures who all found themselves in Zurich in 1918: Lenin, Joyce, and the Dada artist Tristan Tzara. Fact can attest to their presence in Zurich that year; an imaginative process on the part of Stoppard and the play's protagonist, the invalid soldier Henry Carr, reanimates their conjectural meeting. Here political history and personal memory make comic and often awkward bedfellows but Carr, like Stoppard, refuses to apologise for the fragmented text that makes up the play, 'constant digression being the saving grace of senile reminiscence'.[18] The world events that have brought them to Zurich suggest a meeting that is both accidental and pivotal to the years that follow. Their hermetic existence in the politically neutral Switzerland – 'even when there is war *everywhere else*, there is no war in Switzerland' (p. 9) as Carr reminds us – raises further questions about the responsibilities of art. How to balance the writing of Joyce, depicted here trying to complete *Ulysses*, with his responsibilities to his fellow man? Is Joyce right, as he claims, to 'attach no importance to the swings and roundabouts of political history' (p. 32)? The framing circumlocutory narrative of Henry Carr evokes the memory play, famously explored in Tennessee Williams's *The Glass Menagerie* (1944), with the central character recollecting his world to the audience while participating in it, making him half character, half onstage director. Stoppard further complicates the notion of the memory play by introducing Henry's own memories of a particular play, more specifically his starring role in Oscar Wilde's *The Importance of Being Earnest* (1895). Wilde's comedy of mistaken identities and misplaced children is echoed in various strands in the plot, as in the scene where all the characters unintentionally exchange their letters in the library. Yet the intertextual reference asks Stoppard difficult questions, too: Wilde could dismiss the need to be earnest with a flick of the epigrammatic wrist, but how might Stoppard and the postmodern playfulness of his early work answer the same charge? Tzara's critique of Joyce's draft for *Ulysses* pre-empts this reading of Stoppard's play:

> As an arrangement of words it is graceless without being random; as a narrative it lacks charm or even vulgarity; as an experience it is like sharing a cell with a fanatic in search of a mania. (p. 69)

Here Joyce's *Ulysses*, the supreme attempt to render interiority, is dismissed as graceless. Stoppard's own work attempts to answer this charge. Although the play is centred around a single man's recollections, it forgoes an interest in unreliable subjective memory for an exploration of political and intellectual history. Here, the individual memory is a structural expedient rather than a subject of discussion.

Philosophies of Theatre

Despite the influential writings of Artaud, Brecht, or Stanislavski, who pioneered method acting, Beckett, Pinter, and Stoppard were reluctant to define themselves via manifesto or critical practice. Beckett famously quipped that if he had known what Godot represented he would have said so in the play; Pinter refused to defend or explain the silences and cruelties of his early work; and Stoppard littered his plays with a series of conflicting metatheatrical languages.* This was a new stage that deliberately downplayed the role of the author as locus of meanings, even if the playwrights often demanded more directorial control. Yet Pinter, Stoppard, and Beckett offer theatrical worlds that even in their idiosyncrasies and intransigence, suggest, for example, recognisably Pinteresque or Beckettian perspectives. As Raymond Williams has argued, 'the more general pattern of unreality, failure to communicate, and meaninglessness is indeed now so widespread that it is, virtually, in itself, a dramatic convention.'[19] Beckett's *Endgame* (1957), like much of his work, gives its audience empty ritual in the place of conventional plot development. The double pairings of *Waiting for Godot* are recalled in the duos of Hamm and Clov, who cannot stand or sit down respectively, and Nell and Nag, Hamm's legless parents who inexplicably live in dustbins. The nonreferential stage seems post-apocalyptic, with only a small black window at the back offering the characters any point of exit or possibility of acknowledging the world outside the suffocating stage space. Nell's death towards the end of the play occurs with little comment; the nihilism of her existence seems no more preferable to the inevitably of her demise. As Nell suggests, 'it's like the funny story we have heard too often, we still find it funny, but we don't laugh any more'.[20] The consolations of comedy become both parodic and deadening through continual repetition.

While Beckett's theatre hovers between parody and nihilism, Stoppard's work takes a parallel interest in absorbing a range of contesting

---

* For a discussion of meta-literature, see Part Three: 'The Postmodern Novel'.

theatrical traditions. His play *Jumpers* (1972) begins with a faded music-hall performer who is announced as the 'incomparable, magnetic Dorothy Moore' but confesses to the audience her qualifying adjectives are more probably 'unreliable, neurotic'.[21] In this intimate displacement of her promised brilliance, she at once points up a tension between the expected and the actual and pledges her fidelity to the audience by the very fact of her admission of being 'unreliable'. Like a postmodern version of Osborne's Archie Rice in *The Entertainer*, her fragments of song and half-forgotten melodies suggest the gradual erosion of a civic, community theatre. She is supposedly magnetic, yet all she attracts is an increasingly bizarre and contradictory stage world, as suggested by the ambivalent stage direction 'her bedroom forms around her' (p. 14). She is married to George Moore, a moral philosopher intent on proving the existence of God. Their marriage, with its familiar pattern of an academic intellectual neglectful of his beautiful, deranged wife, suggests comparisons with Ibsen or Chekhov, and the psychological realism of late nineteenth-century drama. Yet this, too, is an influence that is rejected: in place of psychological realism, Stoppard offers us mental and physical gymnastics, a world where, as Archie suggests, the truth is an 'interim judgement' (p. 89).

The plot centres on a wayward team of amateur gymnasts, one of whom has been murdered while they were practising a human pyramid formation in Moore's study. Their physical agility is called into question by their shabby appearance and aging physiques, while the Professor's mental capacities are similarly tested by his inability to solve the murder. His debates on materialism and human existence offer him little when faced with a need for empirical evidence. The jumpers themselves, with their mixture of burlesque and farce, introduce a competing theatrical genre onto the stage. Stoppard flirts with yet another genre in the detective plot, which tracks incompetent attempts to identify the murderer. Here, the conventions of the well-made play or the neat denouements of J. B. Priestley's *An Inspector Calls* (1945) or Agatha Christie's *The Mousetrap* (1952) are invoked only to be rejected. In a world that is at once madcap and subject to continued philosophical scrutiny by its strutting professors, Stoppard operates a theatrical heteroglossia (literally, 'many languages'), constructing a porous space full of competing narratives and generic modes.

In a profoundly destabilised world, all Archie can offer the audience by way of concluding consolation is the promise that 'one of the thieves was saved' (p. 89), echoing the theological musings of Vladimir and Estragon in *Waiting for Godot*. The drawing-room-cum-gymnasium setting of *Jumpers* is an apt metaphor for the postwar stage. All three playwrights manipulate the apparent openness of the stage world – the 'empty space' that Peter Brook evoked in 1968 – to create dramas of elision, omission, and evasion. Characters are blinded, physically immobile, unable to speak, or denied the possibility of leaving the stage. Even their memories are found wanting, unravelling before them. Yet while the nihilistic and unsettling stage worlds of Stoppard, Beckett, and Pinter might suggest inertia, their influence on postwar British drama was vital.

Extended Commentary: Pinter, *The Room* (1960)

Pinter's play *The Room* (1960) was the first he ever wrote, completing it in 1957, three years before its first professional production at the Hampstead Theatre Club in London. It provides an early distillation of his 1950s and 1960s works, but also gestures to the shared formal concerns of a generation of postwar playwrights. The stark title immediately invites comparison with the absurdist works of Ionesco, whose plays *The Lesson* (1952) and *The Chairs* (1948) offer elliptical clues to their often baffling onstage dialogues. This is an everyday space or object subjected to *reductio ad absurdum*. In Pinter's case, it is both a very particular room in a working-class area of London, all rooms and anything denoted by the signifier 'room', and a fictionalised room that cannot exist outside a single moment on stage. The disorientating shifts between these three different rooms means that, although the action never leaves the titular space, its location is continually undermined. The social milieu of the play, as in many of Pinter's early works, aligns it with the British New Wave and the kitchen-sink realism of Osborne or Bond; the room of the play's title is a dingy 1950s living room in a two-storey London house. Like many of Pinter's rooms, its ownership is contested: Rose appears to be a tenant to Mr Kidd's landlord but throughout the play, intruders, strangers, and anticipated visitors all come to stake their claims. These interruptions and intrusions are also interruptions to the New Wave genre: although the locales and accents on stage suggest an affinity with Jimmy Porter, the verbal violence inflicted on various characters in Pinter's play forgo Osborne's stagey diatribes for ominous precision and unsettling repetition; Pinter's world suggests social disintegration rather than social tension.

The play begins with Rose talking to an apparently indifferent and unlistening character called Bert Hudd before he drives off in a van. Her monologue appears phatic and banal, but hints at a danger that Hudd has narrowly escaped: 'It's good you weren't down there, in the basement'.[22] Through her speech, she creates the room as a refuge and safe house, as if it were a fall-out shelter from some unspecified catastrophe. Yet Bert's silent presence makes it unclear whether they share the room or whether either one of them might be an unwilling prisoner – Rose's ambiguous switch between plural pronouns and the singular evade the issue of occupation: 'we're all right … You're happy up here' (p. 87). Eventually they are revealed to be a married couple, but subsequent events undermine their pairing. Their room is occupied, but barely inhabited. Even in Rose's apparently innocuous patter, she offers flat contradictions which further unsettle our reading of Bert's silence: she praises her lovely weak tea despite telling Bert she's left it standing in the pot; she repeatedly declares that 'nobody bothers us' (p. 87) while looking anxiously out of the window for the next intruder. Like the silent Lucky in *Waiting for Godot* or the ominous auditor in *Not I*, Pinter uses the onstage presence of Bert to ensure none of his characters finds respite from the anxiety of surveillance. Rose's inconsistencies echo the apparently bald statements made throughout the play. People say they are leaving only to stubbornly remain on stage; they claim not to have met only to share a furtive reminiscence. The onstage characters are at once obtuse and suspicious of these contradictions. Even the Sands, a couple who come in looking for a spare room, describe the basement only to insist they have walked down from the attic. The room oscillates between a desolate bed-sit and an eerily voyeuristic space.

Throughout the play, Pinter elides the deictic (or direct) language of the stage with the characters' verbal contradictions. A good example of this comes in the use of the word 'vacant'. The Sands have been told that the room is vacant by Riley, but Rose assures them it is 'full up' and 'occupied' (p. 102). When Rose questions the landlord, he avoids answering her directly by offering another kind of vacancy in its place:

> ROSE. Mr Kidd, what did they mean about this room?
> MR KIDD. What room?
> ROSE. Is this room vacant?
> MR KIDD. Vacant? (p. 103)

Throughout the play, the vacancy of the characters becomes as unsettling as the stark presentation of the room. The frequent pauses, gaps, and silences create another kind of absence. When reading the play script, the contest between the conclusive stage directions and the often dissembling statements by characters about where they are going and why creates another sort of textual contest: here it is consensus which is absent.

The entrance of Mr Kidd the landlord heightens the ambiguity of the stage space rather than reclaiming it. He prompts a series of exchanges which use evasion and omission to make their menace unmistakable, even if their particulars are vague, as in Mr Kidd's reminiscence of his dead sister:

> MR KIDD. She had a lovely boudoir. A beautiful boudoir.
> ROSE. What did she die of?
> MR KIDD. Who?
> ROSE. Your sister.
> *Pause.*
> MR KIDD. I've made ends meet.
> *Pause.*
> ROSE. You full at the moment, Mr Kidd?
> MR KIDD. Packed out.
> ROSE. All sorts, I suppose?
> MR. KIDD. Oh yes, I make ends meet. (p. 92)

Here we find a language where, as Pinter has commented 'under what is said, another thing is said'.[23] Kidd's refusal to answer Rose's question about his sister's death makes his digression into a euphemism. The colloquialism of 'making ends meet' is reinvested with a latent terror: his own sister's unspecified 'end' is confessed to here and ignored. He is both scrimping and saving, and exploring any brutal action which will help him to continue doing so. Each subsequent phrase – 'packed out' – is haunted by a displaced threat, while each repetition of the phrase 'I make ends meet' builds on its ominous implication. The unsettling tribute to his sister's 'beautiful boudoir' hints both at forced prostitution and murder, but these are possible crimes never confirmed, uncovered, or brought to justice. Throughout the play, apparently innocuous dialogue ensures that the audience come to fear both the room and the unspecified world beyond it. As Mrs Sands nervously remarks of the weather, 'it's murder out' (p. 95).

The unspoken crime committed by Mr Kidd is mirrored in the play's conclusion. A blind black man called Riley who lives in the basement demands to see Rose, claiming he has a message for her. When he forces his way into the room he addresses her as Sal and asks her to 'come home' (p. 109). When Bert returns and finds them embracing, he kicks Riley to the floor, possibly to death. The play ends with Rose declaring she has gone blind. Yet the blindness that Riley seemingly 'transfers' to Rose engulfs the play in other ways, too: the death of Mr Kidd's sister is an event the audience never sees, but is invited to imagine; the death of Riley is an event that apparently occurs onstage, but is never verbally confirmed by any of the characters. With speech itself a subversive act, the audience relies on their visual impressions only to find that they, too, are impossible to read. Like the baffled artists at the opening of Stoppard's *Artist Descending A Staircase* who must piece together a death from a tape recording, or the party-game turned intimidation tactic that is the blind man's bluff played onstage in *The Birthday Party*, Pinter makes his play ambivalent while further undermining our own subjective powers of reasoning. His conversations, which move between menace and inertia, are the only refuge against the ever-present threats of darkness and silence. The silent blackout which finishes *The Room* finds its characters subsumed by both.

Notes

1   Samuel Beckett, *'Proust' and Three Dialogues* (London: John Calder, 1965), p. 19.

2   Vivian Mercier, *The Irish Times*, 18 February 1956, p. 18.

3   Martin Esslin, *The Theatre of the Absurd* (Harmondsworth: Penguin, 1968), p. 26.

4   Raymond Williams, *Drama from Ibsen to Brecht* (London: Chatto & Windus, 1968), p. 342.

5   Samuel Beckett, *Not I*, in *The Complete Dramatic Works* (London: Faber, 1990), p. 375.

6   Harold Pinter, *The Birthday Party* (London: Faber, 1993), p. 39.

7   Jeanne R. Malkin, *Verbal Violence in Contemporary Drama* (Cambridge: Cambridge University Press, 1992), p. 54.

8   Tom Stoppard, *The Real Thing* (London: Faber, 1984), p. 22.

9   Samuel Beckett, *Krapp's Last Tape*, in *The Complete Dramatic Works*, p. 215.

10   Tom Stoppard, *Artist Descending A Staircase*, in *Stoppard: The Plays for Radio 1964–1991* (London: Faber, 1990), p. 122.

11   Harold Pinter, *The Homecoming* (London: Methuen, 1965), p. 8.

12   Samuel Beckett, *Waiting for Godot*, in *The Complete Dramatic Works*, p. 12.

13   Tom Stoppard, *Rosencrantz and Guildenstern Are Dead* (London: Faber, 1967), p. 76.

14   Harold Pinter, *The Caretaker*, in *Plays: Two* (London: Faber, 1991), p. 11.

15   *'Proust' and Three Dialogues*, p. 15.

16   Samuel Beckett, *Happy Days*, in *The Complete Dramatic Works*, p. 143.

17   Harold Pinter, *No Man's Land*, in *Plays: Four* (London: Faber, 1991), p. 84.

18   Tom Stoppard, *Travesties* (London: Faber, 1975), p. 6.

19   Raymond Williams, *Modern Tragedy* (London: Hogarth Press, 1992), p. 153.

20   Samuel Beckett, *Endgame*, in *The Dramatic Works of Samuel Beckett* (London: Faber, 1986), p. 101.

21   Tom Stoppard, *Jumpers* (London: Faber, 1973), p. 17.

22   Harold Pinter, *The Room*, in *Plays: One* (London: Faber, 1991), p. 87.

23   Harold Pinter, 'Writing for the Theatre', *Various Voices: Poetry, Prose and Politics 1948–1998* (London: Faber, 1998), p. 56.

Part Four
Critical Theories and Debates

Nostalgia and National Identity

The Midlands are coming, Birmingham coming nearer
Past grey sheep chewing
At scrubland fields. *That's England for you,*
This table-cloth should be absolutely white.

Alan Brownjohn, 'In the Trade'[1]

Alan Brownjohn's image of a uninterested long-distance commuter surveying England's shabby landscapes in his poem 'In the Trade' is as particular in its Britishness as its speaker seems vaguely indifferent. Its dismissive *'That's England for you'* expects little better than scrubland fields, and the nonchalant sheep are as passively part of this landscape as the humans who inhabit it. Soon their attention turns from the exterior back to the railway carriage, where the speaker's pedantic cleanliness hints at racial anxieties about his Britain and its makeup. His whining conditional 'should' also suggests a nation that somehow fails to meet the speaker's already low expectations. Each geographical signpost on this journey is noted with a sense of inevitability rather than mythic ritual.

Britain has often been a landscape viewed through the window of a train. With a characteristically Victorian belief in progress, the nineteenth-century poet Alfred Lord Tennyson felt the 'ringing grooves of change'[2] as he took his first steam railway journey in 'Locksley Hall' (1842). Here was a technology promising new possibilities for high-speed travel, and one which offered another way of viewing the nation's landscape. It symbolised British confidence and a sense of national superiority; the country was now traversable from East to West in a little over two hours, and as its architectural wonders flew by it was difficult to argue with its claim to greatness. In twentieth-century literature, the train journey offered a more haunted ambivalence just as its buildings, as Nikolaus Pevsner's mammoth *The Buildings of England* (1951–74) shows us, suggest an architectural history that has been squandered and neglected. Edward Thomas's 'Adelstrop' (1917) describes a memory of passing a branch line station, the image underwritten with a sense of fragility. The poem begins with an affirmation and ends with the enraptured noise of all the birds of Oxfordshire and Gloucestershire. Yet within this comforting frame of memory, continuity, and nature, the speaker remembers too that no-one boarded or left the train at the stop: even in his celebration of its solitude, he hints at its eventual destruction.

In fact it was domestic politics, rather than wartime deprivation, that destroyed the world Thomas glimpses fleetingly through his train window. In the 1950s and 1960s, Sir Richard Beeching advised the government to overhaul the national rail system through a process known as 'rationalisation'. Smaller branch lines were closed, and over a third of the nation's rail network was shut down. This drive towards efficiency and modernisation was in keeping with Tennyson's notion of progress, yet stripped the railway of the pastoral possibilities it offered for viewing the nation.

It is no accident then that Larkin, the postwar poet so often associated with a nostalgic English past, sets his most memorable poetic speakers in transit, looking from train windows into worlds they neither understand nor inhabit. In 'I Remember, I Remember', we are taken back to Larkin's home town, Coventry, where a fascinated friend questions him on its significance to him as writer. The title also returns us to Edward Thomas's aforementioned poem, where the opening refrain, 'I remember', celebrates the poetic act as one of memorial and the landscape as a haunting possibility. Yet, by the time we reach Larkin's England, memory is a blank. Unlike Thomas's poem, now we know why the landscape should be significant to the viewer – it is his birthplace.

We are only struck by how far it falls short of our expectations. Larkin's poetic eye, as it takes in the weary postwar architecture with the same indifference as Brownjohn's commuter, can only find it in himself to forgive it for its banality. His hometown is not the Romantic point of origin for the poet, or the well-spring for the formative experience. Rather, it is a site of nonformation. If much of Larkin's work suggests a yearning for community, or a 'huge hymn to old England',[3] as Andrew Motion argued, the promised comforts of 'To the Sea' and 'Show Saturday' are not to be found here. Instead, in 'I Remember I Remember',[4] nostalgia returns us to the place where things did not start. Through its dialogue with Thomas's line, the poem highlights the rupture between the two halves of the twentieth century. While the Victorian train journey offers progress, and the early twentieth-century train journey signifies memorial, the postwar equivalent suggests only an anxious dialogue with tradition. Larkin identifies the space where the past should be, and finds aporia,* a blank space. If nothing happens anywhere, Larkin's line suggests, it might just as well happen everywhere.

This nihilistic attitude to the environment, and the landscape's refusal to offer up individual identity or easy points of reference, complicates what we might at first read as part of the wave of postwar nostalgia that swept Britain in the early 1950s. This was a country that took civic pride in the crowning of a new monarch in 1953. This, commentators assured the public, was a new golden age. Just as Elizabeth I's reign had ushered in a period of economic growth, political stability, and artistic flowering, so too would Elizabeth II's rule see the transformation of an austere Britain, still on postwar rationing, into a great nation.

It is partly this public rhetoric of nostalgia that accounts for its uneasy thematic treatment in the literature of the period. Even as, formally, much literature treads a conservative path that tacitly privileges traditional methods over the possibilities of modernism, the world it surveys is both in danger of modernising itself into oblivion and memorialising its past into absurdity. At the comic climax of *Lucky Jim* (1954), the protagonist

---

* An aporia is a technical device where a speaker expresses doubt or uncertainty about something, often for rhetorical effect. It is also used in deconstructionist theory to describe an impossible path, or a 'non-way' (Jacques Derrida).

Jim Dixon gives a drunken lecture on Merrie England. His disdain for the subject and for cosy English nostalgia is matched only by the irreverence of his delivery, which provides grotesque mimicry of the professor he is trying to impress. Yet whether this sharp-eyed satire is diagnosing a problem inherent in British culture or is a farcical parody is more difficult to establish. A. S. Byatt's novel *Still Life* (1978) attempts to examine 1950s nostalgia via the world-weary Frederica, but her double-edged response tells us more about the difficulty of deciphering this mood than defining it: Frederica considers that there had been 'some sort of innocence about the rejoicing at that time (when she was a sharp but observant seventeen). There was no duplicity, only a truly aimless and thwarted nostalgia, about the pious enthusiasms of the commentators' and recalls weeping with 'hysterical glee over Jim Dixon's bludgeoning animosity towards Merrie England'. Once older, however, Frederica comes to 'feel nostalgia for what at the time she diagnosed boldly as bleary illusion' and how the Coronation 'tried and failed to be now and England'.[5] Frederica tellingly moves from cynical disillusion to nostalgia rather than vice versa in this retrospective account of the period, but attempts to chip away at the iconography of the Coronation only for her analysis to peter out into monosyllabic indecision: 'it *was* now, and England. Then'.

Byatt's conflicted response to the early 1950s and its sense of national identity offers a starting point for reassessing Larkin's England: can it be recovered if it never existed? Larkin's England is a place of conditionals, subjunctives, and missed opportunities. He stubbornly resists, for example, the badge of parochial regionalist that has often been bestowed on him. Only the shimmering American freedoms of jazz offer him escape from Britain's despised coasts and disappointed horizons, Sidney Bechet's trumpet falling on his ears in a great affirmation.[6] The nation's religion does little to shore up Britain's identity; in 'Church Going', the church can be entered only when its speaker is sure there's nothing going on inside.[7] The 'goings on' are ambivalent here; they could refer to a religious service or, more widely, the presence of God. If the speaker is more of a religious sceptic than an atheist, he remains fearful in the equivocation of agnosticism. Place can be celebrated only when it insists on its difference, like the strange loneliness of Ireland which offers a comfort in its unfamiliarity that can never be found in England.[8]

Any sense of home is similarly opposed to its notional ideal. In invisible ten-line pentameters, Larkin constructs a squared container for his misery – 'Home is so Sad' – yet the poem's controlled grieving for its aspiration stammers on to the final line, where the metre breaks down completely into a series of simple, mournful objects:

> Look at the pictures and the cutlery.
> The music in the piano stool. That vase.[9]

It never delivers what its promises, but its giddy expectations must be fought for and preserved, as a later Larkin observes in 'Going, going', imagining 'England gone':

> The shadows, the meadows, the lanes,
> The guildhalls, the carved choirs.[10]

Yet even here, when Larkin pens an ecological polemic fearful both of town planning and nuclear annihilation, he can present us only with a series of snapshots. No figures or actions animate the lost landscape Larkin memorialises, only a scattered inventory, as if the world he is intent on preserving has already disappeared, or if to imagine it as a living landscape would be to question its legitimacy. As David Gervais notes of these lines, 'there is no living sense of the tradition the poem purports to defend'.[11] The ever-disappearing rural world must be mourned, but can be imagined only in fitful recollections.

Rural England

In 1949, the government passed the National Parks and Access to the Countryside Act. In response to the mass suburban sprawl of the 1930s and 1940s which many feared would destroy rural England altogether, the Act introduced conservation and preservation as organising principles behind agricultural management. Urban expansion was now carefully managed so as not to encroach on specific rural areas, designated as National Parks, and specific rights were given to walkers to allow them access to rural areas. While the Act was welcomed by the majority of citizens, it legislated for the urban day-tripper as much as the rural labourer. The countryside was now the collective property of the people and the state, to be enjoyed by all. This seismic shift in ways of thinking about the countryside came in part as a result of the widespread destruction of many of Britain's cities in the war. Here was a part of British heritage that, at last, could be salvaged, and the power of preservation was strengthened in 1968 with the Countryside Act, which bound planners to consider the 'natural beauty and amenity' of the land. This was a landscape with aesthetic as well as national and historical significance. Yet, as Raymond Williams's *The Country and the City* (1973) made clear in its study of rural and urban literary representations in earlier British literature, these were also steps which reaffirmed the oppositional categories of rural and urban without pausing to define them. For the poet John Betjeman, at least, government policies did nothing to stem the process of urbanisation and the rise of indifferent middle-class suburbanites who cared little for the land that lay under their feet. Unspoiled countryside was merely an opportunity for a new power station, as his poem 'Inexpensive Progress' suggests.[12] The notion of a 'protected' landscape only hints at the horrors that will be meted out to anywhere that falls short of gaining the badge of immunity. Access to the countryside, in Betjeman's eyes, will just bring another slew of goggling tourists.

A fascination with war narratives in part explains the interest in nostalgic autobiographical writing in the immediate postwar period, with works such as Robert Graves's revised *Goodbye To All That* (1957), Maureen Duffy's *That's How It Was* (1962), and Barbara Comyns's harrowing comedy of 1930s London bohemia, *Our Spoons Came From Woolworths* (1950). Yet the most popular reminiscences from the period trade specifically in rural nostalgia for their explorations of a writer's past. Laurie Lee's autobiographical trilogy is most successful in its opening volume *Cider with Rosie* (1960), where he retraces a rural idyll. Here, the war comes as the inevitable answer to the innocent joy of childhood, and

Lee can only confess frankly that 'I was not surprised when I heard of the end of the world. Everything pointed to it'.[13] Peace, when it finally comes, brings no 'angels or explanations' (p. 28) and the final days of Lee's childhood see the traditional village life he knows crumbling around him, a casual historical accident that finds he 'belonged to that generation which saw, by chance, the end of a thousand years' life' (p. 262). Readers devour these works, and continue to return to them, as the narrative consciously immerses itself in a world it advertises to its reader is no longer available to them except mediated through the page. The literary voice might fail in its polemical entreaties to politicians and town councillors to rethink their plans for expansion, but it is more sure-footed when carrying out its own form of rural preservation. The war irrevocably cuts readers off from the past world offered to them in the text, hermetically sealing childhood into a pastoral neverland.

While the countryside did not suffer in the Second World War in the same way as the bombed-out cities of Bristol or Coventry, it needed to be hidden to be preserved. As Grevel Lindop's poem 'White Horse' recalls, the landmarks of England were often covered over for fear of enemy navigation assisted by the 'moon's betrayal', as in the titular 'White Horse' of Berkshire, a piece of ancient art carved into the rural landscape. Yet if the process of deception and concealment begins as a necessary expedient to win a war, it prompts a longer process of covering over that is harder to unpick:

> And how much more
> of England, of us, stayed buried after
> those years, those wars?[14]

Like Lee's sequestered childhood in *Cider with Rosie*, the hidden landscape cannot be returned to without fear of intrusion. The sense of a silent space here, like the absence hovering over Larkin's return to his childhood town, seems typical of a period that, despite its promise of consensus and consolidation, often seems wary and unstable in the literature it produces. Ten years after the war, Louis MacNeice's *Autumn Sequel* (1954) finds the country still feeling its way with tentative ambivalence, not yet sure if it is the time to be merry.[15] If Merrie England is an object of mockery for Jim Dixon, it is also at once a condition to aspire to and to look back on.

The Country House

The English rural landscape as a synecdoche for national identity is often centred on the country house. Almost a genre in itself, the country house novel has often sought to mimic political, social, and national upheavals, from the continual threat of improvements in Jane Austen's *Mansfield Park* (1814) to the ever-present possibility of the workhouse at Woodview in George Moore's *Esther Waters* (1894). Novelists such as Elizabeth Bowen, H. G. Wells, and John Galsworthy continued to mine its literary potential in the first half of the twentieth century in what Mark Girouard identifies as the Indian summer of the country house.[16] Yet as costs of preserving the country house grew ever higher, the 1930s and 1940s saw many rural seats sold, let, or falling into decay. By the time of Evelyn Waugh's *A Handful of Dust* (1934), Tony Last's country house has fallen into the hands of obscure (and untitled) relatives. He is, quite literally, the last in the line. Virginia Woolf's posthumous *Between the Acts* (1941) focuses on a village pageant representing the history of England which is staged at Pointz Hall, but as aeroplanes fly overhead, the watching audience is distracted from the comfort of its national heritage by the threat of an oncoming war. Evelyn Waugh's *Brideshead Revisited* (1945) similarly seems to signal the end of the country house as a viable symbol of English culture; like many country houses during the Second World War, Brideshead is requisitioned for use as a headquarters by the army. As Simon Schama notes, Waugh's apparent elegy for a golden age is in fact 'a long graveside oration for the death of faith, love, dynasty, England itself'.[17] The rural seat, so often synonymous in British literature with national concerns, becomes consumed by the overpowering pull of politics.

The literature of a newly egalitarian postwar Britain might seem an unlikely place for the country house novel to continue. Yet, in keeping with the period's interest in, and dissection of, national image as a nostalgic ideal, writers return again and again to the rural seat to explore the state of the nation. The famous opening of L. P. Hartley's *The Go-Between* (1953) is often invoked to suggest English quietism and conservatism, and the tendency for postwar literature to look backwards: 'the past is a foreign country: they do things differently there'.[18] Here is a book that offers a golden return to the English country house, and uses its first sentence to dismiss charges of anachronism by asserting that this is a world that operates with an unfamiliar, but consistent set of rules. Yet if the country house novel from Austen to Waugh finds the apparent privacy of its aspect and grandeur of its surroundings undermined by the threat of war, the incursion of politics, and the rumblings of change, a similar unease operates here. The novel narrates in retrospective first person the story of Leo Colston, a middle-class schoolboy staying with his wealthy friend Charles at Brandham Hall in the long hot summer of 1900. As the daily thermometer reading suggests, the novel's world is as stifling as the hall's rooms are plentiful. Drawn to Charles's sister Marion, Leo unwittingly becomes the go-between of the novel's title, carrying notes between her and the farm worker Ted with terrible consequences. Yet for all the promises of nostalgia, the novel is as much about the devastating consequences of returning to the past as the comforting melancholy of its memories; as Colston admits on finding the diary that will provide the catalyst for his narrative: 'I should be sitting in another room, rainbow-hued, looking not into the past but into the future: and I should not be sitting alone' (pp. 10–11). It is an anxious, rather than a fervent, return to the prewar innocence of 1900, and one that finds its protagonist in isolation and traumatised by the past. The two wars that separate the action of the novel from the date of composition cast their invisible shadows throughout the text.

Mervyn Peake's *Gormenghast* trilogy (1946–59), meanwhile, satiates the postwar appetite for an ornate fantasy world that resolutely refuses to carry the burden of politics or national anxiety. In three exquisitely crafted novels, Peake vivifies an intricate gallery of freaks and oddities all contained within Gormenghast's walls, the decrepit and intricate centre of Peake's imaginative world. This is a place of stagnation and empty, obsessive ritual. The opening volume *Titus Groan* (1946) centres around the upstart Steerpike, a kitchen hand, who rallies the unthinking workers (the Grey Scrubbers) under the clarion call of equality. Yet this is not a series interested in revolution. Although Steerpike is the only character to question feudalism and inherited privilege, he is also the most Machiavellian figure of the novels, and his egalitarian war is an expedient bid for power rather than a new vision of how society should be run.

Kazuo Ishiguro's *The Remains of the Day* (1989) confirms that the English country house is much more than a site of uncritical nostalgia by making its narrator entirely subservient to its charms. Structuring the narrative around a tour of the South England countryside, his evasive protagonist Stevens reflects on the relationship between landscape and national identity. In pinched and supercilious prose, Stevens claims the English landscape possesses a quality unmatched by any other nation, no matter how dramatic its mountains or canyons. The word he returns to, obsessively, to describe its appeal is greatness: '[w]e call this land of ours *Great Britain* … Yet I would venture that the landscape of our country alone would justify the use of this lofty adjective.' To Stevens, 'it is the very *lack* of obvious drama or spectacle that sets the beauty of our land apart. What is pertinent is the calmness of that beauty, its sense of restraint.'[19] As with the landscape, so with the narrative itself. Ishiguro makes the '*lack* of obvious drama' the captivating centre of the novel, as Stevens the pedantic butler unknowingly tells the story of the decline of the English country house. Set in 1956, when the Suez Crisis further unsettled notions of English empire, Stevens's blind belief in the greatness of Britain colours every decision in his life. This is a belief that ultimately comes at the cost of his personal happiness, as he recounts his past loyal service to Lord Darlington. Although either unvoiced or unperceived in Stevens's narrative, the reader becomes aware of Lord Darlington's right-wing and anti-Semitic tendencies, and the desperate political consequences of his attempt at gentrified diplomacy leading up to the war; Stevens's reverent participation in these events unwittingly sides him with the Nazi party. The seclusion of the country house offers no hiding place from the machinations of Empire, or what the poet Geoffrey Hill termed the 'flawless hubris of heroic guilt'.[20] In other words, it cannot exonerate its masters from their roles in history. By the time of Stevens's retrospective narration, his noble profession has become absurdly redundant. He has become a museum piece, the symbol of a heritage that, if explored further, is not quite as glorious as the American visitors to the Hall suspect. Hartley's retrospective narrator is all too aware of the painful legacy of the past, while Stevens's shortsighted deference to his superiors is an equally crippling example of how allegiance to an ideal makes us fallible.

Postwar literature returns to the country house not with nostalgia but as a kind of psychological and historical detective, excavating its stairwells and gardens for clues that link its empty rooms to our own drab world, mining its archaic traditions to explore the possibility of ritual in a modern society. The dream of owning and possessing the country house is always a folly – from the despotic carer in B. S. Johnson's *House Mother Normal: A Geriatric Comedy* (1971) who attempts to make the reclaimed country house into her 'Empire',[21] to the gleeful awfulness of the spoiled writer-protagonist Angelica Deverell in Elizabeth Taylor's *Angel* (1973). Taylor's novel begins with Angelica (the 'Angel' of the title) as a precocious young girl, fabricating a life for herself at Paradise House where her aunt works as a cook. To her mother's disbelief, Angel's outlandish novels eventually provide her with the means to purchase it. Yet as the novel follows Angel's life through its whims and petty tantrums, it documents the gradual decay of Paradise House with equal acuity. With the walls crumbling around her, Angel dies with a typically romantic flourish. Her faithful servant mourning at her deathbed is told that he will get used to her loss, before he realises there is now nothing left to get used to.[22] Angel's servant, like Stevens, has become a symbol without a purpose. The nothings, silences, evasions, and empty rooms of these novels, like the blank space where Larkin's fond reminiscence of his birth-place should be, create a past that is absent rather than idealised.

Country, Region, Province

If the country house offered a site of recent heritage to investigate Britain's crumbling empire, telescoping the last fifty years of political upheaval into the drama of a single building, other literature looked to a much older Britain, navigating its changing international status by returning to Celtic and Anglo-Saxon myth. The publication of W. G. Hoskins's *The Making of the English Landscape* in 1957 heralded the birth of landscape history. This influential work shared with the work of writers such as Betjeman the view that 'since the year 1914, every single change in the English landscape has either uglified it or destroyed its meaning, or both',[23] yet alongside this disdain for the utilitarian and pragmatic economics that defined land use in the postwar period, Hoskins also awoke the country to a much wider sense of its past. 'Everything in this landscape is older than we think',[24] he asserts at the beginning of his study, and, tracing the country's geography from pre-Roman landscape through the Black Death and the Industrial Revolution, he maps a nation whose roots stretch endlessly backwards. Alongside Nikolaus Pevsner's forty-six volume *The Buildings of England* for Penguin, the book repositions Britain, depicting its varied rural landscapes and its provincial towns with more detail than its dominating cities.

Some of the most powerful literature of the period responds directly to this recovered Britain, defined by its ancient centres of power rather than its current population hubs. Basil Bunting's masterful long poem *Briggflatts* (1966) takes its topographical inspiration from the author's native Northumbria, its name recalling a Quaker community Bunting visited as a boy in Sedburgh. He draws on two competing cultural influences on the land around him: St Cuthbert of Lindisfarne, the medieval English saint, and the tenth-century Viking Eric Bloodaxe, the last king of Northumberland. Bunting's poetic speaker hovers between Cuthbert's ascetic religious fervour and Bloodaxe's ruthless hunger for power, as the Norse and the Anglo-Saxon struggle to define what it is to be English, British, and Northumbrian. The act of writing is itself dissected here and haunted by the need to return to the past:

> The mason stirs:
> Words!
> Pens are too light.
> Take a chisel to write.[25]

The modern world, like the modern word, finds only levity in its depiction of England's heritage and history. Only by returning to an older Britain can its inhabitants make sense of the present day. Bunting's poem is one of the first works published by Bloodaxe, the phenomenally successful Northumbrian independent poetry press that takes similar inspiration from its ancient surroundings for its name. The publisher of this poetry, like the work itself, reroutes the London-centric model of English writing.

Britain is plagued by questions of nationality and identity. The 1960s ushered in thirty years of terrorist violence in Northern Ireland as Nationalists and Unionists clashed over the question of a United Kingdom. Poets who track this conflict – from Seamus Heaney to Paul Muldoon and Tom Paulin – must also explore the efficacy of Celtic, British, or Irish identities, often returning, like Bunting, to the prehistorical as a site of first negotiation.* Thomas Kinsella can only find locale in the personal rather than the public or the political – only the intimate relationship can:

> receive our lives' heat
> and adapt in their mass, like stone.[26]

The period also saw a new generation of Welsh and Scottish poets navigating their national positions, from Liz Lochhead and Edwin Muir to Lynette Roberts. This is a choice which, for Welsh poets at least, also determined the language in which they wrote. Yet, tellingly, the work of Welsh poet R. S. Thomas, for example, shares Larkin's sense of historical stasis, with his confession that Wales has no present or future, but only a past 'brittle with relics'.[27]

If these questions of national identity are often articulated with grave seriousness, Basil Bunting's charge of levity highlights the flippancy or self-effacing comedy which characterises much English writing about its provinces, counties, and internal divisions. While Betjeman mutters darkly of 'Hertfordshire' that 'one can't be sure where London ends',[28]

---

* The relationship between British and Irish identity is explored more fully in Part Three: 'The Bardic Line'.

other poets meet the reactionary response with the glib. Fleur Adcock waxes lyrical about the genius of Surrey with its gift for the suburban,[29] or mocks the ideological and cultural divide between the North and South by commenting on regional variations in match brands:

> Somewhere across England's broad
> midriff, wonderingly drawn
> from west to east, there exists a line
> to the north of which the shops provide
> (catering for a sudden switch
> of taste) superior fried fish, runnier
> yoghurt, blouses cut for the fuller northern
> figure; and the northern match.[30]

The poem is entitled 'England's Glory', but its humour pokes fun at any form of provincial pride. Meanwhile, London-born Wendy Cope finds similar satirical mileage in imagining herself as a provincial poet, wistfully 'writing a lot about nature'.[31] Yet if London perspectives on England's regions and dialects can be reductive, London's sense of itself also underwent radical transformation during the period.

London Ruins

Like Bunting's reimagined Northumbria, the literary London of the postwar era often attempts to replace its burnt-out buildings and the hastily erected replacements with an older sense of itself. In Rose Macaulay's *The World My Wilderness* (1950), the city's derelict wastelands are a 'symbol of loathsome things, war destruction, savagery; an earnest, perhaps, of the universal doom that stalked, sombre and menacing, on its way.'[32] The human attempts to excavate the past and rebuild its social and political structures are tentative and always threatened by the immutable power of anarchy. Personal stories or intimate human relationships can do little other than locate themselves around this site of ruin. As the workmen attempt to restore order to London's streets, wilderness makes continual attempts to reclaim the civilised city for its own, to return it to 'the primeval chaos and odd night which had been before Londinium was, which would be when cities were ghosts haunting the ancestral dreams of memory' (p. 253). Unlike the grounding that Cuthbert and Bloodaxe offer Bunting and his Northumbria, here the sense of a pre-city landscape suggests a world unravelled into nothingness.

The emotional landscapes of Rosamund Lehmann's postwar novels are similarly imperilled by the ugly scenes of desolation that surround her characters. Like Macaulay, this is a sense of the past that is nearer to nihilism than nostalgia. In *The Echoing Grove* (1953), the love triangle of Rickie Masters, his wife Madeleine, and her sister Dinah is prevented from taking centre stage by a recurring sense of horror that paralyses thought and action, or what the narrator describes as 'time refertilised, sown with a transfiguration, a ruin-haunting, ghost-spun No Man's crop of grace.'[33] Unfolding in flashback, the novel's images of a barren London become symbolic of the hidden centres of the characters' lives: Dinah nearly dies after a stillborn pregnancy with Rickie, a fact Madeleine never comes to know; while Rickie offers us a first-person narrative only for us to learn that he is already dead by the time of the novel's opening. Elizabeth Bowen's masterful *The Heat of the Day* (1949) finds a Blitz London reduced to fleeting sense impressions, as if the poetry of its description will shore up its own ephemeral state. Her self-possessed protagonist Stella Rodney can no more navigate her way around the crumbling city than she can her London flat, the awkwardly placed furniture of which is neither a refuge nor a comfort.

National Character

These worlds of fragile national histories, divided provincial loyalties, and devastated cities might offer one reason why so many British writers moved to the United States after the war, or set their novels in the jet-setting world that leapfrogged between the two, as if by looking to a country with a much clearer sense of its national identity Englishness itself might be rethought. The poet W. H. Auden, the most famous of Anglo-

American literary voices, moved to New York in 1939 and lived there for the majority of the time until his death in 1973. It was from the safety of America that he imagined a limbo tribe, a band of people 'much like ourselves' who love inexactness, and have a wide vocabulary to express their equivocation.[34] In the satiric vein of Jonathan Swift in *Gulliver's Travels* (1726), Auden articulates the English position as one of evasion. For the novelist John Fowles, too, this is the defining characteristic. A digression by the narrator of his 1977 novel *Daniel Martin* dissects the difference between American and English notions of national identity by highlighting the English 'genius for compromise, which is really a refusal to choose'. This gift for equivocation finds the English wallowing in the discrepancy between ideas about themselves and the reality. All we are left with, argues Fowles, is a blind tolerance for 'national decay' and for 'muddling through',[35] echoing the diagnosis of Nikolaus Pevsner. While this is a damning indictment of British national character, perhaps it only skirts round the more terrible truth that, as Aubrey Menen argues, 'there are no national virtues ... a nation cannot make our souls for us'.[36]

The restless hopping between London and New York in a series of 1970s and 1980s novels also hints at an anxiety that the English-language novel can be saved from this national decay and linguistic equivocation only by uprooting itself altogether. Martin Amis's *Money* (1984) overdoses on booze, drugs, pornography, and travel, its protagonist John Self addicted to the twentieth century. The flying time between London and New York is all the time Amis's protagonist has to compute where and who he is; he ends the novel no more sure of either, as the unravelling plot places Self's genealogy and paternity in question. The allure of America's assured identity proves to be another false horizon. While John ends the novel cautiously optimistic about his future, the hedonistic allure of the global age makes his quest for self-identity yet more vexed and elusive. In a similar vein, David Lodge's *Changing Places* (1975) swaps Morris J. Zapp's bustling academic life at Euphoric State University for Philip Swallow's at the provincial British university of Rummidge, as if to point up the crippled state of the current university system. Rummidge is caught between the old and the new and is consequently 'disgruntled and discouraged'.[37] The capitalist confidence and patriotic pride of America again underpins the fumbling British attempts at personal autonomy and national consciousness.

Public figures who leave England's shores also seem to be the few who can hold forth on its failings without falling into stereotypical self-effacement. In *An Englishman Abroad* (1989), Alan Bennett recreates the world of Guy Burgess, one of the Cambridge four who betrayed Britain while working for the British Secret Service and defected to Russia during the Cold War. Bennett imagines the figure of Burgess in the late 1980s, after the Falklands War, the last military offensive of the century that attempted to recreate the rhetoric of a great Empire. Far from occupying the position of the outsider, Burgess's reflections on his knotty relationship with his native country seem oddly typical of a country marked by qualified patriotism: 'So little, England. Little music. Little art. Timid, tasteful, nice.' He finds he can say 'I love England. But I can't say I love my country. I don't know what that means.' [38] Here, the evasive 'one' stands in for a declaration of nationalism – 'one loves [England]' – and the emphatic embrace of his country comes at the expense of the personal pronoun. The displaced Burgess is exceptional, the defecting Englishman, but also emblematic, as Bennett's knowing title suggests, playing on the national stereotype of the bumbling English tourist. Burgess's displacement is here attributed to a knotty personal history, but equally it suggests a nation that, as Fowles suggests, looks to an ideal while castigating the distance between its notional promise and its everyday reality.

Burgess's defection points to a host of literary characters who show their devotion to their native country by deserting it. The precocious narrator of Colin MacInnes's *Absolute Beginners* (1959) thrives on the jostling multiculturalism of postwar London with its jazz, bohemianism, and sexual freedoms. Yet when race riots break out, he can no longer square his personal experience of Britain with its imagined gift for tolerance. The novel ends with him abandoning England; at the airport, he meets an African immigrant, and suggests that it is only in this exchange of native for immigrant that the segregated hatred and small-mindedness of Britain can ever change. His bristling narrator informs us with self-righteous indignation at the close of the novel that he has fallen out of love with both London and England:

As far as I was concerned, the whole damn group of islands could sink under the sea, and all I wanted was to shake my feet of them, and take off somewhere and get naturalized, and settle.[39]

Here, even the geography itself – the 'group of islands' – is divided and isolated, unwilling to merge into a coherent whole. Yet in other ways, the outsider's perspective on British identity is no clearer than the narrator's facile rejection of responsibility for his country. Early on in the novel, the unnamed narrator completes some photography work for Mickey Pondoroso, a Latin American researcher who is completing a study on notions of Britishness in the middle of the century. Only half-way through their shoot does Mickey bashfully confess: 'I've got very few interesting ideas about them' (p. 24). Here, yet again, where we would expect statement and hypothesis, we reach a blank nothingness. We return once more to Larkin's railway station, and have nothing to say.

In *Trawl* (1966), the experimental novelist B. S. Johnson attempts to investigate identity and national consciousness by setting his autobiographical protagonist off on a journey across the Baltic Sea in the trawler of the title. He must leave England entirely to free himself from the trappings of his London life, and to come to know himself and his country in more tangible ways. Yet in terms of the novel's narrative progress, he flounders. 'No, this is ludicrous, this out-of-placeness is only a reminder of what was,'[40] he tells us. While Larkin's alienating trips to Ireland are enough to tell him that foreignness brings comfort to the already displaced, Johnson's narrator finds no such escape. A further complication in Johnson's novel is that the journey is double edged; just as his protagonist flees England to renegotiate his relationship to the past, so does Johnson flee from the conservative and traditional form of the postwar British novel. Making free use of ellipsis, stream-of-consciousness, and graphic techniques to represent the mental map of his protagonists' journey, Johnson hopes to leave behind not only a nostalgic version of England, but a nostalgic version of the English novel. To keep writers focused on English shores is to contain and limit the innovative possibilities of their craft.

Form and Nostalgia

Johnson's formal and geographical dilemma is shared by a number of writers from the period. Donald Davie is another English poet who moved to the United States, staying for twenty years after settling there in 1968, yet his poetic eye strayed homewards with the publication of *Shires* in 1974, which offers a poem for each of England's forty counties. Yet it is less a landscape that Davie is describing, more a literary heritage, as he moves through the map of England. His poem 'Dorset' identifies it as 'Thomas Hardy's country',[41] recalling the vividly imagined rural Wessex of novels such as *The Mayor of Casterbridge* (1888) and *Tess of the D'Urbervilles* (1891). Yet this nostalgic vision of English agrarianism has been lost, argues the poem, through works such as John Fowles's *The French Lieutenant's Woman* (1969), which use pastiche and intertextuality to question the efficacy of memorialising landscape in fiction. Fowles's parodic Victorian recreation of Dorset's Lyme Regis mimics Jane Austen's *Persuasion* (1818), but in a way that suggests rupture rather than continuity. The landscape itself becomes distant, ironic, and knowing; the ethics of representation always militate heavily against the possibility of a personal relationship with it. We know the land through literature rather than personal experience. Meanwhile, Davie's eulogy to Surrey begins with a literary *ubi sunt*: 'Who now reads Thomson or Collins?' (p. 319, l. 1).* These are landscapes lost to the motorways and literary worlds lost to the indifferent reader. To build a literary heritage from the English landscape is to run the risk of parody, or to risk being bricked in by a decaying tradition.

If Alan Bennett's depictions of outsiders such as Guy Burgess present them as ambivalent about their relationship with the country they've left behind, his more establishment figures remain similarly vexed; how can one be modern and English, if it is an identity founded on nostalgia and marked by an obsessive return to the past? The brisk pragmatism of the headmaster in Bennett's play *Forty Years On* (1968) dismisses the experimental threads of modern British literature as the work of

---

* *Ubi sunt* is a Latin phrase, meaning 'where are they?', and gives its name to a medieval lyric genre which laments the absence of something. The poets Davie refers to are James Thomson (1700–48) and William Collins (1721–59) whose work falls between the Augustan and Romantic traditions. They are often referred to as the poets of sensibility.

'highbrow layabouts'.[42] His pupils enact a school revue of British literary history, but are forced to excise authors or trends that do not fit the headmaster's stable, venerable notion of tradition and heritage. His teaching stooge, Franklin, is similarly disinclined to admit to a literature worth commemorating since the 1920s: '[i]t had seemed such a nice little going on in 1919. Novels full of the lost meals of childhood, new baked scones and fresh churned butter' (p. 19). The novel's job is to preserve an England that no longer exists or to restage a world where motives, identities, and causal relations are opaque. As Franklin might say of the postwar period, 'the lost meals of childhood' offered by the reminiscences of Laurie Lee are preferable to the dark and shapeless modern world depicted in the work of B. S. Johnson.

Bennett's late 1970s work, such as the play *The Old Country* (1978) still finds its bewildered and starched upper-middle classes raking over the coals of Englishness, Empire, and Elgar. As three couples come together for an evening, discussing the current problems of government and everyday living seems an obligation rather than an interest. As Duff remarks to his wife Hilary: '[i]t is sad to find oneself so often striking the elegiac note when one is by temperament and inclination a modernist'.[43] Duff, like Burgess, is unable to move from the evasions of 'one' to the proclamations of 'I'. While Bennett's own theatrical worlds are defiantly realist and traditional, his characters' language always brushes up against the limitations of their chosen forms of expression. The implicit irony of Duff's assertion here is that even as he confesses and disavows his English tendency towards nostalgia and conservatism, his melancholy realisation only heightens the elegiac quality of his statement. This is a way of speaking which is self-aware but also cyclical and self-perpetuating, unable to move beyond its inertia. Perhaps the only way of looking backwards with a critical eye that neither muffles the past nor rarefies it is the method articulated by the painter Stephen in Timberlake Wertenbaker's depiction of 1980s London in *Three Birds Alighting on a Field* (1992). Stephen consciously paints what is vanishing as it vanishes, or a memory of something that was there long ago. As he points out:

We drool over the aborigines because they hold their land sacred. But we must have all done that once. Even the English. Particularly the English.[44]

In Stephen's eyes, at least, the lack of continuity with the past doesn't make it impossible to recover.

England for Sale

If England is a country that postwar writing either memorialises, mourns, or abandons, it also tracks its emergence as a brand. Even Betjeman tells with piquant humour of villagers who fabricate quaint tales of rural England for a tourist who keeps them in drinks.[45] The dual role of preservation and recreation that the English landscape was signed up for in the 1949 National Parks and Access to the Countryside Act was further capitalised on by the National Heritage Act of 1983. The Act's principle objective was to form English Heritage, a government quango given the responsibility of managing the historical built environment of England. Together with Natural England, which sought to conserve the rural landscape, these powerful organisations redrew the status and stature of the country. Yet by focusing on preservation, the Act implicitly asked England what monuments, buildings, and environments constituted its heritage, and which of these were important enough to a sense of Englishness to override the necessity of house-building and urban development.

Much literature of the period responds to this challenge with a coruscating dissection of English iconography. In David Edgar's play *Destiny* (1977), the racist agitator Paul stirs up tension and hatred via his ironic reading of England's rural branding as a green and pleasant land. He recalls a war poster reading 'This Is Your England, Fight For It', with a picture of a village green and thatched cottages, and points out with bitterness that few English soldiers who ended up giving their lives for the war effort had ever seen a thatched cottage.[46]

The English landscape of the past is an easy symbol for arousing national pride, but offers only jarring absurdity when placed alongside the lived environment of a heavily industrialised and densely populated nation. Michael Frayn's 1980s satire *Benefactors* (1984) is similarly unforgiving in its depiction of capitalist Thatcherite developers who know that the unspoiled countryside is a way to sell a property, even if that very property destroys the countryside it gives access to. As a delighted David boasts to Sheila in Act One, from the top of his skyscrapers workers will be able to see the Chilterns over the hills of Hampstead Heath.[47] Theirs is a pushy London world simultaneously anxious about the scarcity of resources and propelled by the limitless capacity to make money and spend it. The tattered and tense world of 1980s London is on shabby display throughout Michael Hofmann's first collection *Acrimony*, which takes in the 'Game spirits, tat, and service industries' of 'Albion Market'[48] and peers through windows full of 'potplants like a jungle dawn',[49] while the radio crackles with BNP election campaigns and 'their fiction of an all-white Albion'.[50] The English countryside is both out of focus and acutely rendered, as in the airbases of Cornwall where 'the picturesque collides with the strategically / important'.[51]

By the time of novelist Alisdair Gray's *Something Leather* (1990), nostalgia itself has become another sort of brand. In a chapter entitled 'Culture Capitalism', the Scottish artist Harry finds her work appropriated and sold through the British culture and heritage industry. A cynical London art dealer asks her to redirect her work specifically towards this market. As he assures her, 'nostalgia and grotesque infantilism are booming in many places, but especially Britain', and with a celebrity-written catalogue written by a 'brainier than usual popular writer', her sculptures can make the leap to bestseller, television series, and feature film.[52] Culture is also seen through the lens of period Britain in Malcolm Bradbury's *Cuts* (1988). As the protagonist Henry Babbacombe, a university lecturer, struggles to survive the government's continual cuts in higher education spending, he works on a television script which is proving equally susceptible to the red pen. The directors are determined to make his script into a chocolate-box England story that will outstrip *Brideshead Revisited* and *The Jewel in the Crown* for nostalgic national appeal.*

---

* The early 1980s television adaptations of these novels were phenomenally successful, and are often voted among the best British television programmes ever made.

Henry's artistically compromised position offers some useful analogies for the writing of the postwar period, which often finds itself looking back without any sense of its relationship to the past. As the aging inhabitant of a Lancashire street splutters in Jim Cartwright's play *Road* (1986): 'I don't see how that time could turn into this time'.[53] The rebuilding of a new, efficient, functional Britain in the aftermath of the Second World War, and the Thatcherite revolution of the 1980s that redrew the social and geographical map of the country both leave a series of fissures in the sense of the literature's national continuity. Yet, tellingly, Henry Babbacombe's frustrated rewrites of his scripts finally become comforting. He begins the task with resignation, mindful of how the directors will mangle his version of the story in the interests of giving the television audience a neat and prettified version of England. However, watching 'the ever-unrolling tale of misery, violence, despair, obscenity, greed and conflict that is called the news'[54] in his hotel room, he is forced to accept the benefits of writing an ordered and elegant version of the truth rather than addressing the problems of the present. Quietism and elegy fit better with the world he wants to inhabit than conflict and upheaval. While the strain often shows, a significant strand of postwar British literature turns its attention away from that same troubling news broadcast with a similar relief.

Notes

1   Alan Brownjohn, 'In the Trade', *Collected Poems* (London: Hutchinson, 1988), p. 166, ll. 20–3.
2   Alfred Lord Tennyson, *Tennyson: A Selected Edition*, ed. Christopher Ricks (Harlow: Longman, 1989), p. 46, l. 182.
3   Andrew Motion, *Philip Larkin: A Writer's Life* (London: Faber, 1993), p. 437.
4   Philip Larkin, 'I Remember, I Remember', *Collected Poems* (hereafter *CP*) (London: Faber, 1988), p. 68, ll. 34–6.
5   A. S. Byatt, *Still Life* (London: Chatto & Windus, 1991), pp. 318–19.
6   Philip Larkin, 'For Sidney Bechet', *CP*, p. 87, l. 14.
7   Philip Larkin, 'Church Going', *CP*, p. 58, l. 1.
8   See Philip Larkin, 'The Importance of Elsewhere', *CP*, p. 105, l. 12.
9   Philip Larkin, 'Home is So Sad', *CP*, p. 88, ll. 9–10.
10   Philip Larkin, 'Going, going', *CP*, p. 134, ll. 44–5.

11   David Gervais, *Literary Englands: Versions of 'Englishness' in Modern Writing* (Cambridge: Cambridge University Press, 1993), p. 217.

12   John Betjeman, 'Inexpensive Progress', *Collected Poems* (hereafter *CP*) (London: John Murray, 2006), p. 287.

13   Laurie Lee, *Cider with Rosie* (London: Hogarth Press, 1960), p. 23.

14   Grevel Lindop, 'White Horse', *Tourists* (Manchester: Carcanet, 1987), p. 10, ll. 12–14.

15   Louis Macniece, *Autumn Sequel*, in *Collected Poems* (London: Faber, 2007), p. 434, Canto xxv, ll. 14–15.

16   Mark Girouard, *Life in the English Country House* (Harmondsworth: Penguin, 1978), p. 299.

17   Simon Schama, *Landscape and Memory* (London: Harper Collins, 1995), p. 519.

18   L. P. Hartley, *The Go-Between* (London: Hamish Hamilton, 1953), p. 9.

19   Kazuo Ishiguro, *The Remains of the Day* (London: Faber, 1989), pp. 28–9.

20   Geoffrey Hill, 'An Apology for the Revival of Christian Architecture in England', *Tenebrae* (London: Andre Deutsch, 1978), p. 25, l. 53.

21   B. S. Johnson, *House Mother Normal: A Geriatric Comedy, in Omnibus* (London: Picador, 2004), p. 9.

22   Elizabeth Taylor, *Angel* (London: Chatto & Windus, 1973), p. 252.

23   W. G. Hoskins, *The Making of the English Landscape* (London: Hodder and Stoughton, 1992), p. 239.

24   W. G. Hoskins, *The Making of the English Landscape*, p. 12.

25   Basil Bunting, *Briggflatts* (Newcastle: Bloodaxe, 1966), p. 5, ll. 113–16.

26   Thomas Kinsella, 'Personal Places', *Collected Poems* (Manchester: Carcanet, 2001), p. 283, ll. 2–3.

27   R. S. Thomas, 'Welsh Landscape', *Collected Poems: 1945–1990* (London: J.M. Dent, 1993), p. 37, l. 23.

28   John Betjeman, 'Hertfordshire', *CP*, p. 225, l. 29.

29   Fleur Adcock, 'The Genius of Surrey', *Poems 1960–2000* (Newcastle: Bloodaxe, 2000), p. 165.

30   Fleur Adcock, 'England's Glory', *Poems 1960–2000*, p. 164, ll. 37–44.

31   Wendy Cope, 'Pastoral', *Serious Concerns* (London: Faber, 1992), p. 45, l. 2.

32   Rose Macaulay, *The World My Wilderness* (London: Virago, 1982), p. 252.

33   Rosamund Lehmann, *The Echoing Grove* (London: Collins, 1984), p. 12.

34   W. H. Auden, 'Limbo Culture', *Collected Poems* (London: Faber, 1976), p. 616, ll. 9–11.

35   John Fowles, *Daniel Martin* (London: Jonathan Cape, 1977), pp. 83–4.

36   Aubrey Menen, *Dead Men in the Silver Market: an Autobiographical Essay on National Prides* (London: Chatto & Windus, 1954), p. 126.

37   David Lodge, *Changing Places* (London: Secker & Warburg, 1975), p. 9.

38 Alan Bennett, *An Englishman Abroad*, in *Plays: One* (London: Faber, 1998), p. 292.

39 Colin MacInnes, *Absolute Beginners* (London: Allison & Busby, 2001), pp. 197–8.

40 B. S. Johnson, *Trawl*, in *Omnibus*, p. 179.

41 Donald Davie, 'Dorset', *Collected Poems* (Manchester: Carcanet, 2002), p. 305, l. 3.

42 Alan Bennett, *Forty Years On*, in *Plays: One*, p. 75.

43 Alan Bennett, *The Old Country*, in *Plays: One*, p. 226.

44 Timberlake Wertenbaker, *Three Birds Alighting on a Field*, in *Plays: One* (London: Faber, 1996), p. 414.

45 John Betjeman, 'The Dear Old Village', *CP*, p. 191.

46 David Edgar, *Destiny*, in *Plays: One* (London: Methuen. 1994), p. 390.

47 Michael Frayn, *Benefactors* (London: Methuen, 1984), p. 38.

48 Michael Hofmann, 'Albion Market', *Acrimony* (London: Faber, 1986), p. 33, l. 26.

49 Michael Hofmann, 'From Kensal Rise to Heaven', *Acrimony*, p. 34, l. 12.

50 Michael Hofmann, 'Campaign Fever', *Acrimony*, p. 37, l. 17.

51 Michael Hofmann, 'Aerial Perspective', *Acrimony*, p. 24, ll. 1–2.

52 Alisdair Gray, *Something Leather* (London: Picador, 1991), p. 177.

53 Jim Cartwright, *Road* (London: Methuen, 1990), p. 43.

54 Malcolm Bradbury, *Cuts* (London: Arrow, 1984), p. 89.

Immigrants and Exiles

In Michael Frayn's early novel *Towards the End of the Morning* (1967), the journalist John Dyson is invited to speak on a television programme about race relations. For Dyson, this is merely an opportunity to gain media exposure; his contribution to the programme rarely goes beyond the minimal positive response, and his later assessment of his performance focuses on his facial gestures over his rhetoric. For Dyson, race is a platform, rather than an important point of discussion. This pointed omission evades an issue that has helped shape modern Britain as much as the postwar reorganisation of its education system. The period from 1950 to 1990 is marked by a sea change in attitudes to multiculturalism as well as a paradigm shift in the country's racial demography. After Indian independence was granted in 1947, Britain finally let go of its 'jewel in the crown'; one year later, the Nationality Act gave equal residency rights to all inhabitants of Britain's colonies. While immigration to Britain had been going on for hundreds of years, 1948 was a turning point in its history; for many, the most iconic symbol of the period is the photograph of the SS *Windrush* docking in Tilbury with the majority of its passengers immigrants from the Caribbean. For the government, immigration was an attractive prospect, a solution to the massive job of rebuilding Britain after the war using a cheap labour force. For many immigrants of the *Windrush* generation, the move to

Britain seemed to promise a return to the 'mother country',* and the opportunity for economic stability.

Yet, as literature of the period suggests, arrival in Britain and gradual acceptance into its society would be far more painful and protracted than the crossing itself. The author Caryl Phillips in *The Atlantic Sound* (2000) recounts his mother's journey to England with its alternating sense of danger and disappointment, and that divided response continued when she reached dry land. In 1958 race riots broke out in Nottingham and Notting Hill, London, as white youths clashed with local immigrant communities. By 1962, the government had passed the Immigration Act, responding to the mood of civic unrest with the first attempt to cap numbers of foreign immigrants to Britain. It was only in 1976, by contrast, that the Race Relations Act finally outlawed racial discrimination. This double-edged process of welcome and exclusion, of assimilating and demarcating racial categories, meant that debates about Britishness and the notion of nationalism often centred on race. If immigrants imagined a return to the mother country, their white British neighbours were often reluctant to treat them as anything other than visitors. Sheila Patterson's 1963 sociological study of West Indian immigration in Brixton articulates the series of prejudices accompanying this 'dark stranger', including 'alienness ... savagery, violence, sexuality', but also 'athletic, artistic and musical gifts, and an appealing and childlike simplicity which is in no way incompatible with the remainder of the image.'[1] Here Patterson's roll-call of prejudice and racial hatred is curiously agentless. These are attitudes which are inherited, fostered, and passed on, but rarely spoken of or explored. The dangerous consequences of making racism an inevitable problem or a natural phenomenon can be seen in Britain's changing political map of the period. It was during the Second World War that the first version of the British National Party was formed from the British Union of Fascists. By 1983, the National Front sponsored enough electoral candidates to gain airtime on national television.

---

* The phrase 'mother country' was used by the first Puritan settlers in America to refer to Britain, the country they had left behind. It has come to mean more generally the land of one's ancestors, or a country in relation to its colonies and dependencies. These two discrete definitions mean the phrase has a special relevance when used by British immigrant writers, although it is usually used to describe Britain rather than an ex-colony.

If the forty years since the *Windrush* docked saw a process of gradual integration and a growing wave of anti-immigrant feeling in Britain, it was the 1980s and the birth of Thatcherism that saw race and representation become a key intellectual, as well as political issue. While the early postwar period saw the rise of sociology and a society preoccupied with dissecting and commenting on itself, the growing influence of Marxism in British intellectual thought saw the formation of cultural studies in the 1980s, spearheaded by thinkers such as Stuart Hall. This was a critical movement that examined race, gender, and nationality through a Marxist lens, analysing representation as a series of negotiations with the dominant power structures of society. For Hall, one of Britain's foremost black intellectuals, the country's postcolonial settlers were the pawns in its ongoing 'quarrel with itself'.[2] This quarrel has refocused itself around a series of key moments of postwar literary and political history.

In April 1968, the MP Enoch Powell addressed the Conservative Association in Birmingham with a speech that, for all the wrong reasons, would become one of the most famous in British political history. In an address now known as the 'Rivers of Blood' speech, Powell attempted to explain the disillusion of the working-class white man and his intolerance of immigrants. Using racist language of invasion and miscegenation, Powell imagined the ultimate dominance of the black man in Britain, referring to the Civil Rights movement in the United States as:

> that tragic and intractable phenomenon which we watch with
> horror on the other side of the Atlantic but which there is
> interwoven with the history and existence of the States itself [and
> is] coming upon us here by our own volition and our own neglect.[3]

Yet if neglect had swept the country, it showed more in the unchecked rise of institutional racism than in the political implications of the Black Power movement; Powell was, however, sacked from the Shadow Cabinet after giving this speech.

By the 1980s, the ruling Conservative party had long since eradicated that racist rhetoric from its manifestoes. Thatcher's statecraft necessitated a language of nationalism that would include immigrant and nonwhite communities, and she returned to the vexed category of 'Englishness' in a renewed attempt to absorb all ethnicities under its banner. Hall notes that this all-embracing term 'stabilizes so much of the dominant political and cultural discourses' it purports to represent no ethnicity at all.[4] Yet redefining Englishness was not as simple as it seemed. One of the most controversial literary works of the period, Salman Rushdie's *The Satanic Verses*, was published in 1988 during Thatcher's third term as Prime Minister, and fictionalises her negatively as 'Mrs Torture'. Beginning with two Indian immigrants arriving in Britain, the novel offers a playful but complex dissection of the relationships between language, nation, and ethnicity. The religious uproar the book provoked in Muslim communities meant that by 1989 groups of British immigrants were burning the book, and Rushdie had gone into hiding after being issued with a fatwa by Ayatollah Ruhollah Khomeini. One of the most in-depth explorations of the postwar British immigrant experience became simultaneously the most reviled by the community it depicted.

The Pleasures of Arrival

If a whole series of postwar authors politely looked elsewhere, the literary voices that captured the *Windrush* generation took on some of the most prominent political questions of the period. One of the earliest depictions of a mixed-race relationship comes in Shelagh Delaney's play *A Taste of Honey* (1958), where the tomboy protagonist, Jo, sleeps with a black sailor named Jimmy. Yet, tellingly, Jimmy is only a transient part of the play's landscape, his ship docking briefly in Manchester before it sails on to the next port. We see the shocked reactions of Jo's mother at the prospect of a mixed-race child, but the play ends before Jo's labour. The play is both groundbreaking for the period in its depiction of Jimmy and Jo's relationship and curiously emblematic of the national attitudes towards the nonwhite presence. Even when the black man is only passing through Britain, racist notions of contamination haunt the characters long after his departure.

Jimmy's position as a sailor is typical in other ways, too. A strand of literary responses to and representations of race in the postwar decade focuses on the immigrant's journey to and early experiences of the mother country; a voyage to an alien land that is also a return home. Fictional accounts from the period, as with documentary testimonials, chronicle an optimism that soon gives way to resignation on disembarkation. George Lamming's journey from Barbados is reimagined in *The Emigrants* (1954) by viewing his earlier self through the eyes of the incredulous British immigration officials as the newcomers pass through customs.[5] Here the racial assumptions made by the customs officials are confirmed not by the appearance of the West Indian immigrants or their behaviour but by their choosing to come to England. In a deliberate strategy that subverts the reader's expectations of the narrative and the way it should be told, Lamming's immigrants are viewed with suspicion not because of the threat they pose to their destination island but for the fuzzy logic of abandoning their homeland. The very title of his work, *The Emigrants*, reads his characters through their departure rather than their arrival and here, it is the native English who are forced to give up their fictions – the 'tragic farce' of the situation, or the movies that sell the dream of the brave explorer – for the mundane reality of their own nation as a destination. In this sense, Lamming's is a fiction of reconciliation, in that his West Indian immigrants must similarly give up their tall stories of the mother country for the banal reality of a London that is dirty, crowded, smelly, and chaotic.

In later representations of the journey 'home', the narrative resists regular chronology, as if the trip has made a mockery of linear progression and the causal relationship between destination and origin, or past and present. In contrast to Lamming's displaced story which views the false expectations of the new arrivals through English eyes, Caryl Phillips's *The Final Passage* (1985) offers an account of the 'naturalised' protagonist Leila before an account of her original journey. This structural device means that the journey, when it comes, is overshadowed by its retrospective significance. Leila's first bleak assessment of England makes her realise 'she would have to learn a new word; overcast'.[6] The knowledge of how this country will change her is with her even as she has her first glimpse of it. Her observations are always governed by the understanding of herself in a world she does not belong in, as in her description of the white person's face, criss-crossed with veins that are 'scratched all over it like a map with only the smallest rivers marked on it' (p. 194). The half-finished map that Leila sees in the white face suggests the continuing difficulty of locating herself in this strange environment.

This is also a journey to a place which is already known to its voyagers from the colonial depictions of England they have studied at school. It comes secondhand via the rural idylls that have peppered their childhood reading. Descriptions of this familiar but alien land are often underlined by this pre-existing knowledge. The narrator of V. S. Naipaul's *The Enigma of Arrival* (1987) is aware in his description of rural England that everything is seen 'with the literary eye, or with the aid of literature'. He is a stranger, but one with 'a knowledge of the language and the history of the language and the writing.'[7] In this imaginative space he is permitted a freedom to roam, although in actuality he is reluctant to explore, preferring to stay indoors and imagine the England he has come to rather than find it not to his liking. When he eventually travels to London from the 'literary' rural England, there is also a wrenching gap between the metropolis he expects and the world he surveys, increasingly aware that 'the grandeur belonged to the past; that I had come to England at the wrong time; that I had come too late to find England, the heart of empire, which (like a provincial, from a far corner of the empire) I had created in my fantasy' (p. 120). The unnamed writer-protagonist of Naipaul's novel makes continual frustrated attempts to rewrite this England in his own novel, to excavate this lost history, and to reject the experience of the postcolonial immigrant as an admissible part of his fictive world. However, even as he attempts to avoid making his experiences of racism part of his writing, he is forced to admit he is 'hiding my experience from myself; hiding myself from my experience' (p. 117).

In an apocryphal story, the Caribbean writers Sam Selvon and George Lamming were said to have argued over the use of a typewriter on their journey to England. Yet this anecdote, which suggests an energetic competition for literary production, seems less typical of other immigrant authors' experiences. The sense of a literary past that immigrant writers know but cannot access recurs in much fiction of the period. On arriving in a wintry London in the 1950s, the characters in

Phillips's *The Final Passage* have 'nothing to declare except their accents' (p. 143). Echoing Oscar Wilde's famous aphorism on arriving in America that he had nothing to declare but his genius, Phillips replaces Wilde's dandyish confidence in literary excellence with a resigned admission of inevitability. These people own nothing, and will always be viewed via their otherness. The journey narrative is an eye-witness account but one which continually interrogates its own authority. Zulfikar Ghose's autobiography *Confessions of a Native-Alien* (1965) is, as its title suggests, similarly conflicted. In a narrative which moves from Bombay to Keele to London, even the point of origin remains contested. As Ghose notes, his first seven years were spent in part of India which would become Pakistan, and he suggests that:

> the distinction between the two countries of my early life has been the schizophrenic theme of much of my thinking: it created a psychological conflict and a pressing need to know that I do belong somewhere and neither the conflict nor the need has ever been resolved.[8]

Second-generation responses to the immigrant journey are similarly complex. In Caryl Phillips's novel *State of Independence* (1986), the protagonist Bertram returns to his native Jamaica after twenty years in England, as it prepares to celebrate its independence. However, he is looking for home, rather than self-determination, and struggles to find it in either place. Phillips's play *Strange Fruit* (1980) similarly makes the journey home as dispiriting as the difficult voyage to the mother country. The drama centres on the brothers Alvin and Errol, second-generation immigrants whose mother, a schoolteacher, urges them to establish themselves as successful 'naturalised' British citizens. Alvin attends university and plans to be a writer, but after returning to his mother's native West India he is crippled by the discovery of his island heritage. There, his 'chalkie' mother is held in contempt for never having returned from England, and Alvin's own notions of ethnic identity are irrevocably split as a result. This crisis of origin is symbolised in the first novel Alvin now cannot write. Hoping to pen 'that first classic of decolonization',[9] his island voyage instead uncovers a place full of corruption and a family who are reluctant to acknowledge him as their own. Ultimately, he is too ashamed of his people to record his impressions on the page. Alvin has clung to the affirmative identity of the 'decolonized' writer, but is unable to square this notion with the disconnect he feels on returning to the place he has claimed as a spiritual home. This continual tension between the journey, its destination, and its subsequent depiction creates a link between the immigrant voyage and the literature it produces; the question of where the immigrant is travelling to becomes synonymous with those whom they are writing for. Both questions produce contradictory responses that shape not only the travel narrative, but the subsequent literature of assimilation. As Phillips succinctly put it in 1987, 'Europe's current "problem" relates directly to the permanence of our presence, not our continued arrival.'[10]

Liming in London

In 1960, George Lamming's *The Pleasures of Exile* first articulated the problem faced by the West Indian migrant writer. To compose fiction was to anticipate an audience for that fiction, yet writers' knowledge of their native West India told them that 'the West Indian of average opportunity and intelligence has not yet been converted to reading as a civilised activity'.[11] This makes the decision to write one that must come with a concomitant decision about how to write and for whom; it further suggests migrant writers are forced to choose a culturally alien audience, and that this choice will make tacit decisions for writers about the shape, form, and perspective of their work.

These problems are explored with deceptive comedy in Sam Selvon's *The Lonely Londoners* (1956). The novel begins with the protagonist, Moses Aloetta, coming to meet Galahad at Waterloo station. Just as the immigrant journey to England is often represented as a flashback or marked by a change in narrative perspective, here the opening arrival scene is characterised by the weary realities of veteran immigrant Londoner Moses rather than the bounding enthusiasm of Galahad. The shock of the newcomer's impression of London is supplanted by Moses's unexpected rush of nostalgia. The voice and form prioritise the immigrant tradition rather than the British literature that Naipaul's narrator longs for in *The Enigma of Arrival* (1987). Selvon writes in the creolised English of the Trinidad immigrant; the various characters use a shared dialect combining features of both languages, as well as colonising various areas of London itself. Bayswater becomes 'the Water', and Notting Hill becomes 'the Gate'; the act of naming their own London is a key part of the naturalising process, as Moses suggests in his description of Galahad:

> He had a way, whenever he talking with the boys, he using the names of the places like they mean big romance, as if to say 'I was in Oxford Street' have more prestige than if he just say 'I was up the road'. And once he had a date with a frauline, and he make a big point of saying he was meeting she by Charing Cross, because just to say 'Charing Cross' have a lot of romance in it.[12]

If here Moses gently mocks Galahad's preference for 'Oxford Street' over 'up the road', he also acknowledges the importance of language in building new communities. Imported words for women ('frauline') and, elsewhere, the characters' preference for 'liming' (hanging around the streets), reassert the Caribbean immigrants' control over voice and perspective. This is a nonstandard English that echoes the rhythms of lived experience.

The novel similarly rejects linear plot for a series of anecdotes about Moses's fellow immigrants as they gather on Sunday mornings in his flat to share their stories. The structure of the book mirrors the socialising act of 'making a big ballad'; this is a culture in which the storytellers always try to outdo each other with their narratives of daily life. In the central passage describing the sultry summer parks of London, Selvon's preference for the big ballad comes close to modernist stream-of-consciousness in its riotous celebration of city life and its confusing series of sensory experiences. Selvon finds other affinities between Trinidad and British tradition, too, in the comic verve that runs through the work. The immigrant experience of poverty and extreme hunger is mediated through a humorous anecdote about Galahad attempting to eat a dead pigeon. While the novel's titular emphasis suggests the characters' loneliness, their own community is often in sharp contrast to the isolated rich white figures they rub shoulders with, prompting Moses to observe that 'people in this world don't know how other people does affect their lives' (p. 262). Until the final reflective passage recounting Moses's sense of displacement, it remains uncertain which Londoners remain the loneliest.*

Yet while Selvon successfully uses Trinidadian oral traditions to frame his work, the reception of the novel raises questions about its audience. If contemporary British reviewers found it an unusual, comic work, relieved that its difficult questions about immigration and British identity were hidden under generous and lighthearted prose, recent postcolonial critics have been equally keen to see its comedy as a sort of performance hiding a dissection of white notions of otherness. Moses himself is always alert to the temptations and complexities of performing black identity – as he writes of the women he meets, 'the cruder you are the more the girls like you' (p. 100) – and there is a sense that the novel's own critical heritage falls into the same difficulties. Is the current trend to downplay the novel's comedy similarly misguided, an attempt to wrench from the text a reading which will conform with current critical debates about postcolonial identities? One of the novel's most memorable passages finds a frustrated Galahad addressing his skin colour as an object, a limiting abstract he must cajole and reason with:

> So Galahad talking to the colour Black, as if is a person, telling it that is not *he* who causing botheration in the place, but Black, who is a worthless thing for making trouble all about. 'Black, you see what you cause to happen yesterday? I went to look at that room that Ram tell me about in the Gate, and as soon as the landlady see you she say the room let already. She ain't even give me a chance to say good morning. Why the hell you can't change colour?' (p. 77)

This disavowal of identity is both terrifying and absurdly comic, but also describes the same process that both immigrant writers and their audience must go through before identity can finally be not isolated, removed, or absorbed, but owned.

---

* Andrea Levy's 2004 novel *Small Island* also depicts the experience of immigrants in London. It is discussed in another volume in this series, *New Directions: Writing Post 1990*.

Recolonising Literature

A different kind of process was at work in the postwar literature that looked to Britain's legacy of Empire, or charted countries' transitions from colonial outposts to autonomous and independent nations. Attia Hosain's *Sunlight on a Broken Column* (1961) charts the divisive split between Sunni and Shia Muslims in 1930s India. Religious conflict is mirrored by competing notions of home and allegiance. For Laila, the protagonist, her aunt's decision to school her children in England seems designed to alienate them from their culture. The keenly felt and sharply observed conflicts in Laila's Anglo-Indian world are played for parody in G. V. Desani's *All About H. Hatterr* (1948), where Selvon's bravura energy meets *Tristram Shandy*.* A dazzling mock-biography, and an often overlooked influence on Salman Rushdie's *Midnight's Children* (1981), Desani's novel questions notions of cultural origin in its depiction of a bragging Anglo-Indian. The hero Hatterr dismisses the absence of his mother with a casual 'who cares?', fascinated instead by the 'clowning and vaudeville-turning' of his own literary project. He situates himself in the 'frisky fraternity of autobiography-makers' rather than worry about his cultural heritage;[13] hybridity for Hatterr is a cause for celebration more than concern. Yet other writers carried the mark of their journey with more solemnity, unable to escape into the refuge of literary creation. Doris Lessing arrived in Britain in the late 1940s with her first semi-autobiographical novel already written but rejected by numerous publishers in Rhodesia, and its journey from an untouchable manuscript to a British bestseller suggests a public ready to listen to its unflinching account of South African slave-ownership. Yet a Conservative manifesto from 1951 was still happy to sell its party as the pallbearers of Empire, and pledged that the party would 'strive to promote [the Empire's] unity, its strength, and its progress'.[14] This was a nation that was apparently content to give up its colonial conquests, withdrawing from many of its African colonies before Portugal, France, or Spain, yet culturally and politically, seemed reluctant to let go.

---

* *Tristram Shandy* (1759–66) by Laurence Sterne tells the story of its eponymous protagonist through digressions, diversions, and playful narrative devices that have often been echoed by modern writers.

This curious mixture of nostalgia for Empire and a need to reassess its legacy can be seen in a series of novels which look back not only to the colonial past, but the literary representation of that past, from Ruth Prawer Jhabvala's Booker Prize-winning *Heat and Dust* (1975), which flits between the world of the 1920s British Raj and the present day, to William Boyd's *A Good Man in Africa* (1981), which casts its hapless protagonist Morgan Leafy as a diplomat in West Africa. Paul Scott's popular *Raj Quartet* (1965–75), the four-volume work which straddles the middle decades of the postwar period, explores the final days of British rule in India. Its phenomenally successful television adaptation as *The Jewel in the Crown* in the early 1980s prolonged its cultural hold over the period. The narrative centres on Daphne Manners, a young woman who has arrived in India from England, and her British-educated Indian lover Hari Kumar. Like Lessing's *The Grass is Singing* (1950), which opens with the monotone voice of a news article covering a local murder-by-numbers, the first paragraphs seem to state the case with clarity:

> This is the story of a rape, of the events that led up to it and followed it and of the place in which it happened. There is the action, the people, and the place; all of which are interrelated but in their totality incommunicable in isolation from the moral continuum of human affairs.[15]

The narration opens assured of the facts, and is equally confident in drawing its subsequent analogy between the rape and the relationship between India and Britain, 'locked in an imperial embrace of such long standing and subtlety it was no longer possible for them to know whether they hated or loved one another' (p. 1). Yet the very first word of Scott's quartet of novels is the imperative verb 'imagine' ('Imagine, then, a flat landscape') which suggests a different story, and a different version of events. Here readers construct the text from a postcolonial perspective, giving play to their imagination yet also taking orders from the narrator's voice. The narrator, too, is clear-sighted about the way unfolding events reify and confirm for its bewildered English a sense of identity. As Sarah comments, 'We have acquired dignity. At no other time do we move with such grace as we do now when we feel threatened by violence but untouched by its vulgarity' (p. 163). As the English characters bluster and tiptoe around the story, the reader becomes aware of the text always in the background of this series, E. M. Forster's *A Passage to India* (1924), which tells a similar story amid the Indian independence movement in the 1920s. Forster's novel, too, centres around the alleged rape of an English woman, but unlike Scott's narrative, we are never sure whether the event took place, offering a modernist ambivalence in place of Scott's apparently sturdy grip on the facts. Scott's opening 'imagine' then is also a knowing, dangerous imperative, aware of the previous stories that have been created, or invented, drawing on the propensity of white protagonists to fabricate and project their fears and anxieties onto the colonial subject.

Jean Rhys's *Wide Sargasso Sea* (1966) effects a more deliberate retelling, rewriting the story of Charlotte Brontë's *Jane Eyre* (1847) from the point of view of the first Mrs Rochester, the silent madwoman in the attic who haunts Brontë's narrative. In the original novel, Jane Eyre's planned marriage to her employer Mr Rochester is threatened when she discovers he is already married, and the burden of caring for his deranged wife has driven him to despair. When the unnamed first wife burns down Thornfield Hall and finally kills herself, the unspeakable other is removed and Jane marries him. Only Rochester's blindness from the fire remains as a physical symbol of this silently erased figure. Yet Rhys, in rewriting the novel, seeks to retrain the lazy eyes of the shortsighted white reader. As Caryl Phillips has argued, 'Europe is blinded by her past, and does not understand the high price of her churches, art galleries, and architecture' (*The European Tribe*, p. 128).

Although Rochester is never explicitly named in Rhys's novel, which describes his courtship of Antoinette Cosway and their journey to England after she becomes his bride, the story continually makes its readers aware that this is a narrative preoccupied with subverting the dominant perspective. As Antoinette tells Mr Rochester, there is always another side to the story. By reframing *Jane Eyre*, Rhys makes a story of female empowerment and self-determination into one about the gradual erosion of identity, as Antoinette is left to go slowly mad in the attic of a house in alien England. In one memorable early exchange narrated by Rochester, Antoinette asks him about his mythical homeland:

> 'Is it true,' she said, 'that England is like a dream? Because one of my friends who married an Englishman wrote and told me so. She said this place London is like a cold dark dream sometimes. I want to wake up.'
> 'Well,' I answered annoyed, 'that is precisely how your beautiful island seems to me, quite unreal and like a dream.'[16]

Their perspectival contrast can seemingly never be resolved. Antoinette cannot fathom how the natural world of rivers and mountains could ever be thought unreal, just as Rochester is baffled that a swarming city inhabited by millions could ever be a dream. Antoinette's desire to 'wake up' suggests a wish either to stay in her homeland or to encounter England without a sense of displacement, something which neither he, nor Rhys's narrative, can grant her. Further reframing this excavation of the past, the Caribbean poet Derek Walcott later memorialises Jean Rhys herself, imagining her own early life as a girl in Jamaica as yet another text to be reinhabited and reshaped. There the precocious child sits, 'her right hand married to *Jane Eyre*, / foreseeing that her own white wedding dress / will be white paper'.[17] To excavate the past is also to wed your own future to its dictates. Yet Rhys's determination to return to the Victorian novel here is not symptomatic of a backward-looking work, but suggests a literary responsibility to uncover the colonial history that runs through the most domestic of English classics.

Apparently responding to the tacit acknowledgement both Scott and Rhys make that the novel can hide as much as it reveals, the British playwright David Edgar considers the literary efficacy of racial representation as well as the drama of racial conflict. *The Jail Diary of Albie Sachs* (1978) depicts a white South African writer who has been imprisoned for his anti-apartheid views. Sachs has worked both as a journalist and a novelist but, as he explains, the most effective way to communicate his message is through drama rather than the novel as 'books are flat, controlled. The stuff of life is rolled up flat and sliced in two-dimensional pages'.[18] While Scott and Rhys look to the past to interrogate Britain's colonial history, Edgar uses the spectre of that history to haunt the present. His polemical play *Destiny* (1976) was prompted by the growing support for the National Front in his local constituency of West Bromwich during the 1970s. The play follows four characters in independence-era India in 1947 whose lives intertwine at a British by-election thirty years later. Here is an ideological battle which is fought not as Britain surrenders the colonial crown but in the dirty world of local politics that characterises the postwar period. The unchecked racism of 1970s Britain comes not despite its history as a benevolent Empire, but because of it. While the literature of British immigration often blurs the relationship between cause and effect, or destination and origin, works that explore Britain's colonial past are often at pains to point out the inevitable causal links between now and then. As Hussein explains wryly in Edgar's *Our Own People* (1987), 'we are over here, because, dear Mr Kitchen, you were over there'.[19]

A Multicultural Music

While Edgar's plays hint at the inadequacies of the novel or more traditional literary forms to bridge racial divides, other works look to popular culture as a means of gaining a voice for black Britain. The centrality of dance-hall scenes to novels such as Sam Selvon's *The Lonely Londoners* (1956) or Muriel Spark's *The Ballad of Peckham Rye* (1960) foregrounds music as a means of connection between disparate groups of Londoners; both novels are oddly prescient of the musical story that would unfold in subsequent decades. For the suffocated suburbanite Karim in Hanif Kureishi's *The Buddha of Suburbia* (1990), the late 1970s explosion of punk offers a soundtrack of self-determination as he moves to the big city. Britain's embrace of Caribbean music and hybrid styles, from calypso in the 1950s to ska and reggae in the 1960s, also suggests a youth culture readier to accept a multicultural Britain than its parents' generation.

Colin MacInnes's notion of a utopian liberal London in *Absolute Beginners* (1959) comprised of young, free-thinking white teenagers and Afro-Caribbean immigrants is perhaps idealised, but the enormous success of bands such as the Specials and UB40 in the early 1980s point to a newly politicised and vibrant British music scene. If, as Caryl Phillips suggests, the early 1970s offered only 'a kind of post-Beatles despair' (*The European Tribe*, p. 2) with its third-rate music, the prominence of reggae artists such as Bob Marley in the latter part of the decade helped define a young black Britain that was culturally rich and politically engaged. As successful as home-grown ska and reggae artists were in the British roots scene, a great deal of its energy also came from the imported record. As Paul Gilroy points out in *There Ain't No Black in the Union Jack* (1987), the import record spoke of a counter-culture 'free from the commercialisation which characterised the British music industry'.[20] Here, symbolically, the import was valued above the indigenous which, by association, was bland, orthodox, and mass-produced.

Several writers from this period find their creative catalyst in the black British music scene. Selvon himself described his dialect prose as an attempt to make the blank page into a 'tape recorder',[21] and the next generation of writers literalise his metaphor. The Brixton-based poet and musician Linton Kwesi Johnson first came to prominence in the late 1970s. Born in Jamaica, he became involved in the London dub scene while finishing a degree at Goldsmiths University in London. His work fuses Jamaican patois with dub poetry performance; recordings of his poems recited over bass and drums were included on his first album, *Dread Beat an' Blood* (1978). His work is engaged with politics as deeply as with rhythm, as this extract from his 1980 collection, *Inglan is a Bitch*, suggests:

> di CRE can't set wi free
> di TUC can't dhu it fi wi
> di Liberal Pawty is nat very hawty
> an'di Tory Pawty a noh fi wi party[22]

The organisations Johnson lists here (the Campaign for Racial Equality and the Trade Unions Congress) remain socially impotent for all their political clout, their phonic similarity only emphasising their inability to promote change. His often vitriolic protests at the racism of Britain at the turn of the 1980s is no more than a clear-sighted prediction of the years that followed. In the 1960s, Sam Selvon had returned to his lonely protagonist Moses only to find him affluent and indifferent to political agency in *Moses Ascending* (1963).[23] As Black Power protests march outside, Moses, now a wealthy landlord, is most worried about the damage to his properties. For Johnson, such evasions are no longer possible. In April 1981, Brixton was the scene of Britain's worst ever race riot, as local people clashed with police over the enforcement of the 'sus' law, a new decree which allowed police to stop and search citizens simply on suspicion. Although the rioting had subsided by the following day, the police and government alike were reluctant to learn lessons from the protests.

The dub poet Benjamin Zephaniah found early fame both with his album *Rasta* (1982) and with his first collection *Pen Rhythm* (1980). His work has at once helped postwar British poetry maintain visibility outside the academic community and also brought the concerns of black Britain to a white audience. Yet his assimilation into mainstream literary culture has not tempered his outspoken voice; a recent poem 'The Race Industry' suggests that even though racial discrimination is now acknowledged by the British government as unacceptable, it pays lip service to diversity only to make a profit from the minorities it claims to support:

> Without Black suffering they'd have no jobs.
> Without our dead they'd have no office.
> Without our tears they'd have no drink.
> If they stopped sucking we could get justice.
> The coconuts are getting paid.
> Men, women and Brixton are being betrayed.[24]

Here, Brixton, the word that is now a synecdoche for British racial tension, police brutality, and governmental indifference, offers a symbol which no-one can read or respond to. For Zephaniah, the need to promote racial equality has become merely a means of personal promotion for a new generation of government careerists. His work, along with Johnson's, suggests that popular music and dub poetry offer black British culture widespread visibility, but also a critical platform that is pointedly political. For the popular Guyana-born poet John Agard, rhythm itself is a political tool. His demotic (everyday speech) provides a necessary deconstruction of Standard English; as he warns an Oxford don, 'I dont need no axe / to split / up yu syntax'.[25] If it is music, rather than literature, that shows the greatest potential for an indigenous multicultural art, it is also when poetry takes to the stage that the black British voice is at its most strident.

Conflict and Censorship

The riots of 1981 highlighted the growing racism of inner-city London. Yet the government's apparent indifference came in marked contrast to its preoccupation one year later with a conflict apparently much further from its waters. In April 1982, Argentinian forces occupied the historically disputed territory of the Falkland Islands. Thatcher's government responded with a swift military reprisal which eventually recaptured the islands and resulted in nearly a thousand Argentine deaths. The patriotic fervour which swept the country after the British military victory prompted Thatcher's return to government with an increased majority. Yet the sense that only a nostalgic return to Empire could fuel national feeling worried some: as Stuart Hall pointed out in 1982:

> as the country drifts deeper into recession, we seem to possess no other viable vocabulary in which to cast our sense of who the British people are and where they are going, except one drawn from the inventory of a lost imperial greatness.[26]

This debate re-emerged later in the decade with the controversial reception of Salman Rushdie's *Satanic Verses* (1988). Muslim leaders condemned the book as blasphemous, leading to book-burnings throughout Britain. Yet the intricate, messy, and shifting voices of the novel are as preoccupied with nationhood and language as with religion. The novel, like Lamming's or Selvon's thirty years earlier, begins with an immigrant journey to England, but then confounds expectations. The two protagonists, Gibreel Farishta and Saladin Chamcha, are travelling in a plane which is hijacked and eventually explodes, yet both characters are miraculously saved and plummet to Britain from the sky. The immigrant narrative is hijacked by Rushdie in other ways, too; Farishta is a superstar in his native India rather than an economic migrant, whereas Chamcha has already emigrated to England.

Rushdie's energetic brand of magic realism* continually disrupts the linear narrative that leads us from origin to destination: as Farishta and Chamcha fall to earth, they are transformed into the devil and an archangel. Yet, in other ways, the novel's generic hybridity is also a way of exploring issues of identity and cultural genealogy. The policeman who discovers Chamcha suspects him of being an illegal immigrant, prompting a ribald display of racist British law enforcement. The novel's tonal variations and interweaving narratives stretch the coherence to breaking point, and its characters are wracked with similar divisions. Farishta's acting career suggests a playful relationship with plural identities; his friend Bhupen sees him as a positive force, 'an actor from a minority playing roles from many religions, and being accepted'.[27] Similarly, postcolonial theorist Homi K. Bhabha has asserted that acts of cultural engagement are produced performatively.[28] Yet Farishta's growing pathological disorder is continually linked to his vexed questions about his Indian identity, and he eventually commits suicide, while Chamcha finds renewal and reconciliation in his homeland.

Through the other figures that populate Chamcha and Farishta's journeys, Rushdie also complicates the narrative of immigration. With the Muslim Immam forced to stay in London, for example, Rushdie explores the endless paradox of the exile, whose 'vision of revolution' is of 'looking forwards by always looking back' (p. 205). Meanwhile the gap between the exile and the immigrant stretches as wide as the 'immeasurable distance' between Englishness and Indianness themselves (p. 41). If the novel's reception meant its readers mined the text for absolutist definitions and dogmatic stances, Rushdie's own narrative questions the efficacy of

---

* Magic realism describes literature that combines a realist framework with fantastical elements.

such binary oppositions, suggesting doubt, rather than blasphemy, as the opposite of faith and questioning textual authority as much as religious doctrine. However, perhaps its most arresting claim lies with its newfound confidence in an English-language novel that needn't be from England, about England, or by an English writer.

New Spaces

In the short story 'The Devastating Boys' (1972) by Elizabeth Taylor, an elderly middle-aged couple from rural England agree to look after two inner-city black children for a summer holiday volunteer scheme. The wife, Laura, awaits their visit with mild bewilderment rather than foreboding, but her own bafflement mirrors Benny and Sep's as they arrive into this unknown world. Their rowdy energy unravels Laura's life and puts it back together again.[29] This is a vignette rather than a genre, yet it suggests some tentative links between the novels of nostalgic rural England explored in the previous chapter and Britain's postcolonial literature of change and uprooting. Caryl Phillips stages a similar meeting point in his screenplay for the film *Playing Away* (1980), which imagines a Brixton cricket team of West Indian descent asked to play in a rural English village. As Phillips's preface points out, West Indian immigrants gave up a largely rural life to live in the concrete and glass of urban London. This is, like the journey that Benny and Sep make to rural England, a journey to an unfamiliar world, but it is also reminiscent, for all its alienness, of home.

For the Caribbean poet Derek Walcott, who now lives in the United States, writing itself is a means of excavating, interrogating, and complicating notions of home. In Walcott's collection *The Fortunate Traveller* (1981), he goes on a series of journeys by sea and air, as if to finally see the world he inhabits with an objectivity not bestowed on the land-bound. Drunk on whisky in a ship's cabin, he watches England recede into the distance until it is an indistinct line on the horizon.[30] Yet even then, he must think on its history, and remind himself that Albion, too, was once a colony. The sea is a recurring image in his work. Not hemmed in by land borders, it is the perpetual in-between space. Its surfaces have seen a series of political and national battles played out, but only in its depths do we finally find a place free from the human histories of faith, emancipation, and lamentation. Here, Walcott, reminds us, is the sound 'like rumour without any echo / of History, really beginning'.[31] For Walcott, the immigrant writer's journey is not one from alienation to assimilation, or from isolation to integration, but rather a continual process, a movement that finds journeys beneath journeys, and destinations beyond its end points. In the poem 'Codicil', at least, the journey ends not with a return home but with a hard-fought right to keep travelling. Trudging an endless beach in the moonlight, the poet knows this is his destiny as an exile.[32]

Notes

1   Sheila Patterson, *Dark Strangers* (Harmondsworth: Pelican, 1963), p. 87.
2   Stuart Hall, 'Black Men, White Media', *Savacou* 9/10, 1971, pp. 97–100.
3   See, for example, 'Enoch Powell's 'Rivers of Blood' speech', *The Telegraph*, 6 November 2007, p. 23.
4   Stuart Hall, 'New ethnicities', in David Morley and Kuan-Hsing Chen (eds), *Stuart Hall: Critical dialogues in cultural studies* (London: Routledge, 1996), pp. 441–9, p. 447.
5   George Lamming, *The Emigrants* (London: Allison & Busby, 1980), p. 107.
6   Caryl Phillips, *The Final Passage* (London: Faber, 1985), p. 142.
7   V. S. Naipaul, *The Enigma of Arrival* (London: Penguin, 1987), p. 22.
8   Zulfikar Ghose, *Confessions of a Native-Alien* (London: Routledge, 1965), p. 2.
9   Caryl Phillips, *Strange Fruit* (Ambergate: Amber Lane Press, 1981), p. 80.
10   Caryl Phillips, *The European Tribe* (London: Faber, 1987), p. 123.
11   George Lamming, *The Pleasures of Exile* (London: Michael Joseph, 1960), p. 23.
12   Sam Selvon, *The Lonely Londoners* (London: Penguin, 2006), p. 71.
13   G. V. Desani, *All About H. Hatterr* (Penguin: Harmondsworth, 1969), p. 47.
14   British Conservative Party Manifesto, 1951.
15   Paul Scott, *The Raj Quartet* (London: Heinemann, 1976), p. 1.
16   Jean Rhys, *Wide Sargasso Sea* (London: Penguin, 1997), p. 49.

17   Derek Walcott, 'Jean Rhys', *The Fortunate Traveller* (London: Faber, 1980),
      p. 47, ll. 72–4.

18   David Edgar, *The Jail Dairy of Albie Sachs*, in *Plays: Two* (London: Methuen,
      1994), p. 48.

19   David Edgar, *Our Own People*, in *Plays: One* (London: Methuen, 1994),
      p. 71.

20   Paul Gilroy, *There Ain't No Black in the Union Jack* (London: Routledge,
      2002), p. 219.

21   '"Interview with John Thieme", "Oldtalk": two interviews with Sam
      Selvon', in Martin Zehnder (ed.), *Something Rich and Strange: Selected
      Essays on Sam Selvon* (Leeds: Peepal Tree Press, 2003), p. 11.

22   Linton Kwesi Johnson, 'Independent Intavenshan', *Inglan is a Bitch*
      (London: Race Today, 1980), p. 19, ll. 22–5.

23   See Samuel Selvon, *Moses Ascending* (London: Allen Wingate, 1963).

24   Benjamin Zephaniah, 'The Race Industry', *Too Strong, Too Black*
      (Newcastle: Bloodaxe, 2001), p. 43, ll. 20–5.

25   John Agard, 'Listen Mr Oxford don', *Mangoes & Bullets* (London: Pluto,
      1985), p. 44, ll. 8–10.

26   Stuart Hall, 'The Empire Strikes Back', *The Hard Road to Renewal:
      Thatcherism and the Crisis of the Left* (London: Verso, 1988), p. 68.

27   Salman Rushdie, *The Satanic Verses* (London: Viking Penguin, 1988), p. 54.

28   Homi K. Bhabha, *The Location of Culture* (London: Routledge, 2004), p.
      4.

29   Elizabeth Taylor, 'The Devastating Boys', *The Devastating Boys* (London:
      Chatto & Windus, 1972).

30   Derek Walcott, 'The Fortunate Traveller', *The Fortunate Traveller*, p. 92,
      l. 113.

31   Derek Walcott, 'The Sea is History', *Selected Poems* (London: Faber, 2007),
      p. 125, ll. 79–80.

32   Derek Walcott, 'Codicil', *Selected Poems*, p. 35, ll. 2–3.

Class and Education

Parents who can barely afford it
Should not send their children to public school ill will reward it
Stevie Smith, 'Parents' (1957)[1]

Stevie Smith's pithy homily for the aspiring middle-class parent suggests the pervasive links between class and education in postwar Britain. The nineteenth-century class debate begun by poet and schools inspector Matthew Arnold in *Culture and Anarchy* (1869) re-emerged with a fervency few could have foreseen in the early part of the century. For Arnold, the middle-class anxiety about the working class and their political enfranchisement had been a means of propagating cultural philanthropy. Culture, defined in contrast to 'the ordinary popular literature', was a way of 'doing away with classes';[2] a utopian solution to social unrest. The adoption of Arnold's ideas in postwar Britain was both more pragmatic and driven more by economics than social cohesion or aesthetic aim. Britain after the Second World War was an impoverished nation, many of its cities in ruins and its population depleted. From the ashes of a costly war came the Attlee government's creation of the modern Welfare State, a range of measures designed to offer cradle-to-grave support for all British citizens. William Beveridge gave Britain its first system of social security, while the National Health Service was set up in 1947. Yet of all the measures designed to create a skilled workforce that could move

216

Britain back to economic prosperity, the overhaul of secondary education left the most lasting legacy in postwar writing and culture.

Welfare Fictions and Social Theorists

The 1944 Butler Education Act redrew the map of state education, ensuring free schooling for all children up to sixteen. The new system envisaged a tripartite model of education, offering state-supported grammar schools for academically gifted children, secondary modern schools for the less able, and technical colleges for vocational training courses. A standardised national exam known as the 11-plus determined students' route through the system. Yet this apparently egalitarian model which promised social mobility and the abolishment of traditional class hierarchies was not without its social engineering. When it became clear to the government that girls regularly outperformed boys in the 11-plus, grammar school entries were skewed towards male applicants.[3] The social and economic implications of a child's performance in this single exam taken at eleven years old were far reaching; successful authors from the period who failed the 11-plus are few and far between. The state's attempt to remodel society also created painful chasms between generations: the working-class boy given an education unimaginable in his parents' day was often isolated both from his origins and from the unfamiliar world of the grammar school, which was dominated by middle-class students. Yet it is difficult to overestimate the impact of the Butler Act on the literature of the 1950s and 1960s. Its assumed symbiosis of class and education meant that the first generation of writers to benefit from it were also more conscious than ever before of class difference and the tensions implicit in moving between differing social categories.

The state presented itself as a benevolent provider of opportunity, building a society founded on merit rather than inherited privilege. As Edward Hallett Carr had agued in *The New Society* (1951), 'mass democracy calls just as much as an individualist democracy for an educated society'.[4] Critics of this model were, in the 1950s at least, relatively scarce. Michael Young's *The Rise of the Meritocracy* (1958) gave us the word meritocracy as we know it today yet, ironically, the book is a satire, imagining a dystopian state in 2011 where the principles of selection and social engineering have moved from meritocracy to eugenics. In attempting to promote equality, Young argues, the state will merely create a new upper class who are shored up by the certainty of having earned their place, rather than feeling a social responsibility from the guilt of familial inheritance.[5] Tony Crosland, too, noted in *The Future of Socialism* (1956) that 'a hereditary society, denied the opportunity to rise, avoids also the sense of failure at having risen'.[6] A large body of literature from the postwar period testifies to Crosland's concerns; the rural schoolchildren in Penelope Fitzgerald's *The Bookshop* (1978), for example, 'would remember nothing more painful or more decisive than the envelopes waiting on the desks',[7] parcelling them off either to a grammar school or the local secondary modern. John Dyson in Michael Frayn's *Towards the End of the Morning* (1967) reflects that failure has become 'the secular equivalent of sin', creating a society built 'not of laws and duties, but of tests and comparisons'.[8] The 11-plus exam was both a sign of social mobility and an arbitrary incision in children's education, a barometer of intellectual aptitude that would have dramatic and irreversible consequences for their lives. For many autobiographical works looking back on the period, such as Lorna Sage's *Bad Blood* (2000), it is the pivot on which the narrative turns, offering escape from a cosseted and parochial life.

The 11-plus was not the only feature of the Welfare State that gave commentators of the period cause for anxiety. For author and theologian C. S. Lewis, the emphasis on progress and efficiency enslaved individuals to a 'world-wide paternalism', raising the question of whether there was any possibility of 'getting the super Welfare State's honey and avoiding the sting'.[9] Other Welfare State critiques are more knowing, or more affectionate, as in the comical portrayal of National Service in David Lodge's *Ginger, You're Barmy* (1962), which describes it as 'the last surviving relic of feudalism in English society'.[10] Jonathan Browne's liberal education finds him ill-equipped for the mysterious hierarchies of the army, where 'intelligence, critical judgement, culture' are 'liabilities rather than assets in applying for a commission' (p. 76). If the world of the army seems atypical in the postwar literary landscape, the comic mismatch between Browne's education and the subsequent society it equips him so badly for is less so; this is an allegedly tailor-made education that rarely seems to survive the tests of experience and practical application.

The radical liberal politics of the 1960s would question the efficacy of state welfare with its emphasis on conformity and consensus; Herbert Marcuse was one of many cultural critics to see the postwar Welfare State as a malignant force, threatening individual choice and freedom.[11] Yet, in keeping with the conservative and anthropological tendencies of the period, the most influential cultural critique was more sociological study than polemic. Richard Hoggart's *The Uses of Literacy* (1957) explores the impact of postwar social policy on working-class culture. Hoggart, born in a working-class area of Leeds before progressing through the grammar school system to become a university lecturer, is perhaps the archetypal model of the 'scholarship boy', yet remains ambivalent about the working-class culture he has left behind. His highly influential work hovers between autobiography and sociology, supporting his detached observations of working-class life with the authenticity of lived experience.

The Scholarship Boy

The most influential material in Hoggart's study remains that on the scholarship boy, who he identifies as a figure confused about his origins and inheritance, perpetually self-effacing and anxious in his own body; 'like transplanted stock, he reacts to a widespread drought earlier than those who have been left in their original soil'.[12] His notion offers a revealing fit with key 1950s protagonists from Jimmy Porter in John Osborne's *Look Back in Anger* (1956) to Jim Dixon in Kingsley Amis's *Lucky Jim* (1954). Both of these characters offer different responses to the same internal conflict: Dixon, a university lecturer, carries a shoulder-shrugging disdain for academia only just balanced by the class chip on his other shoulder, whereas Jimmy rages at the complacency and lack of intellectual curiosity of those around him. In both cases, this manifests itself in physical as well as verbal violence; their anxiety about their class status and the threat of an emasculating upper-class gentility result in aggressive displays of masculinity. Yet, for all their occasional brawling, their targets are predominantly intellectual. Jimmy groans with disdain at the Sunday papers, and the way their reviews of French literature are designed to make their readers feel stupid; Jim's baffled antipathy towards his academic research finds only comic relief in the way his lectures throw no light on nonproblems.

In fact, 1950s and 1960s literature is awash with portrayals of the scholarship boy, the often reclusive, angry, and displaced individual who must wade through a world of snobbery and class prejudice. Dennis Potter's series of plays following the life of semi-autobiographical Nigel Barton memorably find him in the Oxford University debating chamber speaking on the importance of working-class culture. Nigel argues that '[n]o one who has been brought up in a working class culture can ever altogether escape, or wish to escape, the almost suffocating warmth and friendliness of that culture', but goes on to say that 'as soon as you cross the frontiers between one class and another you feel – I feel – as though you are negotiating a minefield. Even one's own parents feel that you are judging them, scorning them even.' At this point the president retorts that '[t]he honourable member may feel that he knows what he's talking about. I wish we had the same privilege! (*Laughter*)'[13] Here, the mocking Oxbridge president recasts the word 'privilege' and returns it from the upper class back to Nigel, son of a coalminer. His cruelty rests on the fact that Nigel can have the 'privilege' of authenticity, or social mobility, but never of inherited wealth. Potter's use of military metaphors is telling here, with Nigel's mention of class 'frontiers' and the 'minefield' of communication between social groups. Like Jimmy Porter's struggle to find a 'brave new cause', vitriolic class war becomes a rallying cry to those uprooted individuals who have neither political allegiance nor conflict to mobilise them. The 1950s, the much touted age of affluence, threatened its inhabitants with apathy rather than conflict. Without a Spanish Civil War or Nazi Germany to fight, the blurring of class boundaries may yet remove the final dividing line that allows the continuation of hostilities, and Jimmy's furious rants or Barton's beleaguered protests struggle to keep the borders between themselves and the world they inhabit clear.

This need to cling to class divisions even as the state attempts to dissolve them offers up many of these texts to Marxist readings. Frequently, individuals struggle to hold onto their identity in the face of rapid social changes. The drive for economic prosperity and commercial expansion dictates the supposed choices of postwar protagonists in their 'liberation' from class shackles. D. M. Black's poem 'The Educators' (1969) describes a shadowy set of teachers who 'dismantle' their students before passing their limbs and entrails around.[14] As a metaphor for the state's dissection of the individual, it remains chilling and suggestive. More famously, in *Lord of the Flies* (1954), William Golding recasts the myth of a good education into a study of animalistic savagery. Marooned on an island, the abandoned school-children move from community survival to barbaric violence.

The playwright Willy Russell mines his teaching career in Liverpool for comic pathos in *Educating Rita* (1981), which explores the relationship between a cynical and disaffected English lecturer, Frank, and Rita, a working-class hairdresser seeking a literary education through a university access scheme. Here self-improvement and auto-didacticism (self-education) offer more challenges to the cynical don than to the sharp student. Rita's bullish wit and keen intelligence seduce Frank from his studied ennui, and challenge his assumptions about what and how he teaches. Rita brings a natural Marxism to the literature she studies; the hierarchies of E. M. Forster's *Howards End* (1910) frustrate her sharp sense of fairness, with the narrator's pithy dismissal of the poor. If the issues of status and class are explored here with generosity rather than antagonism, Russell retains an anxiety about the play's subject and its possible audience. Frank suggests a trip to the theatre early on in their lessons, only to have Rita insist she hates theatre. She is being represented in a medium she does not rate. Here, the playwright retains the sense of working in a culture alien to his class origin, a knowing echo of Larkin's poem 'A Study of Reading Habits', which has its speaker dismiss books completely.[15] If Larkin receives an Oxbridge education only to pour scorn on Spenser and Chaucer, who might the final audience for his poetry be? The point of tension comes here from a nagging sense that the authors are estranged from their audience through birth and their origins through education.

If sustained antagonism to social mobility informs characters such as Jim Dixon or Jimmy Porter, others simply cast off the legacy of entitlement altogether. For the protagonists of Allan Sillitoe's *Saturday Night and Sunday Morning* (1958) or John Wain's *Hurry on Down* (1953), a refusal of the state's munificence becomes a political gesture: in *Hurry on Down*, Charles Lumley trains as a hospital porter rather than take up the graduate position his university education dictates. When ridiculed by his friends for challenging the state's model of aspiration and economic ambition, he claims that a porter is as important in civic society as a lawyer or a lecturer. Jimmy Porter, whose 'white-tile' university education has landed him a job running a sweet shop, would most likely agree. Charles finds little release in disobeying the educational narrative provided for him by the state. Instead, he is left to reflect that he has 'become a parasite on the world he detested'.[16] The apparent mobility enshrined by the Butler Education Act instead creates a generation only too aware of the painful gaps between the haves and the have-nots. Educational and social theories of the time often used the ladder as a metaphor for social mobility. Yet, as cultural theorist Raymond Williams argues, 'the ladder will never do; it is the product of a divided society, and must fall with it'.[17] For Charles, who has ascended the ladder only to try to climb down again, the metaphor no longer holds. In its place, he sees only:

> a web, sticky and cunningly arranged. You were either a spider,
> sitting comfortably in the middle or waiting with malicious joy
> in hiding, or you were a fly, struggling amid the clinging threads.
> (p. 84)

The 'clinging threads' and social anxiety of the scholarship boy substitute education for identity; the fiction about him finds a series of protagonists who are both harangued and haunted.

Working-class Dramas

At the same time that the new social make-up of the university in the 1950s created fictional characters marked by uprooting and alienation, the literary spotlight on working-class life and community offered a radical shift in social representations. On the stage, the work of Joe Orton, John Osborne, and Shelagh Delaney rewrote the middle-class drawing-room comedy of Noel Coward and Terence Rattigan; on screen the popular New Wave movement saw popular culture rallying around the working-class anti-hero, from Arthur Seaton in the 1960s adaptation of Alan Sillitoe's *Saturday Night and Sunday Morning* to Frank Machin in the 1963 adaptation of David Storey's *This Sporting Life* (1960). This new brand of matinée idol was iconoclastic, rebellious, and usually working class; the films eschewed London for the mining towns of Yorkshire (*This Sporting Life*) or the canals of Manchester (*A Taste of Honey*, 1958). While the writers of these novels, screenplays, and dramas were themselves often working class, the immense popularity of these films also set the agenda for other depictions of contemporary British life. Doris Lessing, who was born in the former Rhodesia but came to London after the war, records with ironic distance the glamorisation of working-class experience by the intelligentsia. Here, the modern interest in sociology combined with a renewed interest in a societal group that had been often fictionalised but more often patronised. As she comments, 'not one truthful word could ever be written until it was first baptised, so to speak, by the working class'.[18] The working class become both subject and consumer, although in a framework still controlled by middle-class tastes and sensibilities.

This sentimental promotion of working-class life as authentic and honest is common even within the social study or documentary report. Richard Hoggart attempts to describe his upbringing with sociological objectivity, but admits that he, too, cannot help but romanticise the working-class home: 'like any life with a firm centre, it has a powerful hold ... working-class people themselves are often sentimental about it'.[19]

In his simultaneous distancing from and comparison to the working-class people he describes, he articulates the troubling space left by his educational privileges. Other works find working-class culture buffeted by idealised projections on the one hand and disdain on the other. In Stephen Berkoff's play *East* (1975), the absent-minded mother asks her son what a proletariat is, but for the purposes of a crossword puzzle rather than a protracted debate on the political apathy of her own class.[20] The notion of the 'authentic' working-class community is mocked, too, in David Edgar's *Enjoy* (1980). As an elderly couple wait for their council estate to be demolished, they are sent a government leaflet which admits that previous redevelopments have destroyed working-class communities. The leaflet promises them a visit from a registered sociologist who will observe them and help them preserve their intrinsic qualities of 'self-reliance, neighbourliness and self-help'.[21] Here, the state is unable to conceive of a self-governing or self-generating community. It expects the working class to endure a series of expedient interventions in their lives, and supports their community more in the interests of sociology than compassion.

Philip Larkin's massed working class and 'cut-price' crowds have their desires defined for them by adverts in cheap magazines, and remain hemmed in by knick-knacks, commodities, and objects that take the place of feelings, as he describes in the poem 'Here'.[22] Yet those without the money for cheap commodities find little else to replace the silences of their lives. Edward Bond's *Saved* (1965) offers a stuttering dialogue of monosyllables to articulate what journalists called the 'new poor' as if to detach them from the comfy sentimentality which prevented middle-class voters from worrying about them. Meanwhile, Mike Leigh's actor-improvised dramas replace the mournful silences of Pinter with the tinny chatter and nagging persistence of Beverley in *Abigail's Party* (1979).[23] Here, the superficial life of the nouveau-riche is laid out for painful comedy as Beverley's long-suffering husband dies from a heart attack at the climax of a dreadful dinner party. Although sexual politics resurface throughout the evening's excruciating dialogues, it is the war between the popular and the middle-brow that provides the play's final battle-cry, as Laurence's love of Van Gogh is ridiculed by Beverley's crude pornographic ideas of erotic art. Personal taste or discriminating judgement are replaced by a middle-class obsession with cultural status or the commodified world of the working class.

Meanwhile, the playwright Arnold Wesker gave the postwar period some of its richest depictions of working-class culture in works such as *Chicken Soup with Barley* (1958) and *Chips with Everything* (1962). His political commitment to socialism extended to the programming and production of theatre as well as composition; in the late 1950s, he set up the Centre 42 group in London, attempting to promote a series of socialist and socially committed theatre projects. Yet if he saw in theatre a dynamic and culturally revivifying form which might engage with and preserve a way of life he saw as being under threat, his plays are less confident of the existence of a listening, engaged audience. The final scene of *Roots* (1959) finds the usually silenced Beatie offering a defiant defence of education and the need for a sceptical and politically engaged working-class culture 'asking questions, all the time'.[24] The common culture called for by commentators such as Richard Hoggart and Raymond Williams is expressed here in resigned complaint. Beatie rails against the seduction of the working class by prurient magazines, yellow-back fiction, and entertainments of the lowest common denominator. Yet the silence her soliloquy is met with onstage suggests a reluctance to answer those questions. Instead, we find a drama of victimhood or apathy. As the raging protagonist of Howard Barker's *Claw* (1975) has it, all are defenceless in the face of the government's 'great claw, slashing us, splitting our people, their great claw ripping our faces and tearing up our streets'.[25]

Private Passions

While class struggle and the education system are synonymous in much literature of the period, it's telling that one of the best-selling novels of the 1960s was Muriel Spark's *The Prime of Miss Jean Brodie* (1961). This is a novel of education that refuses to make the classroom a study of social realism, taking place in a hallowed and traditional private girls' school in Scotland. Yet if Spark's caustic and enigmatic comedy is far from the impassioned brow-beating of Nigel Barton or Jimmy Porter, its interest in legacy makes it nearer to its angrier counterparts than it seems. The highly idiosyncratic teaching methods of Miss Jean Brodie, her students' fierce and unswerving devotion to her, and the eerily possessive notion of them as 'her girls'[26] suggest a parallel with the state's ownership of education and its investment in students as economic products, yet the novel's reluctance to take itself seriously undermines these parallels. In sharp and acerbic prose, Spark offers an alternative to the grey disappointments of the scholarship boys. The 1980s prompted a revival of more traditional educational depictions too. In Julian Mitchell's *Another Country* (1982), the 1930s boys' public school is returned to with a more articulate eye for its internal ructions. In the midst of its totalising hierarchies and systems of privilege are the voices of two outsiders: Guy Bennett, who grapples with his homosexuality, and Tommy Judd, a principled Marxist. The fear of both *Das Kapital* and same-sex relationships make their presence too threatening for the school to contain. This is a system that must reject dissenters rather than restructure itself. Similarly, public school life in William Boyd's television dramas *Good and Bad at Games* (1985) and *Dutch Girls* (1985) seems cruel and sadistic.

Iris Murdoch's training as a philosopher maps out another way of viewing education in the period. If Philip Larkin and Kingsley Amis made names for themselves as Oxbridge iconoclasts, exchanging letters that ridicule classic literature and instead muse on the relative benefits of pornography and jazz, Murdoch's long-time devotion to Oxford highlights a literature of moral seriousness that remains unafraid of the novel of ideas (see Part Three: 'The Moral Novel'). Throughout her fiction, protagonists struggle to teach themselves about the world or to learn from their moral weaknesses. Most notably in *The Sandcastle* (1957), she introduces a prestigious private school, but one where the shifts in public education have begun to influence the teaching staff, unlike Spark's hermetically sealed world in *The Prime of Miss Jean Brodie*. The novel's catalyst for action is the arrival of a revolutionary new headmaster whose pupil preference is for the 'mediocre boy'[27] who can be coached to excellence rather than the star pupils who can glide effortlessly through the system. Murdoch's interest here is less in the changing admissions policies of private schools than in the psychological role of the teacher and how it informs moral choice, but her setting is suggestive of how the state's interventions had made incursions even on schools outside its remit.

Yet the Butler Act and its subsequent reorganisation of secondary education gave novelists, dramatists, and poets of the period more than a shared thematic concern. Hoggart's *The Uses of Literacy* does not stop at providing critics with a new literary anti-hero, the scholarship boy, but also details the implications of mass literacy and its effect on art and culture. Examining the cheap yellow-back fodder provided to the working class in the guise of entertainment, Hoggart constructs an argument linking literary craft to social responsibility. The newly literate masses are worthy of more than the savvy media serves up for them, he suggests, and calls for an Arnoldian return to a literature which will engage and provoke. As it stands, 'popular writing cannot genuinely explore experience' (p. 188). If modernism's aesthetic considers form over audience, never worrying about charges of exclusivity or elitism, postwar literature often offers conscious appeals to the scholarship boys of the future. In this way, educational changes can help explain literature's formal conservatism in the postwar period. To experiment is also to risk alienating the growing body of working-class and middle-class readers new to literary fiction. Pamela Hansford Johnson fretted in 1949 that the 'ordinary reader' is 'seriously worried' by the baffling experiments of 'arid' modernism; challenged by the critic to find something to admire in a literature they do not appreciate, Johnson argues, they will instead 'take refuge, more often than not, in the detective story'.[28] This is a literature that must talk to its new audience, without talking down, a balancing act which creates a rich source of tension in many postwar works.

A Formal Education

This may go some way to explaining why experimental fiction of the period is often self-questioning and fraught in its quest for innovation, mindful of the audience it is leaving behind. It is significant that one of the most sustained depictions of postwar education comes in B. S. Johnson's formally radical *Albert Angelo* (1964). Johnson was a novelist out of time, a formal experimenter whose techniques included publishing chapters in random orders for the reader to shuffle and reorganise (*The Unfortunates*, 1969) and making holes in the pages of his books to allow readers to look forward to future plot twists. His frustrated career and eventual suicide in 1972 suggest the difficulties of sustaining dissent against the move to formal conservatism.

Albert Angelo's protagonist is a struggling architect who supports himself with supply teaching. Much of the narrative follows Albert through a series of inner-city London schools where the students' apathy and casual violence is by turns dispiriting and terrifying. Yet rather than sketch out these shabby classrooms and streets in the everyday language of New Wave realism, Johnson employs an ever-shifting range of narrative techniques. The novel switches between first, second, and third person, before finding its most experimental voice in the schoolroom scene, where the page divides in two to give us the lesson Albert is teaching on the right hand side and the wandering pattern of his thoughts on the left. Albert's eventual death at the hands of his mindlessly violent students links the breakdown of the education system with the formal rupture of the novel, which ends with a frustrated authorial intrusion. To turn your back on the dictates of the Welfare State and the formal responsibilities of the novelist was a risk that few writers in the period would take. One of Johnson's final pieces of writing before his suicide was an essay called 'Education and Training', which aimed to explain his life based on the teaching he'd received at various institutions, in particular his failing of the 11-plus and his frustrated life at his local secondary modern.[29] If Potter's and Larkin's experiences at Oxford form their disdain for the intelligentsia and their keen sense of class conflict, Johnson's educational story creates a narrative of intellectual neglect and public indifference to his work.

Meanwhile, novelists such as James Kelman and Angela Carter followed Johnson in their use of the classroom to explore issues of form. The narrator of Kelman's *A Disaffection* (1989) is the alcoholic twenty-nine-year-old teacher Patrick Doyle, who comes to believe that school is a malevolent agent of the state controlling the poor it claims to be empowering. The structure of the novel itself relies on the heavy repetition of inculcation, as the subversive Doyle asks his students to repeat after him: 'we are being fenced in by the teachers'.[30] The relationship between narrator and reader comes to mirror the contract between teacher and pupil, novelists' unquestioned power a corrupting influence they finally use for their own advantage. Angela Carter's *Heroes and Villains* (1969) offers an educational meritocracy that is half way between Huxley's *Brave New World* (1932) and Michael Young. Post-apocalypse, the Professors live in towns of glass and steel while the Barbarians roam the jungle. The novel focuses on a Professor's daughter, Marianne, who is carried away to be a captive bride. Even before her capture, she inhabits a world that has become hermetically sealed from experience and communication is effectively impossible. She spends her days leafing through dictionaries, searching for incomprehensible words which she can only define through their use in other books, as words have ceased to describe the world around her and 'now only stood for ideas and memories'.[31] When the meritocracy seeks to separate people by intelligence, the novel suggests, there will ultimately be no dialogue between the human mind and the world of experience.

Trouble on Campus

While the farce and social anxiety of *Lucky Jim* was co-opted on publication into the expedient media shorthand of the Angry Young Man, its more lasting literary legacy was the establishment of the campus novel. This genre borrows both Amis's university setting and comic mode, and its popularity continued into the 1970s and 1980s, with writers such as David Lodge and Malcolm Bradbury. Despite, or perhaps because of, growing concerns about the relevance of academic debate to national culture, the protagonists of the campus novel continued to fret about their relationship to the world around them. For the liberal and left-leaning Professor Treece in Bradbury's *Eating People is Wrong* (1959), the arrival of the scholarship boy into his lecture halls and onto his faculty is a fact his social conscience welcomes, but his own self-doubt chews over:

It could not be denied that all forms of social stratification, once solid, were liquefying in the torrid heat engendered by reforming zealots like himself. Treece had to admit that, if it became a choice between being respected too much and not at all he would, in spite of his liberal pretensions, rest easier in spirit under the former regime.[32]

The changing social make-up of the academic elite is something Treece simultaneously wants to take credit for and to worry about. Anita Brookner's early heroines are similarly disrupted and discomfitted by their literary education and the demands of a world that expects professional seriousness. Kitty Maule's university teaching job in *Providence* (1982) is a 'temporary and rather pleasant way of filling in the time until her true occupation should be revealed to her'.[33] Dr Ruth Weiss in *A Start in Life* (1982) is a female Quixote who blames the romantic promises of literature for having ruined her life by inflicting a moral education where she should 'ponder the careers of Anna Karenina and Emma Bovary, but … emulate those of David Copperfield and Little Dorrit'.[34] Even in the university lecture hall, literature offers the same false promises as it does for Larkin's crabbed old man in 'A Study of Reading Habits'.

The chivalric quest for knowledge or romance has, by the time of David Lodge's novel *Small World* (1984), been reduced to a poorly attended conference in a snowy provincial campus of 'cracked and pitted walls'.[35] The high-flying transnational world of academic conferences provides comic respite from tedious term-times, but the promise of escape only brings with it pasts that cannot be abandoned and names people would rather forget. Yet in Lodge's *Nice Work* (1988), the campus novel is momentarily returned to its roots in class anxiety rather than rarified theoretical debate. The novel's premise centres on a cultural exchange between academia and industry. The feminist lecturer Robyn Penrose is encouraged to spend one afternoon a week with Vic Wilcox, who manages an engineering firm. If the novel makes repeated references to Elizabeth Gaskell's *North and South* (1848), an industrial novel which unravelled the class prejudices of its southern heroine, it also delights in the contradictions of an academic whose apparently liberal stance assumes she will be immune from undergoing a similar process. Instead, as in her first visit to the foundry, she panics at being so far from her comfort zone:

> How she wishes she were back in her snug little house, tapping away on her word-processor, dissecting the lexemes of some classic Victorian novel, delicately detaching the hermeneutic code from the proairetic code, the cultural from the symbolic, surrounded by books and files, the gas fire hissing and a cup of coffee steaming at her elbow.[36]

Lodge mocks the hermitical comforts of university life and its stubborn indifference to the political systems that shape it. As the narrator dryly notes:

> while Robyn had been preoccupied with the issues of contemporary literary theory and its repercussions on the Cambridge English Faculty, the Conservative Government of Mrs Thatcher, elected in 1979 with a mandate to cut public spending, had set about decimating the national system of higher education. (p. 29)

Lodge's own position both as a novelist and as a professor of English literature raises further points of tension. Is the university another kind of factory, producing anaesthetised thinkers who determinedly avoid the pragmatics of real life? If the immediate postwar period rejuvenates literature by expanding access to education, do subsequent generations see literature being produced only by and for educational establishments themselves?

The increasing professionalisation both of the English academic and the writer in the postwar period means it is the educational establishment, as much as the ordinary reader, that will most likely decide the future of a literary work. Peter Porter, once a contender for Oxford Professor of Poetry, is cynical about the efficacy of creating a literary canon via an educational institution. In his poem 'Tipp-Ex for the Oscar', the satiric bile that, in previous periods, might have been reserved for the professional reviewer or the disloyal patron is transferred to the larger institution of the university. The poet and former teacher U. A. Fanthorpe is anxious, too, about the centralised process of education and its impact on the way we read literature. Her poem 'Knowing about Sonnets' shows how the act of teaching might imperil texts and their interpretation, even as Fanthorpe herself signs up to be a 'set text'. The poem enacts a classroom discussion of Rupert Brooke's 'The Soldier', combining lines from the poem with prescriptive words from the teacher. Yet if Brooke's sonnet is written as an act of poignant courage in a bloody war, the interpretation, Fanthorpe suggests, is cowardly, fully subservient to the demands of critical theory and formalist approaches. A quotation from Terry Eagleton's *Criticism and Ideology* (1976) opens the poem, as if the student's direct response to the text must defer to the authority of theory. The barked instructions for reading the poem turn interpretation into a dry exercise of obedience:

> The next step is telling the sonnet
> What it is trying to say. This is called Interpretation.[38]

The poem dramatises the balancing act between context and pretext in reading literature. Has the pluralist and relativist approach of contemporary theory reduced literature to another source text to be scrutinised, mummified, or discarded?

The work of Carol Ann Duffy, another poet and former teacher, suggests that the complex intersection of class and education in British society is a dynamic that no amount of social engineering can solve. Her poem sequence 'Comprehensive' offers seven monologues by characters at a comprehensive school, from the Arsenal supporter who supports 'the National Front' to Muslim immigrants whose 'families face Mecca'.[39] In stuttering phrases and monosyllables, identity politics becomes subsumed in the brutal fact of inclusion. Yet if socialism is, for Duffy, the 'tree that never grew',[40] the energising friction that characterises social and educational debates during the period creates a literature that, even in its form, considers its audience before its aesthetic.

Notes

1 Stevie Smith, 'Parents', *Collected Poems* (Harmondsworth: Penguin, 1978), p. 363, ll. 1–2.

2 Matthew Arnold, *Culture and Anarchy* (Cambridge: Cambridge University Press, 1960), p. 56.

3 For contemporary accounts of the social impact of the Butler Act, see C. A. R. Crosland, *The Future of Socialism* (London: Jonathan Cape, 1956) and Brian Jackson and Dennis Marsden's anthropological study *Education and the Working Class: some general themes raised by a study of 88 working-class children in a northern industrial city* (London: Routledge, 1962).

4 Edward Hallett Carr, *The New Society* (London: Beacon Press, 1957) p. 543.

5 See Michael Young, *The Rise of the Meritocracy* (London: Transaction Publishers, 1994), p. 106.

6 C. A. R. Crosland, *The Future of Socialism* (London: Robinson, 2006), p. 65.

7 Penelope Fitzgerald, *The Bookshop* (London: Duckworth, 1989), p. 101.

8 Michael Frayn, *The End of the Morning* (London: Fontana, 1986), p. 95.

9 C. S. Lewis, 'Willing Slave of the Welfare State', *Undeceptions: Essays on Theology and Ethics* (London: Geoffrey Bless, 1971), p. 263.

10 David Lodge, *Ginger, You're Barmy* (London: Penguin, 1982), p. 76.

11 See Herbert Marcuse, 'Liberation from the Affluent Society' in David Cooper (ed.), *The Dialectics of Liberation* (Harmondsworth: Penguin, 1968), p. 132, where Marcuse describes the Welfare State as a 'Warfare state'.

12 Richard Hoggart, *The Uses of Literacy* (Harmondsworth: Penguin, 1957) p. 293.

13 Dennis Potter, *The Nigel Barton Plays* (Harmondsworth: Penguin, 1967), p. 32.

14 D. M. Black, 'The Educators', in Edward Lucie-Smith (ed.), *British Poetry Since 1945* (Harmondsworth: Penguin, 1986), p. 176, l. 26.

15 Philip Larkin, 'A Study of Reading Habits', *Collected Poems* (hereafter *CP*) (London: Faber, 2003), p. 102, l. 18.

16 John Wain, *Hurry On Down* (Harmondsworth: Penguin, 1971), p. 81.

17 Raymond Williams, *Culture and Society: 1780–1950* (London: Chatto & Windus, 1958), p. 332.

18 Doris Lessing, *In Pursuit of the English: A Documentary* (London: MacGibbon and Kee, 1960), p. 29.

19   Richard Hoggart, *The Uses of Literacy*, p. 39.
20   Steven Berkoff, *East*, in *The Collected Plays* Vol 1. (London: Faber, 1994).
21   David Edgar, *Enjoy*, in *Plays: Two* (London: Methuen, 2003), p. 271.
22   Philip Larkin, 'Here', *CP*, p. 136, ll. 17, 15–16.
23   Mike Leigh, *Abigail's Party / Goose-Pimples* (London: Penguin, 1983).
24   Arnold Wesker, *Roots*, in *Plays: One* (London: Methuen, 2001), p. 156.
25   Howard Barker, *Claw*, in *Collected Plays: Volume One* (London: Calder, 1994), p. 71.
26   Muriel Spark, *The Prime of Miss Jean Brodie* (London: Macmillan, 1961), p. 9.
27   Iris Murdoch, *The Sandcastle* (London: Vintage, 2003), p. 19.
28   Pamela Hansford Johnson, *The Listener*, 42:235, 11 August 1949, p. 11.
29   Extracts from this essay are reprinted in Jonathan Coe, *Like A Fiery Elephant: The Story of B.S. Johnson* (London: Jonathan Cape, 2004).
30   James Kelman, *A Disaffection* (London: Vintage, 1999), p. 7.
31   Angela Carter, *Heroes and Villains* (London: Penguin, 1990), p. 7.
32   Malcolm Bradbury, *Eating People is Wrong* (London: Secker & Warburg, 1986), p. 51.
33   Anita Brookner, *Providence* (London: Panther, 1983), p. 32.
34   Anita Brookner, *A Start in Life* (London: Panther, 1982), p. 19.
35   David Lodge, *Small World* (London: Secker & Warburg, 1984), p. 3.
36   David Lodge, *Nice Work* (London: Secker & Warburg, 1988), p. 65.
37   Peter Porter, 'Tipp-Ex for the Oscar', *Collected Poems 2: 1984–1999* (Oxford: Oxford University Press, 1999), p. 61, ll. 34–9.
38   U. A. Fanthorpe, 'Knowing about Sonnets', *Collected Poems 1978–2003* (Calstock: Peterloo, 2005), p. 167, ll. 6–7.
39   Carol Ann Duffy, 'Comprehensive', *New Selected Poems 1984–2004* (Basingstoke: Picador, 2004), p. 4, l. 16.
40   Carol Ann Duffy, 'Politico', *New Selected Poems*, p. 51, l. 15.

Sex and Identity

The opening description of the female foil to Amis's protagonist Ronnie in his novel *I Want It Now* (1968) suggests the complex intersection of sexuality and gender in postwar British writing.[1] From a structural perspective, Amis is keen to communicate that this woman's beauty transcends that of any woman Ronnie has seen before. At the level of plot, she is the necessary catalyst that will motivate the protagonist from this point on. Yet the only way to express this exceptional beauty is to introduce her as an ambivalently gendered figure. The social trappings of dress and cosmetics suggest a masculine or hermaphrodite presence, from the 'corrugations' of the sweater to the lack of make-up. Yet, paradoxically, it is this very lack of make-up which enables the protagonist to see her face's essential femaleness, or at least its total rejection of male characteristics. Nevertheless, the passage remains anxious about its momentary attraction to maleness, or something close to it; the crude knee-jerk misogyny of the final lines, which contrasts his endless capacity for forgiveness with the arrogant confidence that he would possess her suggests a desperate need to reassert his authority after the emasculating power of desire. The anxiety continues throughout the scene: Ronnie's first overtures to her are momentarily disrupted when she begins a conversation with a male producer (p. 27). A momentary suggestion of a homosexual impulse becomes literalised in this producer, who becomes a passing rival for her attentions. By diverting her attention back to him, Ronnie manages to eradicate the troubling homosexual presence at the margins of their love narrative.

Men and Misogyny

Yet what comes easily for Ronnie in this scene is more difficult for many of the fictional figures of postwar literature. As the above discussion suggests, misogyny and homophobia become linked to a more general anxiety about sexual status and gender roles. Once demarcations between the sexes are questioned, desire itself becomes a dangerous and difficult presence. In the earlier *I Like It Here* (1958), Garnet Bowen's romantic overtures to Sandra keep returning to the anxious subject of homosexuality, albeit with comic self-awareness.[2] As theorist Eve Kosofsky Sedgwick has argued, 'to be feminized or suffer gender confusion within a framework that includes a woman' is 'dire'; 'lust itself (meaning, in this context, desire for women) is a machine for depriving males of self-identity'.[3] In this novel, the female's only means of deflecting this feminisation process is to puncture the male anxiety both through humour, and by reassuring him of his own virility.

The 'machine' that Sedgwick describes was, for a number of historical and cultural reasons, running at full steam in the immediate postwar period. As discussed in the previous chapter, the rise of the scholarship boy and the opening up of tertiary education to the working class had often served to reinforce the class boundaries it sought to break down. Sexual relationships were now a complex negotiation of class and gender. The sociologist Geoffrey Gorer identified a new phenomenon of what he termed 'hypergamy' to describe the emasculation of lower-class men who were having relationships with upper-class women; the alliances formed between them at university meant that the sexual hierarchy (favouring men) and the social hierarchy (favouring the upper class) were at dangerous loggerheads. The Angry Young Man was, for Gorer, an inevitable consequence of postwar social engineering:

> It is very much easier for a working-class man to imperil his status as a male than it is for one of the upper middle class. A light tenor voice, a la-di-da (B.B.C. standard English) accent, an extended vocabulary, restraint in the use of expletives, all carry the stigmas of being a cissy or pansy.[4]

Faced with the already emasculating pull of sexual desire and the anxiety around women deemed their social superiors, scholarship boys 'may feel driven to emphasise their manliness in such ways that are open to them, perhaps by surliness or pugnacity, but certainly by frequent copulation or attempts thereat'.[5] Gorer's sociological explanation finds its literary counterpart in Amis's influential *Lucky Jim* (1954), where the protagonist's disdainful view of his colleague Margaret treats her mental illness with withering contempt and a dismissive diagnosis of female hysteria. Tenderness is a quality he can barely afford. This bravado performance of the hyper-masculine defined Amis's public persona too: as a cynical letter to Philip Larkin recorded.[6] The same anxious and objectifying exchanges characterise Charles's relationships with women in John Wain's *Hurry on Down* (1953). In Charles's doomed return to the working class, misogyny becomes acceptable because 'he no longer came of the class that treated women with deference'.[7] The women in his life are portrayed with crude sexual stereotyping, as with Betty, the 'amiable slut' who 'had never pretended to be anything else' (p. 81); yet if his language here is reductive and objectifying, Betty is still granted an essential authenticity which his own uneasy class-shifting has made impossible for him.

If the scholarship boy was 'psychologically over-determined'[8] towards promiscuity, violence, and misogyny, larger social trends reconfigured the way Britain thought about sexual relations and relationships between the sexes. The war had seen women taking on manual labour, high-level clerical work, and other physically and mentally demanding employment. After the war, the government drive was towards economic stability, and the same women were encouraged to return to the home and reinstate the returning men as bread-winners. This shifting cultural expectation of gender, which always put it in the service of social expediency, led to a second wave of feminists questioning the biological efficacy of these prescriptive roles. As the French feminist Simone de Beauvoir argued in her landmark work *The Second Sex* (1953):

> the relation of the two sexes is not quite like that of two electrical poles, for man represents both the positive and the neutral, as is indicated by the common use of man to designate human beings in general; whereas woman represents only the negative, defined by limiting criteria, without reciprocity … She is defined and differentiated with reference to man and not he with reference to her; she is the incidental, the inessential as opposed to the essential. He is the Subject, he is the Absolute – she is the Other.[9]

De Beauvoir explored the cultural binaries of gender relations only to explode the myth of complementarity or equality. To be a woman, if socially defined, was to be an invisible space, a cipher for whatever male projection suited the cultural moment.

In 1948, the publication of Alfred Kinsey's *Sexual Behaviour in the Human Male* had revolutionised the way people thought about sexual practice. Like de Beauvoir's work, Kinsey broke down the easy assumptions of binary identities. Basing his report on a wide-scale survey of young Americans, he was left to conclude that the safe classifying of sexual categories was culturally convenient rather than biologically accurate:

> Males do not represent two discrete populations, heterosexual and homosexual. The world is not to be divided into sheep and goats … It is a fundamental of taxonomy that nature rarely deals with discrete categories. Only the human mind invents categories and tries to force facts into separated pigeon-holes.[10]

Kinsey's work unsettled many social commentators of the period. Tellingly, the year before, the playwright J. B. Priestley blustered anxiously about the unstable way male and female characters were being depicted on stage, calling for 'more psychological maleness and femaleness, and a good deal less sexiness'.[11] On all sides, Priestley was being confronted with the revelation that male and female were more social and cultural categories than biological ones.

While these seismic shifts in how sex and sexuality were understood promised greater tolerance, the immediate knee-jerk cultural reaction was a desperate clinging to those old, increasingly fragile-looking categories, as the striking misogyny of many postwar texts makes clear. Nowhere is this more apparent than in the representations of pregnancy during the period. The increasing freedom of contraception and the legalisation of abortion in 1967 also promised choice and freedom for women, but as Simone de Beauvoir notes, the gradual cultural acceptance of abortion came with a concomitant antipathy towards women's bodies and their reproductive role:

> this proliferation of cells becomes adventitious and troublesome; it is one more feminine defect ... even when [she] consents to abortion, even desires it, the woman feels it as a sacrifice of her femininity: she is compelled to see in her sex a curse, a kind of infirmity, and a danger.[12]

This reading of the woman's body as 'dangerous' is reflected in any number of postwar texts which situate pregnancy as a terrifying punishment for or malignant consequence of sex. In John Osborne's *Look Back in Anger* (1956), this extends to the sexual life of women altogether: Jimmy's description of his love-making with Alison assumes her inert passivity, yet attributes a cruel masochistic pleasure to her seemingly indifference:

> She has the passion of a python. She just devours me whole every time, as if I were some over-large rabbit. That's me. That bulge around her navel – if you're ever wondering what it is – it's me.[13]

It is a mixture of gross egotism and sexual anxiety that misreads what is actually the early signs of pregnancy for devoured masculinity, trapped in the belly of the ravenous woman. Alison is too scared of Jimmy's response to tell him directly of her pregnancy; his friend Cliff, as go-between, is the first to hear she has been 'caught out' (p. 38), as her euphemism has it. Cliff's own response is no less welcoming. After a guilty pause, he asserts 'I'll need some scissors' (p. 39); though his referent is the bandage he is placing around her wounded arm, their later discussion about 'averting the situation' means the possibility of illegal abortion hangs in the air, a burden the woman must bear alone. As we saw in Part Three, 'Social Dramas', Jimmy's opening curse that Alison should lose her baby, so she might experience first hand the pain of grief, becomes a disturbing prophecy in the second act.

Pregnancy is an equally problematic predicament in Bill Naughton's *Alfie* (1966), where the protagonist shivers at the horror of 'some little thing kicking inside you'.[14] Contraception fares little better, in any form. As Alfie complains early on in his narrative, while the last generation might have suffered wars, poverty, and disease, 'they never had to keep their eye on the calendar' (p. 67). Lily, Alfie's girlfriend, is eventually persuaded into an abortion, prompting one of Alfie's few sympathetic admissions that 'life is definitely loaded against the woman' (p. 102). Yet if Jimmy sees Alison's miscarriage as a cruel requirement for her spiritual growth, perhaps Lily's abortion becomes the only means of stopping Alfie's infantile philandering. The Welfare State had made family life an economic priority of the state rather than an individual choice; while contraception and abortion suggested personal power, the cultural representations of the postwar period suggest a defensive misogyny rather than a considered examination of female roles in a newly egalitarian society.

The Dual Role

A closer examination of that newly egalitarian society might also make us question what immediate benefits it promised for women. For Carolyn Steedman, reviewing her Welfare State upbringing in the 1950s, 'being a child when the state was practically engaged in making children healthy and literate was a support against my own circumstances.'[15] As the title of her autobiography suggests, *Landscape for a Good Woman* (1989), the state intervention in her life was a benevolent force which, far from imposing conformity or rigid social roles, taught her she had 'a right to this earth' (p. 122). Yet other fictional and sociological accounts of the period offer competing views. The two women at the centre of Shelagh Delaney's ground-breaking play *A Taste of Honey* (1958) seem condemned to raise children society has conditioned them into keeping. Jo's gay friend Geoff asserts that 'motherhood is supposed to come natural to women',[16] but Jo's alcoholic mother is the most reluctant of guardians. Notions of the natural are further undermined by Geoff's position as surrogate father to Jo's unborn baby, and Jo's own deeply ambivalent relationship to her pregnancy. While the play's conclusion suggests she will keep the baby, she is closer to being a carrier of state property than a potential mother.

The state's expectations of motherhood, like pregnancy, remained confused. As Viola Klein's 1965 survey of married women workers observed, the housewife's life was characterised by 'frustration and futility', an inevitable consequence of 'the anachronism between the economics of the household and those of society at large'.[17] If the state recognised child-rearing as an essential way of rebuilding the country after the war, it offered little in the way of state support for the women who had given up their jobs to raise a family. Lorna Sage's autobiography *Bad Blood* (2000) finds comic mileage in her mother's inept housekeeping, but there are difficult social systems at work here, too. As Elizabeth Wilson notes, 'the welfare state failed to create a network of social services that could support and legitimate the housemaking role of women'.[18] The postwar period gave women a 'dual role'[19] which went both unrecognised and undercompensated, and the competing demands of wife, worker, and mother created an often impossible balancing act. The tension between these identities is reflected in a range of fiction from the period that finds its female protagonists divided, conflicted, and ambivalent about their position in society.

Patricia Waugh notes that, despite the supposed conservatism of postwar British female writing, its protagonists gradually come to suspect 'the impossibility of being "whole" and, recognizing the ideological purpose of such wholeness, begin to develop a most "postmodernist" awareness of the imaginary identity of the self-determining ego'.[20] Here, the dual role fractures and dislocates, solving the problem of contesting archetypes with a series of fragmented perspectives. Waugh notes that many women writers were now exploring 'how human beings might be able to achieve a sense of identity which consists of accepting both connection *and* separation, so that neither is experienced as a threat'.[21] Perhaps one such heroine is found in Elizabeth Bowen's *Eva Trout* (1969). Eva's paternal inheritance has meant a cosseted life of nannies and governesses. After her father's death, and free from perpetual guardianship, she struggles to identify herself. Tellingly, her own difficulties are often ventriloquised by other characters, such as Doctor Bonnard, who reminds her:

> it is so hard not to comply with [what people think of you], not to fall in love with it – not to be overcome by it in the very battle one has against it. The way one is envisaged by other people – what easier way is there of envisaging oneself? There is a fatalism in one's acceptance of it.[22]

The struggle to reject or, more often, to learn to live with those expectations defines her process of self-discovery.

For the writer-protagonist Anna Wulf in Doris Lessing's seminal work *The Golden Notebook* (1962), this series of competing expectations is transformed into a pre-emptive strike and literary strategy; the four separate notebooks she records her life in are to be combined into one golden notebook, which will unify these fractured selves. Like Eva Trout, Anna is perhaps overcome by disunity in her battle against it, but here the embrace of a divided self comes as an act of courage rather than resignation. Lessing's narrative combines four sections from each of Anna's notebooks with a realist text entitled *Free Women*, which describes Anna and her sister Molly's life. In this text, Anna lacks Molly's ability to change:

> She was, on the whole, satisfied with herself, but she was always the same. She envied Molly's capacity to project her own changes of mood. Anna wore neat, delicate clothes, which tended to be either prim, or perhaps a little odd; and relied upon her delicate white hands, and her small, pointed white face to make an impression.[23]

Her comparatively static features are in contrast to Molly's mercurial disguises, but in her writing life, Anna struggles to achieve the unity that her outward appearance suggests. The boundaries between her writing are arbitrary; nevertheless, the notebooks are symbolically coloured red, to explore her relationship with communism, black, to explore her life in Central Africa, yellow, for her ongoing novel which tracks the collapse of her love affair, and blue, for the journal where she records her dreams and ambitions. If the progress towards the final, unified, golden notebook is often painful, Lessing's novel destroys the limiting binaries of Anna's early life, crafting a deliberate complex collage of selves. *The Golden Notebook* suggests, as theorist Judith Butler has argued, that '*woman* itself is a term in process, a becoming, a constructing that cannot rightfully be said to originate or to end.'[24]

While traditional female archetypes of carer and nurturer clashed with the newly defined positions for women in the workplace, a similar tension arose in contemporary expectations of women writers. Feminist critics often asked for a similar political commitment from the women writers they wrote on, although many stubbornly resisted these terms. Subsequent critical studies, such as Patricia Waugh's *Feminine Fictions* (1989), seem determined attempts to 'recuperate' figures such as Anita Brookner from their qualified attitude to gender politics. Meanwhile, Brookner's well-publicised antipathy to feminism is worked through in her Booker Prize-winning novel *Hotel du Lac* (1984). Its protagonist, the novelist Edith Hope, struggles to avoid being co-opted by the female romance writers and feminists alike, defensively reassuring herself that 'those multi-orgasmic girls with the executive briefcases can go elsewhere'.[25] The confusion friends and fans have about how to read Edith's work, and her concomitant fear about how she might read, leads to a period of self-doubt and ambivalence. Catching herself in a hotel mirror, Edith watches her internal idea of herself mutate and deform against her public persona: 'for a moment I panicked, for I am myself now, and was then, although the fact was not recognized' (p. 10). The novel itself proves to be Brookner's own hotel mirror, the half-private, half-public space where she, like Anna Wulf in her notebooks, might rehearse the possibilities of her writing self.

Permissiveness and Censorship

If the 1950s are often characterised by conservatism, consensus, and conformism, the permissive counter-cultural excitement of the 1960s has become enshrined as a cultural totem. This was the decade of youth culture, of student riots, of revolutionary theories about literature that denied the importance of the author and sought instead to satisfy 'the pleasure of the consumer',[26] as if reading itself were a hedonistic sexual act. This was the period of a liberalising British government, which decriminalised abortion and homosexuality. Literature, too, found a series of public platforms on which to stage its own liberation. The most famous of these came in 1960, when Penguin decided to publish D. H. Lawrence's sexually explicit novel *Lady Chatterley's Lover*. The publishers were taken to court; perhaps a gift given the likely outcome of the trial and the ensuing media interest in the case. Penguin drafted in a series of influential figures to testify to the book's literary merit, from E. M. Forster to Richard Hoggart. Hoggart's testimonial in particular became a symbolic gesture of defiance against the establishment. He argued that the novel's treatment of sex attempted to return purity to an act now only described with leering prurience or nervous laughter. The four-letter words littering the text only contributed to, rather than undermining, its moral position. Penguin's victory over the state ensured that the novel became its most successful ever publication; graphic depictions of the sexual act had become the nation's set text. Theatre staged its equivalent censorship battle in 1965, with a production of the banned play *Saved* by Edward Bond. Unlike fiction, the theatre had been subject to much more invasive and ludicrous legal strictures; until 1968, all plays had to be sent to the Royal Household for approval by the Lord Chamberlain before they could be performed. The absurd survival of this law, passed in the sixteenth century, when anarchic theatre might prove a serious threat to the monarchy, became an easy casualty of the liberal age.

Yet if 1960s legislation tells us a story of liberation, literature set in the period questions its gifts of emancipation and progress. A. S. Byatt's novel *Babel Tower* (1996) fictionalises the Chatterley trial, but her characters find that it ushers in a period of querulous anxiety rather than permissive liberation. Contemporary responses to the liberal era were double-edged, too: the plays of Joe Orton work both as satirical farces on conservatism and consensus and comedies that draw repeatedly on that same conservatism. As Jonathan Dollimore notes in his landmark work *Sexual Dissidence* (1991), Orton's work 'interrogates rather than presupposes the norm'.[27] In *Entertaining Mr Sloane* (1964), the first word of the title is both verb and adjective, blurring the distinction between who is entertaining who. As Ed asks his young lodger Mr Sloane, half way through seducing him: 'are you clean living? You may as well know that I set great store by morals. Too much of this casual bunking up nowadays. Too many lads being ruined by birds'.[28] Here an argument of defensive purity is co-opted into a moral imperative to homosexuality; Mr Sloane must keep himself pure for a man. Yet Orton's farce plays devils advocate and parades permissiveness itself as another lazy liberal creed to be mocked and parodied. *Loot* (1966) finds two young criminals, Hal and Dennis, hiding stolen money in Hal's mother's coffin. Their dream of setting up a brothel with their loot is a curious mixture of the prurient, the tasteless, and the utopian. As Hal tells Fay, 'I'd have a spade bird. I don't agree with the colour bar. And a Finnish bird. I'd make them kip together. To bring out the contrast.'[29]

Here liberal notions of integration and equality generate as many satiric targets as Ed's epigrammatic indignation. Hal and Dennis's identity relies on their criminality; it comes as little surprise, then, that the openly homosexual Orton was reluctant to welcome the legalisation of his promiscuous lifestyle in 1966. The binary set up by permissive and conservative forces creates the dynamic energy on which his farce relies.

If Orton's radical farce remained ambivalent about progressive liberalisation, convinced that anarchy relied on an authoritarian state for its energy, novelists such as Nell Dunn typified the apparently liberal attitudes to female sexuality in the period. A series of 1960s works offered protagonists such as Joy in *Poor Cow* (1967), an impulsive young mother with a husband in jail and an irrepressible survival instinct. Yet, tellingly, the novel's title focuses on the dismissive societal response to her. The narrative is equally unsure whether to identify with her or classify her: third-person insertions assure us that 'often Joy lay awake trying to fathom out the meaning of her existence',[30] yet that existence as recorded in her monologues seems both vapid and sentimentalised. Her unshakeable spirit also seems undermined by newly liberal attitudes to sex rather than invigorated by it. As she comments knowingly, 'sex, it's killing me every day … if I don't have it, let's face it, I'm only human, I don't want to be all my life without, I shall get very perverted in time to come, very perverted' (p. 29). She is made to pay the social price of expedient permissiveness while being forced into a guilty conscience. Sex is both a vital life force and a form of torture. There remains profound narrative ambivalence about Joy's ambitions for 'a man, a baby, and a couple of rooms' (p. 138). The fidelity to Joy's demotic (everyday) speech throughout the novel seems closer to sociological fascination than sexual liberation; Joy is no Molly Bloom.*

The permissive society is easily parodied as a fluke, a myth of its own begetting (as in Larkin's infamous 'Sexual intercourse began / In nineteen sixty-three / (Which was rather late for me) – / Between the end of the *Chatterley* ban / And the Beatles' first LP').[31] Larkin hovers uneasily at the margins of the cultural revolution. John Fowles pointedly returns to the Victorian period in *The French Lieutenant's Woman* (1969) only to reflect that:

> we are the more Victorian – in the derogatory sense of the word – century, since we have, in destroying so much of the mystery, the difficulty, the aura of the forbidden, destroyed also a great deal of the pleasure.[32]

Other characters' journeys towards their sexual identities are less clear. In Shena Mackay's *Music Upstairs* (1965), the impressionable Sidonie O'Neill finds herself seduced by both female and male neighbours, as the couple Pam and Lennie take turns as her confidante and lover. Yet in this love triangle it is Pam's pregnancy which finally tips things over into danger. Just as the traditional nuclear family reasserts itself, as in John Osborne or Allan Sillitoe, the characters buckle and break. Margaret Drabble's *The Millstone* (1956) offers another pointed critique of the

---

* Molly Bloom is the central female character of James Joyce's *Ulysses* (1922). The final chapter is given over to her interior monologue as she drifts in and out of sleep, and ruminates on sexual desire.

liberal postwar period. The notion of freedom for women here becomes a dangerous self-reliance; the novel opens with the protagonist, Rosamund, attempting to abort her own child by giving herself alcohol poisoning. As the narrative records with grim irony: 'Emancipated woman, this was me: gin bottle in hand, opening my own door with my own latchkey'.[33] The door the key opens leads to her parents' flat, not her own; the gin bottle she carries is bought from desperation, not hedonism. This is far from the perpetual happiness glibly inscribed in Larkin's poem 'High Windows'. For Ruth, a character in David Edgar's play *Teendreams* (1979), the feminist Germaine Greer puts it best: 'Liberated? I don't feel liberated. I feel like I just jumped off a cliff without a parachute'.[34]

The move towards a third wave of feminism in the 1970s, which considered language and representation themselves as cultural codes to be cracked, offered new ways of deconstructing the permissive myth. Angela Carter's examination of eighteenth-century pornography and the writings of the Marquis de Sade in *The Sadeian Woman: An Exercise in Cultural History* (1979) explores sexual liberation both as a discrete cultural case-study and a wider means of understanding gender norms. Yet, like the emancipated fictional heroines of the 1950s and 1960s who find the permissive age has become a millstone rather than a milestone, de Sade himself becomes incarcerated by his own sexual desires: '[the] passions he thought would free him from the cage of being become the very bars of the cage that traps him.'[35]

The relentless pursuit of sexual pleasure eventually inures him to orgasm. Meanwhile, the unexplored perversion in a house of bestiality and sado-masochism remains love itself, the only way to truly experience pleasure and pain simultaneously. For Carter it is 'the holy terror of love', rather than sex, which offers 'the source of all opposition to the emancipation of women' (p. 150). Freedom to explore our desires can never release us from the enslaving, nurturing power of love itself. Society's brittle illusions of choice and individual agency can never legislate for our own contradictory needs and drives. Rather than celebrating the opportunities of the permissive age, postwar writers more often reminded readers of the necessity for and inevitability of constraint.

Gay Fictions

As we have seen, the period covered by this volume was ushered in by the Kinsey Report, the revolutionary sociological study of American sexual behaviour which revealed the prevalence of premarital and homosexual sex, and ends with Eve Kosofsky Sedgwick's *The Epistemology of the Closet* (1990), a ground-breaking work of queer theory which began to excavate how far Western literary history had been censored by the cultural policy of *'Don't ask; you shouldn't know*. It didn't happen; it doesn't make any difference; it didn't mean anything; it doesn't have any interpretative consequences'.[36] This interest in current sexual practice, reflected in the increasingly confident treatment of homosexual themes in postwar writing or the liberalising legal reforms of the 1960s, is balanced by the subsequent interest in a gay literary history.

Although the Kinsey report had a larger impact in the United States, the increasingly open discussion about homosexuality, along with the ever-present threat of homosexual blackmail (sex between two consenting males remaining illegal until 1967) led to the publication of the Wolfenden Report in Britain in 1957. This government paper argued for the legalisation of homosexuality, although perhaps more in the interests of pragmatics than liberalisation. Cultural representations of homosexuality from the period support this sense of victimhood over empowerment. Although John Osborne's *A Patriot for Me* (1965) returns to the 1890s and the Austro-Hungarian empire for its portrait of the Jewish homosexual Redl, his desperate double life and eventual suicide offer tentative compassion in the place of tolerance. Basil Dearden's 1961 film *Victim* centres on a closeted gay lawyer Melville Farr, played by Dirk Bogarde, who risks his reputation and career to blow the whistle on the blackmail of homosexual men. Despite Farr's heroism, the title of the film is careful to downplay his strength. As late as 1970, the novelist Francis King had to disavow any autobiographical connection to his gay protagonist in *A Domestic Animal*, declaring in a preface that readers should not be tempted to 'identify the narrator with the author'.[37] While 1971 saw the posthumous publication of E. M. Forster's gay novel *Maurice*, his refusal to publish it during his lifetime tells us much about the response to openly gay writers in the 1950s and 1960s.

248

Less high profile works from the period avoid political sensitivity and social conflict by accentuating their marginality throughout. Maureen Duffy's *Microcosm* (1966) weaves together a series of marginal voices all united by passing through a bar: Cathy, who comes to define herself through the discovery of a lesbian community; Marie, stifled by a sexless marriage; and Matt, the main focaliser,* who finds her lesbian relationship both a sanctuary and a prison. The lesbian bar becomes a microcosm of society, but also a site of otherness:

> Come in. Close the doors behind you. Distil this rarefied atmosphere where we can breathe freely apart from the rest of the world like an ashram in the high Himalayas, or a lost tribe of aborigines buried deep in the heart of the social jungle with its own language and customs, unknown except to occasional travellers through on safari, traders who bring us thin cloth and glass ornaments in return for our silver and gold, slavers from the city who hire our cheap labour for their factories and other cut-rate jobs, scientists in search of strange fauna who will put our brains in pickle, missionaries to educate us and police to see we cause no trouble. We stare at them dull-eyed.[38]

The refuge seems both indifferent to the outside world and implicitly hostile; its opening invitation is immediately qualified by the need for secrecy and circumspection. Yet if the description emphasises the bar as 'apart from the rest of the world', the subsequent similes, which situate it as a cultural oddity for the anthropologist, a rare discovery for the scientist, or a commercial venture for passing traders, point to ways homosexuality would come to make itself part of the mainstream, both through financial visibility and social integration. Matt concludes that a microcosm is something that 'springs from the fragmentation of experience and knowledge' (p. 207); rather than providing a utopian

---

* Focaliser is a term used in narrative theory to describe the figure in a text that orientates the narrative. The narrative presents, and does not transcend, the focaliser's thoughts and impressions. Unlike the first-person narrator, the focaliser may be written in the third person.

analogy for modern society, it represents it through messy disjuncture and conflict.

For this reason perhaps, it was the writers who had abandoned Britain for the urban gay communities of the United States who were first able to speak directly and without anxiety about homosexuality. Christopher Isherwood's penultimate novel *A Single Man* (1964) follows Joyce and Woolf in centring on a day in the life of a single protagonist, the gay middle-aged English professor George, as he makes way through the lecture halls and swimming pools of Los Angeles. His confidence in his own sexuality proves anathema to those around him: his student Kenneth, shocked by his openness, is persuaded by George that rigid definitions and archetypes are finally limiting – 'are we to spend [life] identifying each other with catalogues, like tourists in an art gallery?'[39] Seeking the 'answer' from George, as a man entirely comfortable with his sexuality, Kenneth comes to realise that George's openness must be met with a reciprocal gesture. As George reminds him, 'I'm like a book you have to read. A book can't read itself to you. It doesn't even know what it's about' (p. 149).

Isherwood's novel bravely abandons the neurotic stereotyping of gay characters in numerous British works from the period, such as the histrionic melodrama *The Killing of Sister George* (1964) by Frank Marcus. It avoids easy answers about integration and cultural identity; George challenges his students to question the 'liberal heresy' (p. 58) of valorising minorities and the disenfranchised per se. Yet, as George's exchange with Kenneth suggests, it also underlines the need for reciprocal gestures between minorities and larger sections of society. This is a quasi-autobiographical novel written less as a confession than a spirited engagement with its imagined reader. The poet Thom Gunn, who emigrated from England to the United States in 1954, finds similar solace in the bohemian embrace of San Francisco. His cryptic entreaties in the early poem 'Carnal Knowledge' – 'You know I know you know I know you know'[40] – give way to the furtive pleasure of the stranger of 'Modes of Pleasure',[41] the Arcadian celebration of our 'At the Barriers',[42] or the bawdy excess of 'Punch Rubicundus.'[43] In a poem from *The*

Passages of Joy (1982), 'Talbot Road', Gunn describes a rare return to London, but tellingly the teenage boy he meets who reminds him of himself at that age is recognisable only through his air of self-contempt.[44]

These two competing selves are echoed in the fiction of Alan Hollinghurst. His debut, *The Swimming-Pool Library* (1988), like subsequent work, places a cocksure, young gay protagonist alongside an older, more reflective gay character. Hollinghurst's amoral presentation avoids glib historical generalisation, but even at the opening of the novel, the narcissistic protagonist William Beckwith senses the end of an era: '[m]y life was in a strange way that summer ... I was riding high on sex and self-esteem – it was my time, my *belle époque* – but all the while with a faint flicker of calamity.'[45] His narrative, which begins with casual sex and the expensive boredom of the leisured class, is sure it can resist the incursions of politics and history. This is 1983, a year of rising unemployment, but Beckwith is keen to point out that 'hardship' rarely enters his world; only the runaway black teenager he takes to bed gestures at the deprived London on the other side of the river. Yet the narrative awakens him to past and present, if not race or class. Writing in 1988, Hollinghurst is memorialising the last London summer before the AIDS crisis made casual sex, once again, a moral quagmire. He would return to the same city and the same summer in the Booker Prize-winning *The Line of Beauty* (2004), as if settling his debts to the ravages of the epidemic by coming back to year zero of liberated hedonism. As with Hollinghurst's later novel, the past in *The Swimming-Pool Library* unsettles the present. The novel centres on William's meetings with Charles, Lord Nantwich, an aging man who is keen for William to write his life story. In a series of extracts from Charles's diaries and journals, William learns of gay life before the Wolfenden Report or the legalisation of homosexuality. More specifically, he comes to realise that his own grandfather, Lord Beckwith, was a self-styled moral crusader whose public tirades against homosexuality in the 1950s ultimately led to Charles's six-month imprisonment. Although William ends the novel back in the baths where he began, chasing a 'suntanned young lad' (p. 288), he does not escape the scars of history, as his bruised body suggests.

Even in the gay flâneur's* *'belle époque'*, causal responsibility and societal relationships cannot be entirely excised.

The apparent responsibilities of the gay writer in the 1980s, like the critical expectations for female writers in the 1960s, are felt, too, in the work of Jeanette Winterson. Her debut, the quasi-autobiographical bildungsroman† *Oranges Are Not the Only Fruit* (1985) subverts expectations by refusing to place its lesbian characters in the periphery. Instead, the Pentecostal religious community of Accrington becomes the marginal and restrictive world of Maureen Duffy's *Microcosm*; the love between Jeanette and a female member of the congregation becomes all that is natural and honest. This integrity is emphasised by the novel's confidence in its own satirical targets; Winterson's lampooning of her domineering adoptive mother is comic because of its love for, as well as its antagonism towards, its subject. Jeanette's decision to leave the religious community of her adopted parents releases her into, rather than isolates her from, the rest of the world. Yet if the novel seems codified by the authoritative world it flees, using the Old Testament chapters to structure its narrative, it is also driven by the fantastical incursions of medieval quest narrative and chivalric projections that are introduced as an expression of the girls' love.

This adherence to biblical convention and disruption of its omniscience creates a work that, for some critics, fails to 'explode the binary'[46] it rebels against, but other readers have been more ready to see Winterson's narrative strategies as part of a larger lesbian framework. Considering the Dog-Woman protagonist of Winterson's *Sexing the Cherry* (1989), for example, Marilyn R. Farwell argues that 'her sexual encounters, rather than indicating heterosexuality, imply the impossibility of heterosexuality in a woman who creates her own narrative and claims her own agency'.[47] Certainly, in the Dog-Woman, Winterson has created a protagonist whose sexual ambivalence makes the boundaries of gender or sexuality anomalous. As she confesses to us: 'I am too huge for love … No one, male or female, has ever dared to approach me'.[48] The novel itself, which

---

* A flâneur is someone who walks through a city in order to experience it. The term was first used by the nineteenth-century French poet Charles Baudelaire, and has been an important trope throughout modern literature.

† A bildungsroman is a novel which charts the coming-of-age of its central protagonist.

pivots between male and female narrators, confounds the reduction of the self to sexuality or gender. Running free of expectations, the self:

> is not contained in any moment or any place, but it is only in the intersection of moment and place that the self might, for a moment, be seen vanishing through a door, which disappears at once. (p. 80)

Michel Foucault had argued in 1964 that sexuality was a historical construct;[49] while the postwar period saw a sea change in political, social, and cultural ways of considering gender and sexuality, its most significant development was to acknowledge the terms themselves as socially produced, relativist, and always shifting. By Winterson's third novel *The Passion* (1987), love is stripped of its social contexts and literary pretensions. In its place comes an open declaration of desire: 'I am in love with her; not a fantasy or a myth or a creature of my own making.'[50]

Notes

1   Kingsley Amis, *I Want It Now* (London: Jonathan Cape, 1968), pp. 26–7.
2   Kingsley Amis, *I Like It Here* (London: Victor Gollancz, 1958), p. 35.
3   Eve Kosofsky Sedgwick, *Between Men: English Literature and Male Homosocial Desire* (New York: Columbia University Press, 1985), p. 36.
4   Geoffrey Gorer, 'The Perils of Hypergamy', *The Dangers of Equality and Other Essays* (London: Cresset, 1966), p. 56.
5   Geoffrey Gorer, 'The Perils of Hypergamy', p. 56.
6   See Kingsley Amis to Philip Larkin, 26 November 1953, quoted in Colin Wilson, *The Angry Years: The Rise and Fall of the Angry Young Men* (London: Robson, 2007), p. 56.
7   John Wain, *Hurry on Down* (Harmondsworth: Penguin, 1971), p. 48.
8   Geoffrey Gorer, 'The Perils of Hypergamy', p. 56.
9   Simone de Beauvoir, *The Second Sex*, trans. H. M. Parshley (London: Vintage, 2007), pp. 16–17.
10   Alfred Kinsey, *Sexual Behaviour in the Human Male* (Bloomington: University of Indiana Press, 1998), p. 613.
11   J. B. Priestley, *Theatre Outlook* (London: Nicholson and Watson, 1947), p. 53.

12   Simone de Beauvoir, *The Second Sex*, p. 59.
13   John Osborne, *Look Back in Anger* (London: Faber, 1996), p. 37.
14   Bill Naughton, *Alfie* (London: MacGibbon & Kee, 1966), p. 102.
15   Carolyn Steedman, *Landscape for a Good Woman* (London: Virago, 1989), p. 122.
16   Shelagh Delaney, *A Taste of Honey* (London: Methuen, 1959), p. 55.
17   Viola Klein, *Britain's Married Women Workers* (London: Routledge, 1965), p. 56.
18   Elizabeth Wilson, *Only Halfway to Paradise: Women in Postwar Britain 1945–1980* (Northcote: Tavistock, 1980), p. 40.
19   Elizabeth Wilson, *Only Halfway to Paradise*, p. 80.
20   Patricia Waugh, *Feminine Fictions: Revisiting the Postmodern* (London: Routledge, 1989), p. 128.
21   Patricia Waugh, *Feminine Fictions*, p. 86.
22   Elizabeth Bowen, *Eva Trout* (London: Jonathan Cape, 1969), p. 263.
23   Doris Lessing, *The Golden Notebook* (London: Michael Joseph, 1962), p. 30.
24   Judith Butler, *Gender Trouble* (Abingdon: Routledge, 2006), p. 45.
25   Anita Brookner, *Hotel du Lac* (London: Jonathan Cape, 1984), p. 28.
26   Roland Barthes, *The Pleasure of the Text*, in Susan Sontag (ed.), *A Roland Barthes Reader* (London: Vintage, 2000), p. 413.
27   Jonathan Dollimore, *Sexual Dissidence* (Oxford: Clarendon Press, 1991), p. 317.
28   Joe Orton, *Entertaining Mr Sloane* (London: Methuen, 1965), p. 35.
29   Joe Orton, *Loot* (London: Methuen, 1966), p. 38.
30   Nell Dunn, *Poor Cow* (London: Virago, 1988), p. 28.
31   Philip Larkin, 'Annus Mirabilis', *Collected Poems* (London: Faber, 2003), p. 146, ll. 1–5.
32   John Fowles, *The French Lieutenant's Woman* (London: Fontana, 1969), p. 261.
33   Margaret Drabble, *The Millstone* (London: Weidenfeld and Nicholson, 1965), p. 10.
34   David Edgar, *Teendreams*, in *Plays Two* (London: Methuen, 1991), p. 121.
35   Angela Carter, *The Sadeian Woman: An Exercise in Cultural History* (London: Virago, 1992), p. 149.
36   Eve Kosofsky Sedgwick, *Epistemology of the Closet*, 2nd edn (London: University of California Press, 2008), p. 53.
37   Francis King, *A Domestic Animal* (London: Gay Modern Classics, 1984), p. 1.
38   Maureen Duffy, *Microcosm* (London: Virago, 1988), p. 21.
39   Christopher Isherwood, *A Single Man* (London: Methuen, 1964), p. 148.

40 Thom Gunn, 'Carnal Knowledge', *Collected Poems* (hereafter *CP*) (London: Faber, 1993), p. 15, l. 6.

41 Thom Gunn, 'Modes of Pleasure', *CP*, p. 102, l. 1.

42 Thom Gunn, 'At the Barriers', *CP*, p. 399, l. 64.

43 Thom Gunn, 'Punch Rubicundus', *CP*, p. 398, l. 15.

44 Thom Gunn, 'Talbot Road', *CP*, p. 383, Section 3, l. 15.

45 Alan Hollinghurst, *The Swimming-Pool Library* (London: Vintage, 2004), p. 3.

46 Laura Doan, 'Jeanette Winterson's Sexing the Postmodern', in Laura Doan (ed.), *The Lesbian Postmodern* (New York: Columbia University Press, 1994), pp. 137–55, p. 138.

47 Marilyn R. Farwell, *Heterosexual Plots & Lesbian Narratives* (London: New York University Press, 1996), p. 185.

48 Jeanette Winterson, *Sexing the Cherry* (London: Vintage, 1990), p. 34.

49 Michel Foucault, *The History of Sexuality* (Harmondsworth: Penguin, 1984), pp. 105–6.

50 Jeanette Winterson, *The Passion* (London: Bloomsbury, 1991), p. 253.

Part Five
References and Resources

Timeline

	Historical Events	Literary Events
1950	China invades Tibet; McCarthy witch hunts in the USA	Doris Lessing *The Grass is Singing*
1951	Festival of Britain held in London; general election puts Conservatives in power	Anthony Powell *A Question of Upbringing*
1952	George VII dies; Elizabeth II accedes	Samuel Beckett *En Attendant Godot* (*Waiting for Godot*) premiered in France; L. P. Hartley *The Go-Between*
1953	Coronation of Elizabeth II; USSR explodes the H-bomb; Hillary and Tensing scale Everest	
1954	End of food rationing	Kingsley Amis *Lucky Jim*; William Golding *Lord of the Flies*; Iris Murdoch *Under the Net*
1955	Anthony Eden becomes Prime Minister after Churchill resigns	Samuel Beckett *Waiting for Godot* (first English performance)
1956	Egyptian president nationalises the Suez Canel; UK and France forced to withdraw after US-imposed ceasefire (the Suez Crisis)	John Osborne *Look Back in Anger*; Sam Selvon *The Lonely Londoners;* Colin Wilson *The Outsider*

Timeline

Historical Events	Literary Events
1957 Harold Macmillan becomes Prime Minister; death penalty abolished; Wolfenden Report recommends liberalising laws relating to homosexuality and prostitution; first British H-bomb exploded	Richard Hoggart *The Uses of Literacy*; Ted Hughes *The Hawk in the Rain*; Stevie Smith *Not Waving but Drowning*; Muriel Spark *The Comforters*
1958 CND launched; race riots in London and Nottingham; word 'meritocracy' is coined	Harold Pinter *The Birthday Party*; Shelagh Delaney *A Taste of Honey*
1959 The Mini goes on sale; Conservatives re-elected; first motorway opens	C. P. Snow *The Two Cultures and the Scientific Revolution*
1960 Macmillan predicts 'the winds of change' in a speech to the South African parliament; Cyprus and Nigeria become independent; Penguin cleared of obscenity for publishing *Lady Chatterley's Lover*	D. H. Lawrence *Lady Chatterley's Lover*; Harold Pinter *The Caretaker*; Muriel Spark *The Ballad of Peckham Rye*
1961 CND protests; the Pill is introduced for married women; Caribbean and Asian immigration peaks; Berlin Wall erected	V. S. Naipaul *A House for Mr. Biswas*; Muriel Spark *The Prime of Miss Jean Brodie*
1962 Cuban missile crisis; Commonwealth Immigration Act restricts entry to Britain for Commonwealth citizens	Anthony Burgess *A Clockwork Orange*; Stevie Smith *Selected Poems*
1963 The Profumo affair threatens to bring down the government; Kennedy assassinated; USA officially enters Vietnam; Beatles' first no. 1	Sylvia Plath *The Bell Jar*; Muriel Spark *The Girls of Slender Means*
1964 Zambia and Malta become independent; Harold Wilson's Labour government is elected	William Golding *The Spire*; Philip Larkin *The Whitsun Weddings*; Joe Orton *Entertaining Mr. Sloane*

Historical Events	Literary Events
1965 Race Relations Act passed; Winston Churchill given state funeral; Southern Rhodesia declares independence; Telford council converts its schools to comprehensive system (twenty-eight councils have done the same by 1980)	Harold Pinter *The Homecoming*; Sylvia Plath *Ariel*
1966 Ian Brady and Myra Hindley are given life imprisonment for Moors Murders; 144 killed in Welsh landslide disaster in Aberfan; England wins World Cup	Basil Bunting *Briggflats*; Seamus Heaney *Death of a Naturalist*; Jean Rhys *Wide Sargasso Sea;* Tom Stoppard *Rosencrantz and Guildenstern are dead*
1967 Abortion legalised; homosexuality decriminalised between consenting adults; anti-Vietnam war protests in London; BBC2 launched	*The Mersey Sound* poetry anthology; Angela Carter *The Magic Toyshop*; Ted Hughes *Wodwo*
1968 Student protests in Paris and Prague; precensorship of British theatre ends; Martin Luther King assassinated; Enoch Powell's 'Rivers of Blood' speech	Tom Stoppard *The Real Inspector Hound*; Kingsley Amis *I Want it Now*
1969 Neil Armstrong is first man on the moon; Booker Prize begins; first Concorde flights; rioting in Belfast; Open University founded	Angela Carter *Heroes and Villains*; John Fowles *The French Lieutenant's Woman*
1970 Ted Heath becomes Prime Minister; voting age reduced to eighteen	Tony Harrison *The Loiners*; Ted Hughes *Crow*; Iris Murdoch *A Fairly Honourable Defeat*
1971 Arson attacks in Belfast; India at war with Pakistan over Bangladesh independence; Britain goes decimal	Posthumous publication of E. M. Forster's novel of gay love, *Maurice*; Stevie Smith *Scorpion*
1972 Seven killed in first IRA terrorist attacks; British Asians expelled from Uganda	Tom Stoppard *Jumpers*; Seamus Heaney *Wintering Out*

Timeline

	Historical Events	Literary Events
1973	Britain joins the EEC (European Economic Community)	Iris Murdoch *The Black Prince*
1974	Miners' strike begins; twenty-one killed in IRA terrorist bombs in Birmingham; US President Nixon resigns over Watergate scandal	Muriel Spark *The Abbess of Crewe*; Philip Larkin *High Windows*
1975	Sex Discrimination Act; Margaret Thatcher elected leader of Conservative party	Seamus Heaney *North*; Malcolm Bradbury *The History Man*
1976	Punk emerges on London scene; Harold Wilson resigns; Cod wars; Race Relations Act outlaws discrimination in the workplace	Tony Harrison *The School of Eloquence*
1977	Queen's Silver Jubilee	Barbara Pym *Quartet in Autumn*
1978	First test-tube baby born	A. S. Byatt *Still Life*; Iris Murdoch *The Sea, The Sea*
1979	'Winter of Discontent' as poorly paid public employees strike; Conservatives elected	Seamus Heaney *Field Work*; Caryl Churchill *Cloud Nine*
1980	Zimbabwe becomes independent; Iranian Embassy siege	Julian Barnes *Metroland*; William Golding *Rites of Passage*
1981	Riots in Brixton, Liverpool, and Manchester; Prince Charles marries Lady Diana Spencer; unemployment tops five million	Alisdair Gray *Lanark*; Salman Rushdie *Midnight's Children*
1982	Falklands Conflict begins, with invasion of the Islands by Argentina; Channel 4 introduced	Caryl Churchill *Top Girls*; Julian Barnes *Before She Met Me*
1983	Conservatives re-elected with increased majority; US cruise missiles installed at Greenham Common	Graham Swift *Waterland*; J. H. Prynne *Poems*

Historical Events	Literary Events
1984 Miners' strike; four killed by IRA bomb at Tory conference	Julian Barnes *Flaubert's Parrot*; Angela Carter *Nights at the Circus*
1985 Miners' strike ends; Live Aid concert at Wembley Stadium; WHO declares AIDS an epidemic	Tony Harrison *v.*; Jeanette Winterson *Oranges are Not the Only Fruit*
1986 Chernobyl nuclear reactor explodes; Big Bang on the London stock exchange	Caryl Steedman *Landscape for a Good Woman*; Caryl Phillips *State of Independence*
1987 Thatcher elected for third term; Kings' Cross tube fire; Wall Street crash	Seamus Heaney *The Haw Lantern*; V. S. Naipaul *The Enigma of Arrival*; Jeanette Winterson *The Passion*
1988 An airliner is blown up over Lockerbie and 281 are killed; Liberals merge with SDP to become the Social and Liberal Democratic Party	Alan Hollinghurst *The Swimming-Pool Library*; David Lodge *Nice Work*; Salman Rushdie *The Satanic Verses*
1989 Fatwa passed on Salman Rushdie; Berlin Wall is demolished; Tiananmen Square massacre	Julian Barnes *The History of the World in 10½ Chapters*; Kazuo Ishiguro *The Remains of the Day*; James Kelman *A Disaffection*
1990 Nelson Mandela freed; the Cold War ends; German reunification; poll tax riots; WHO removes homosexuality from list of diseases; Margaret Thatcher resigns	A. S. Byatt *Possession*; Hanif Kureishi *The Buddha of Suburbia*

Further Reading

Further Reading is divided into four sections, all with their own subdivisions. Author-specific works on the eighteen authors explored in Part Three have been incorporated into the first section under the appropriate headings.

Genre and Form

Fiction

Bradbury, Malcolm (ed.), *The Novel Today* (Glasgow: Fontana, 1977)
> A collection of essays by postwar novelists considering the nature of the modern novel, including contributions by Iris Murdoch, Doris Lessing, and John Fowles

Carey, John, *William Golding: The Man Who Wrote 'The Lord of the Flies'* (London: Faber, 2009)
> A critical biography of William Golding, which examines his novels in the context of his life, letters, and unpublished works

Cheyette, Bryan, *Muriel Spark: Writers and their Work* (Plymouth: Northcote House, 2000)
> A concise study of Muriel Spark's work, with a useful bibliography and suggestions for further reading

Connor, Steven, *The English Novel in History, 1950–1995* (London: Routledge, 1997)
> A wide-ranging discussion of postwar prose fiction which considers writers such as A. S. Byatt, Hanif Kureishi, Salman Rushdie, and Margaret Drabble

Conradi, Peter J., *The Saint and the Artist: A Study of the Fiction of Iris Murdoch* (London: HarperCollins, 2001)

> A detailed guide to Iris Murdoch's work, which offers an in-depth reading of each of her novels

Gasiorek, Andrzej, *Postwar British Fiction: Realism and After* (London: Edward Arnold, 1995)

> A lively reading of postwar fiction, which considers the continuing relevance of realism to contemporary writing

Head, Dominic, *The Cambridge Introduction to Modern British Fiction, 1950–2000* (Cambridge: Cambridge University Press, 2002)

> An exhaustive survey of recent British fiction, which is an excellent reference guide as well as offering thoughtful perspectives on class, gender, and national identity

Holmes, Frederick M., *Julian Barnes* (Basingstoke: Palgrave Macmillan, 2008)

> This guide to Julian Barnes' fiction includes a detailed study of literary techniques, and an overview of the critical reception of his novels

Lea, Daniel, *Graham Swift* (Manchester: Manchester University Press, 2006)

> This carefully written study provides a detailed critical analysis of Swift's work, moving chronologically through his novels

Leader, Zachary (ed.), *On Modern British Fiction* (Oxford: Oxford University Press, 2002)

> This engaged and original selection of essays includes a consideration of the postwar Scottish novel, British science fiction, contemporary reviewing, commissioning and editing modern fiction, and comedy in British postwar writing

Lodge, David, *The Novelist at the Crossroads* (London: Routledge & Kegan Paul, 1971)

> This classic study of postwar writing articulates anxieties about conservatism in the modern British novel

McHale, Brian, *Postmodernist Fiction* (London: Methuen, 1987)

> This study argues for postmodernist fiction as a category and situates the British novel in the context of North American metafiction and Latin American magic realism

Sage, Lorna, *Women in the House of Fiction: Postwar Women Novelists* (London: Macmillan, 1992)

> This pioneering study examines fictional strategies in the work of twenty-two British women novelists

— (ed.), *Essays on the Art of Angela Carter: the Flesh and the Mirror* (London: Virago, 2009)

> This edited collection of essays includes contributions by Isabel Armstrong, Margaret Atwood, and Laura Mulvey

Stannard, Martin, *Muriel Spark: The Biography* (London: Weidenfeld & Nicolson, 2009)

> This biography situates Muriel Spark's twenty-two novels in the context of her life and other writings

Waugh, Patricia, *Feminine Fictions: Revisiting the Postmodern* (London: Routledge, 1989)

> This study offers theoretical readings of works by women writers including Margaret Drabble and Sylvia Plath

Poetry

Acheson, James and Romana Huk (eds), *Contemporary British Poetry: Essays in Theory and Criticism* (Albany: State University of New York Press, 1996)

> This edited collection includes essays on Donald Davie, Roy Fisher, J. H. Prynne, Andrew Crozier, John Silkin, Douglas Dunn, Geoffrey Hill, and black women's poetry

Armitage, Simon and Robert Crawford (eds), *The Penguin Book of Poetry from Britain and Ireland* (Harmondsworth: Penguin, 1998)

> An anthology of poetry published in Britain and Ireland since the Second World War

Booth, Martin, *British Poetry 1964–1984: Driving through the Barricades* (London: Routledge, 1985)

> This polemical study argues that the years 1964–1984 represented a discrete renaissance for British poetry and its audiences

Byrne, Sandie, *H, v. and O: the Poetry of Tony Harrison* (Manchester: Manchester University Press, 1998)

> This study examines key motives and themes in the poetry of Tony Harrison

Corcoran, Neil, *English Poetry Since 1940* (London: Longman, 1993)

> This study explores postwar poetry in the context of late modernism, and includes detailed readings of Northern Irish poetry, contemporary women's poetry, and poets including Ted Hughes

Davie, Donald, *Purity of Diction in English Verse* (London: Routledge, 1967)

> This study of diction in English poetry offers a revealing insight into Movement approaches to poetic legacy

—, *Under Briggflatts: A History of Poetry in Great Britain 1960–1980* (Chicago: University of Chicago Press, 1989)

> This work provides a decade-by-decade study of postwar British poetry by one of the most influential poets and critics of the period

Duncan, Andrew, *The Failure of Conservatism in Modern British Poetry* (Cambridge: Salt Publishing, 2003)

> This study considers issues of modernity and aesthetics in modern poetry

Leader, Zachary (ed.), *The Movement Reconsidered: Essays on Larkin, Amis, Gunn, Davie and Their Contemporaries* (Oxford: Oxford University Press, 2009)

> This edited collection offers new perspectives on the Movement poets, exploring their work in terms of reception, postwar cultural debates, and notions of formal conservatism

May, William, *Stevie Smith and Authorship* (Oxford: Oxford University Press, 2010)

> This monograph examines Stevie Smith's poetry in the context of her fiction, illustrations, and book reviews, exploring how her attitude to the reading process shaped her writing and self-promotion

McDonald, Peter, *Mistaken Identities: Poetry and Northern Ireland* (Oxford: Clarendon Press, 1997)

> This book considers issues of nation and classification in Northern Irish poetry, exploring the usefulness of 'Northern Ireland' as a literary category

O'Donoghue, Bernard (ed.), *The Cambridge Companion to Seamus Heaney* (Cambridge: Cambridge University Press, 2008)

> This edited collection draws together a range of contemporary critical approaches to Seamus Heaney's work

Osborne, John, *Larkin, Ideology and Critical Violence: A Case of Wrongful Conviction* (Basingstoke: Palgrave Macmillan, 2006)

> This lively and polemical account of Philip Larkin argues against his apparent conservatism, racism, and provincial outlook

Raban, Jonathan, *The Society of the Poem* (London: Harrap, 1971)

> This examination of modern poetry explores American and British verse alongside each other, suggesting useful links between W. H. Auden, Randal Jarrell, and Ted Hughes

Roberts, Neil, *Ted Hughes: A Literary Life* (Basingstoke: Palgrave Macmillan, 2006)

> This critical biography of Ted Hughes explores his literary influences and the construction of his major poems

—, *Narrative and Voice in Postwar Poetry* (London: Longman, 1999)

> This study considers narrative and dialogic aspects of modern poetry with reference to Derek Walcott, Ted Hughes, and Anne Stevenson

Rose, Jacqueline, *The Haunting of Sylvia Plath* (London: Virago, 1992)

> This classic study of Sylvia Plath examines her cultural significance and suggests the importance of fantasy in her critical reception

Schmidt, Michael and Grevel Lindop (eds), *British Poetry Since 1960: A Critical Survey* (Manchester: Carcanet Press, 1972)

> A collection of essays assessing 1960s poetry, including several pieces on the Mersey Sound and the popularity of performance poetry

Trotter, David, *The Making of the Reader: Language and Subjectivity in Modern English, American, and Irish Poetry* (London: Macmillan, 1984)

> Drawing on reader-response theory, this study considers the readerly strategies used for approaching various contemporary poets

Drama

Aston, Elaine and Elin Diamond (eds), *The Cambridge Companion to Caryl Churchill* (Cambridge: Cambridge University Press, 2010)

> The edited collection draws together a range of contemporary critical approaches to Caryl Churchill's work

Caughie, John, *Television Drama: Realism, Modernism, and British Culture* (Oxford: Oxford University Press, 2000)

> This volume offers a history of postwar television drama to 1990, reading the genre against wider debates about realism and politics

Gilleman, Luc, *John Osborne: Vituperative Artist* (London: Routledge, 2001)

> This study examines John Osborne's work's reception, highlighting the importance of self-construction in Osborne's public persona

Holderness, Graham (ed.), *The Politics of Theatre and Drama* (London: Macmillan, 1992)

> This collection of edited essays explores experimental and political drama of the postwar period

Itzin, Catherine, *Stages in the Revolution: Political Theatre in Britain since 1968* (London: Eyre Methuen, 1980)

> This study argues for the increasingly political nature of theatre since the end of precensorship in 1968

Kelley, Catherine E. (ed.), *The Cambridge Companion to Tom Stoppard* (Cambridge: Cambridge University Press, 2001)

> This edited collection brings together a range of contemporary critical and theoretical approaches to Tom Stoppard's work, and contains useful bibliographical aids for further research

Knowlson, James, *Damned to Fame: the Life of Samuel Beckett* (London: Simon & Schuster, 2006)

> This biographical study of Samuel Beckett situates his drama in the context of his novels, life, and literary interests

Raby, Peter (ed.), *The Cambridge Companion to Harold Pinter* (Cambridge: Cambridge University Press, 2009)

> This edited collection brings together usefully succinct essays on modern approaches to Harold Pinter's work

Rebellato, Dan, *1956 and All That: The Making of Modern British Drama* (London: Routledge, 1999)

> This study deconstructs common assumptions about postwar theatre, re-examining audience response to works from the 1950s and 1960s and exploring representations of masculinity in the theatre

Roberts, Philip, *The Royal Court Theatre and the Modern Stage* (Cambridge: Cambridge University Press, 1999)

> This study considers the role of the Royal Court Theatre in nurturing and producing the works that would define the postwar stage

Shephard, Simon and Peter Womack, *English Drama: A Cultural History* (Oxford: Blackwell, 1996)

> This book offers a comprehensive account of the cultural history of English drama, and situates the postwar theatre alongside a chronological account of English drama since the Medieval period

Spencer, Jenny S., *Dramatic Strategies in the Plays of Edward Bond* (Cambridge: Cambridge University Press, 2001)

> This study examines the formal techniques used by Edward Bond in a variety of his plays

Taylor, John Russell, *Anger and After* (Harmondsworth: Penguin, 1963)

> This account of the postwar stage situates it amidst the Angry Young Man debate, and could be productively read alongside Rebellato's study

Tynan, Kenneth, *Tynan on Theatre* (Harmondsworth: Penguin, 1964)

> This volume collects together Kenneth Tynan's reviews and articles on the English stage, and includes his influential review of John Osborne's *Look Back in Anger*

Social and Historical Context

The Culture Debate

Easthope, Anthony, *Englishness and National Culture* (London: Routledge, 1999)

> This innovative volume examines notions of Englishness with reference to linguistics, cultural icons, and notions of national humour

Hall, Stuart and Paddy Whannel, *The Popular Arts* (London: Hutchinson Educational, 1964)

> This classic cultural studies text examines how far television and popular music can be subject to critical study

Hewison, Robert, *Culture and Consensus: England, Art and Politics Since 1940* (London: Methuen, 1997)

> This sociological account of the postwar period explores how far government-funded initiatives such as CEMA dictated the arts agenda of the late twentieth century

Higgins, John, *Raymond Williams: Literature, Marxism and Cultural Materialism* (London: Routledge, 1999)

> This readable introduction to the writing of the cultural theorist Raymond Williams considers the implications of his work for cultural studies and the way we read literature

Hoggart, Richard, *The Uses of Literacy* (Harmondsworth: Penguin, 1957)

> This classic work combines sociology with autobiography to explore the working-class culture debate

Leavis, F. R., *The Great Tradition: George Eliot, Henry James, Joseph Conrad* (London: Chatto & Windus, 1948)

> Although published outside the range of this study, Leavis's work makes links between form, narrative, and morality in a way that proved influential on the subsequent generation of novelists and critics

Mulhern, Francis, *Culture / Metaculture* (London: Routledge, 2000)

> This concise and thoughtful study outlines how Western society conceives of the notion of culture

Sinfield, Alan, *Literature, Politics and Culture in Postwar Britain* (Oxford: Blackwell, 1989)

> This influential work considers the relationship between literature and other cultural forms, and also explores the influence of American culture on postwar Britain

Snow, C. P., *The Two Cultures and the Scientific Revolution* (Cambridge: Cambridge University Press, 1993)

> This polemic, originally given as the 1959 Rede lecture in Cambridge, argues that literary study has isolated itself from the sciences to the detriment of both disciplines. This edition contains a useful introduction by Stefan Collini

Williams, Raymond, *Culture and Society 1780–1950* (London: Chatto & Windus, 1958)

> This influential work charts the changing perception of English culture over the last two hundred years, making revealing links between the work of Matthew Arnold, F. R. Leavis, and Richard Hoggart

—, *The Long Revolution* (London: Chatto & Windus, 1961)

> This study considers the fiction of postwar Britain in its cultural context, arguing for the re-emergence of realism in the second half of the twentieth century

Politics and History

Bergonzi, Bernard, *Wartime and Aftermath: English Literature and its Background, 1939–1960* (Oxford: Oxford University Press, 1993)

> This study examines fiction and poetry responding to the changed cultural conditions of the postwar period

Conekin, Becky E., *'The Autobiography of a Nation': The 1951 Festival of Britain* (Manchester: Manchester University Press, 2003)

> This study examines notions of Englishness and Empire with reference to postwar British culture

Kynaston, David, *Austerity Britain, 1945–1951* (London: Bloomsbury, 2008)

> This detailed study gives a revealing portrait of Britain in the immediate aftermath of the Second World War

Marwick, Arthur, *British Society since 1945* (Harmondsworth: Penguin, 1982)

> This historical and sociological account of postwar Britain offers useful statistical approaches to the changing cultural conditions

Nairn, Tom, *The Break-Up of Britain: Crisis and Neo-Nationalism* (London: New Left Books, 1997)

> This polemical left-wing account of recent British history considers notions of post-Empire nationality

Nuttall, Jeff, *Bomb Culture* (London: MacGibbon & Kee, 1968)

> This influential counter-cultural work offers an alternative reading of postwar social history and the nuclear question

Sandbrook, Dominic, *Never Had it So Good: A History of Britain from Suez to the Beatles* (London: Abacus, 2006)

> This readable account of 1950s and 1960s Britain offers lively historical analysis alongside a consideration of the key literary events of the period

—, *White Heat: A History of Britain in the Swinging Sixties* (London: Abacus, 2006)

> This work continues Sandbrook's account of the postwar period, focusing on Harold Wilson's government and the cultural moment of the 1960s

Steedman, Carolyn, *Landscape for a Good Woman: A Story of Two Lives* (London: Virago, 1986)

> This autobiographical and sociological work offers an alternative to Richard Hoggart's narrative of postwar Britain, and considers how working-class lives have been misrepresented in literature and by cultural and social criticism

Thompson, E. P., *The Making of the English Working Class* (London: Gollancz, 1963)

> This influential study of the eighteenth- and nineteenth-century working classes argues that posterity has offered condescending readings of their lives

Theories and Methodologies

Postcolonial Literature and Theory

Bhabha, Homi K., *Nation and Narration* (London: Routledge, 1991)

> This volume considers how nationhood is represented with reference to narrative fiction, considering notions of entitlement and representation

—, *The Location of Culture* (London: Routledge, 1994)

> This influential series of essays argues how postcolonial critiques have altered the nature of postmodern discourse

Dabydeen, David (ed.), *The Black Presence in English Literature* (Manchester: Manchester University Press, 1985)

> This edited collection considers the continued presence of black British voices in literary history

Dennis, F. and N. Kahn (eds), *Voices of the Crossing: The Impact on Britain of Writers from Asia, the Caribbean and Africa* (London: Serpent's Tail, 2000)

> This edited collection of essays includes contributions on West Indian writing in Britain, the notion of the exile, and the idea of a vernacular literature

George, R. M., *The Politics of Home: Postcolonial Relocations and Twentieth-Century Fiction* (Cambridge: Cambridge University Press, 1996)

> This study considers the politics of home in postcolonial literature, with reference to authors such as Anita Desai and Salman Rushdie

Gikandi, Simon, *Maps of Englishness: Writing Identity in the Culture of Colonialism* (New York: Columbia University Press, 1996)

> This study of nationhood and postcolonial theory considers the relationship between history, heritage, and identity

Lamming, George, *The Pleasures of Exile* (London: Michael Joseph, 1960)

> This critical work draws on Lamming's own experience as a West Indian novelist to articulate difficulties in the production and reception of West Indian literature

Nasta, Susheila, *Home Truths: Fictions of the South Asian Diaspora in Britain* (Basingstoke: Palgrave, 2002)

> This study considers various fictional accounts of diaspora, with reference to writers such as Sam Selvon and Hanif Kureishi

Phillips, Mike and Trevor Philips, *Windrush: The Irresistible Rise of Multi-Racial Britain* (London: HarperCollins, 1998)

> This is a readable and lucid account of postwar immigration to Britain

Said, Edward, *Orientalism* (London: Penguin, 1978)

> This influential study argues that the West's creation of the 'Orient' in politics and literature has created a cultural and social divide between East and West

—, *Culture and Imperialism* (London: Chatto & Windus, 1993)

> This accompanying study charts the development of imperialism in European culture

Young, Robert, *Postcolonialism: A Historical Introduction* (Oxford: Blackwell, 2001)

> This volume gives a wide-ranging account of postcolonial theories and debates

Postmodernism

Connor, Steven, *Postmodernist Culture: An Introduction to Theories of the Modern* (Oxford: Blackwell, 1997)

> This readable book offers a lucid account of postmodern theory and its application to contemporary art and culture

Jameson, Frederic, *The Political Unconscious* (London: Methuen, 1981)

> This work argues for the importance of historical and Marxist approaches to literary study

—, *Postmodernism, or the Cultural Logic of Late Capitalism* (London: Verso, 1991)

> In this famous study, Frederic Jameson traces notions of postmodernity back to capitalist systems of production and labour

Feminism

de Beauvoir, Simone, *The Second Sex*, trans. H. M. Parshley (Harmondsworth: Penguin, 1972)

> This pioneering feminist work explores gender inequality and the relationship between cultural, biological, and social readings of femininity

Ellman, Mary, *Thinking About Women* (New York: Harcourt, 1968)

> This influential study considers the stereotypical representation of women in literary texts

Firestone, Shulamith, *The Dialectic of Sex: The Case for Feminist Revolution* (London: Women's Press, 1979)

> This polemic by French-Canadian feminist Shula Firestone argues that women can only free themselves from the biological constraints of their sex through the use cybernetic technologies which could carry out human reproduction in a laboratory

Greer, Germaine, *The Female Eunuch* (London: Paladin, 1971)

> This famous study attacks the nuclear family for its suppression of female libido

Kaplan, Cora, *Seachanges: Essays on Culture and Feminism* (London: Verso, 1986)

> This essay collection considers aesthetic and political issues raised by postwar feminist fiction and film

Moi, Toril, *Sexual / Textual Politics: Feminist Literary Theory* (London: Penguin, 1985)

> This offers a useful guide to debates in third-wave feminism and feminist literary theory

Surveys of Postwar Literature

General Guides

Lucas, John, *Moderns and Contemporaries: Novelists, Poets, Critics* (Hassocks: Harvester Press, 1985)

> This study is a useful guide to various poets and novelists of the period in their critical context

Middleton, Peter and Tim Woods, *Literatures of Memory: History, Time and Space in Postwar Writing* (Manchester: Manchester University Press, 2000)

> This study explores the construction of the past and urban space in contemporary British and American literature

Morrison, Blake, *The Movement: English Poetry and Fiction of the 1950s* (Oxford: Oxford University Press, 1980)

> This thoughtful study considers the Movement in poetry and fiction, isolating key authors and literary strategies common to different writers

Stevenson, Randall, *The Oxford English Literary History, Vol. XII, 1960–2000* (Oxford: Oxford University Press, 2004)

> This excellent guide to the period offers author biographies, a detailed discussion of postwar prose, drama, and poetry in its cultural and social context, and a useful consideration of book-buying and changing readership patterns

Reference Works, Bibliographical Aids, and Online Resources

Drabble, Margaret, *The Oxford Companion to English Literature*, 5th edn (Oxford: Oxford University Press, 1995)

> This reference guide includes entries for all major works, authors, and genres of English literature

Fowler, Roger (ed.), *A Dictionary of Modern Critical Terms* (London: Routledge & Kegan Paul, 1987)

> This dictionary offers useful definitions of specialised critical, theoretical, and literary language

Further Reading

Literature Online for HE (LION): http://lion.chadwyck.co.uk

A subscription-based online library featuring nearly half a million works of English and American poetry, drama, and prose and critical articles

The Literary Encyclopaedia: www.litencyc.com

An online resource featuring indexes and bibliographies for major authors, a list of 4,000 internet resources for further study, and profiles of many key authors and individual works

The Poetry Archive: http://poetryarchive.org

An online resource featuring recordings of poets reading their own work, including Tony Harrison, Seamus Heaney, Ted Hughes, Philip Larkin, Sylvia Plath, and Stevie Smith

Index

Index

Index

Acknowledgements

Reprinted by permission of Farrar, Straus and Giroux, LLC, and Faber & Faber Ltd:

1 line from 'Carnal Knowledge' from COLLECTED POEMS by Thom Gunn. Copyright © 1994 by Thom Gunn. Excerpt from FINDERS KEEPERS by Seamus Heaney. Copyright © 2003 by Seamus Heaney. 4 lines from 'Orghast' from SELECTED TRANSLATIONS by Ted Hughes. Copyright © 2008 by Ted Hughes. 5 lines from 'Essential Beauty', 1 line from 'Sad Steps', 2 lines from 'Mr Bleaney', 1.5 lines from 'High Windows', 4 lines from 'Talking in Bed', 4 lines from 'Water', 2 lines from 'Home is So Sad', 2 lines from 'Going, Going', 2 lines from 'Here', and lines from 'Annus Miribilis' from COLLECTED POEMS by Philip Larkin. Copyright © 1998, 2003 by the Estate of Philip Larkin. 3 lines from 'Jean Rhys', and 2 lines from 'The Sea is History' from COLLECTED POEMS 1948–1984 by Derek Walcott. Copyright © Derek Walcott

Fleur Adcock, excerpt from 'England's Glory', from *Poems 1960–2000* (Bloodaxe Books, 2000), reproduced by permission of Bloodaxe Books

John Agard, excerpt from 'Listen Mr Oxford Don', from *Mangoes & Bullets* (Pluto, 1985), reproduced by permission of Caroline Sheldon Literary Agency Ltd

John Ash, excerpt from 'Some Boys (or The English Poem circa 1978)' (1981), from *Collected Poems* (Manchester: Carcanet, 1996), reproduced by permission of Carcanet Press Ltd

Julian Barnes, excerpt from *Metroland* (1990) Copyright © Julian Barnes, 1990. Reproduced by permission of United Agents Ltd (www.unitedagents.co.uk) on behalf of Julian Barnes

Acknowledgements

Excerpt from *Happy Days*, copyright © 1961 by Grove Press, Inc. Copyright renewed © 1989 by Samuel Beckett. Used by permission of Grove/Atlantic, Inc. and Faber & Faber, Ltd

Excerpt from *Not I*, copyright © 1973 by Samuel Beckett. Used by permission of Grove/Atlantic, Inc. and Faber & Faber, Ltd

John Betjeman, excerpt from 'Hertfordshire', from *Collected Poems* by John Betjeman © 1955, 1958, 1962, 1964, 1968, 1970, 1979, 1981, 1982, 2001. Reproduced by permission of John Murray (Publishers)

Edward Bond, excerpts from *Saved* (Methuen, 1969), *Narrow Road to Deep North* (Methuen, 1968), 'Introduction' to *Bingo* in *Plays: Three* (Methuen, 1999), and 'The Rational Theatre' in *Plays: Two* (Methuen, 1998) reproduced by permission of Methuen Drama, an imprint of A & C Black

Elizabeth Bowen, excerpt from *Eva Trout* (Jonathan Cape, 1969). Reproduced with permission of Curtis Brown Group Ltd, London on behalf of the Estate of Elizabeth Bowen Copyright © Elizabeth Bowen 1968

Malcolm Bradbury, excerpt from *Eating People is Wrong* (Secker & Warburg, 1986). Reproduced with permission of Curtis Brown Group Ltd, London on behalf of the Estate of Malcolm Bradbury Copyright © Malcolm Bradbury 1986

Alan Brownjohn, excerpts from 'Scene from the Fifties' and 'In the Trade', from *Collected Poems* (Enitharmon Press, 2006), reproduced by permission of Enitharmon Press

Basil Bunting, excerpt from 'Briggflatts', from *Briggflatts* (Bloodaxe Books, 2009), reproduced by permission of Bloodaxe Books

Acknowledgements

From *Nights at the Circus* by Angela Carter, copyright © 1984 by Angela Carter. Used by permission of Viking Penguin, a division of Penguin Group (USA) Inc.

Caryl Churchill, excerpts from *Softcops* from *Plays: Two* (Methuen, 1990), reproduced by permission of Methuen Drama, an imprint of A&C Black Publishers Ltd

Caryl Churchill, excerpt from *A Mouthful of Birds* from *Plays: Three* (Nick Hern Books, 1998), reproduced by permission of Nick Hern Books

Donald Davie, excerpt from 'Dorset', from *Collected Poems* (Manchester: Carcanet, 2002), reproduced by permission of Carcanet Press Ltd

Extracts from 'Comprehensive' are taken from *Standing Female Nude* by Carol Ann Duffy published by Anvil Press Poetry in 1985

Extract from 'Politico' is taken from *Selling Manhattan* by Carol Ann Duffy published by Anvil Press Poetry in 1987

Maureen Duffy, excerpt from THE MICROCOSM Copyright © 1966 Maureen Duffy. Reprinted by kind permission of Jonathan Clowes Ltd., London, on behalf of Maureen Duffy

U. A. Fanthorpe, excerpt from 'Knowing about Sonnets', *Collected Poems 1978–2003* (Peterloo, 2005), copyright © R. V. Bailey, reproduced by kind permission of the author's estate

John Fowles, excerpt from *The French Lieutenant's Woman* (Fontana, 1969), reproduced by permission of Little, Brown & Company and Aitken Alexander Associates, Ltd

Acknowledgements

Zulfikar Ghose, excerpt from *Confessions of a Native Alien* (Routledge, 1965), p. 2

Tony Harrison, various excerpts from *Collected Poems* (Penguin, 2007) and *Tony Harrison: Plays 2* (Faber & Faber, 2002), reproduced by kind permission of the author's estate

Linton Kwesi Johnson, excerpt from 'Independent Intavenshan', from *Inglan is a Bitch* (Race Today, 1980), copyright © Linton Kwesi Johnson, reproduced by permission of LKJ Music Publishers

Thomas Kinsella, excerpt from 'Personal Places', from *Collected Poems* (Manchester: Carcanet, 2001), reproduced by permission of Carcanet Press Ltd

Doris Lessing, excerpt from THE GOLDEN NOTEBOOK Copyright © 1962 Doris Lessing. Reprinted by kind permission of Jonathan Clowes Ltd., London, on behalf of Doris Lessing

Grevel Lindop, excerpt from 'White Horse', from *Tourists* (Manchester: Carcanet, 1987), reproduced by permission of Carcanet Press Ltd

David Lodge, excerpts from *Nice Work* (Secker & Warburg, 1988). Reproduced with permission of Curtis Brown Group Ltd, London on behalf of David Lodge Copyright © David Lodge 1988

Colin MacInnes, excerpt from *Absolute Beginners* (Allison & Busby, 2001). Reproduced with permission of Curtis Brown Group Ltd, London on behalf of the Estate of Colin MacInnes Copyright © Colin MacInnes 1959

From *The Bell* by Iris Murdoch, copyright © 1958, renewed 1986 by Iris Murdoch, published by Chatto & Windus. Used by permission of Viking Penguin, a division of Penguin Group (USA) Inc. and The Random House Group Ltd

Acknowledgements

From *The Sea, The Sea* by Iris Murdoch, copyright © 1978 by Iris Murdoch, published by Chatto & Windus. Used by permission of Viking Penguin, a division of Penguin Group (USA) Inc. and The Random House Group Ltd

From *A Fairly Honourable Defeat* by Iris Murdoch, copyright © 1975 by Iris Murdoch, published by Chatto & Windus. Used by permission of Viking Penguin, a division of Penguin Group (USA) Inc. and The Random House Group Ltd

From *The Word Child* by Iris Murdoch, copyright © 1958, renewed 1986 by Iris Murdoch, published by Chatto & Windus. Used by permission of Viking Penguin, a division of Penguin Group (USA) Inc. and The Random House Group Ltd

Iris Murdoch, excerpts from 'Against Dryness' (1961) in Malcolm Bradbury (ed.), *The Novel Today: Contemporary Writers on Modern Fiction* (Manchester University Press, 1977), reproduced by permission of Manchester University Press

John Osborne, excerpts from *The Blood of the Bambergs* from *Plays For England/Watch it Come Down* (Oberon, 1999), and *Look Back in Anger* (Faber, 1996) reproduced by kind permission of the author's estate

Excerpt from *The Birthday Party*, copyright © 1959, 1960, 1965 by Harold Pinter. Excerpt from *The Room*, © copyright 1959, 1960 by Harold Pinter. Used by permission of Grove/Atlantic, Inc. and Faber & Faber, Ltd

Excerpt from *No Man's Land*, © copyright 1975 by H. Pinter Ltd. Used by permission of Grove/Atlantic, Inc. and Faber & Faber, Ltd

Excerpt from WIDE SARGASSO SEA by Jean Rhys (Penguin Books, 1968). Copyright © 1966 by Jean Rhys. Used by permission of W. W. Norton & Company, Inc. and Penguin Books Ltd

Acknowledgements

Paul Scott, excerpt from *The Raj Quartet* (Heinemann, 1976), reproduced by permission of David Higham Associates Ltd

Sam Selvon, excerpts from *The Lonely Londoners* (Penguin, 2007) reproduced by kind permission of the Estate of Sam Selvon

Excerpts from 'Not Waving But Drowning', 'Parents', and 'To School!' by Stevie Smith, from COLLECTED POEMS OF STEVIE SMITH, copyright © 1957 by Stevie Smith. Reprinted by permission of New Directions Publishing Corp. and the Executors of James MacGibbon

Excerpts from 'A Dream of Comparison', 'I love …', 'My Muse' and 'The Best Beast of the Fat-Stock Show at Earls Court' by Stevie Smith, from COLLECTED POEMS OF STEVIE SMITH, copyright © 1966 by Stevie Smith. Reprinted by permission of New Directions Publishing Corp. and the Executors of James MacGibbon

Excerpts from 'Childe Rolandine', 'Cock-a-Doo', 'Every lovely Limb's a Desolation', 'How Do You See?', 'Oh Christianity, Christianity', 'Pretty', 'The House of Over-Dew', 'The Songster' and 'The Person from Porlock' by Stevie Smith, from COLLECTED POEMS OF STEVIE SMITH, copyright © 1972 by Stevie Smith. Reprinted by permission of New Directions Publishing Corp. and the Executors of James MacGibbon

By Muriel Spark, from *The Abbess of Crewe*, copyright © 1974 by Copyright Administration Ltd. Reprinted by permission of New Directions Publishing Corp., and David Higham Associates Ltd

By Muriel Spark, from *Loitering with Intent*, copyright © 1981 by Copyright Administration Ltd. Reprinted by permission of New Directions Publishing Corp., and David Higham Associates Ltd

By Muriel Spark, from *The Comforters*, copyright © 1957 by Copyright Administration Ltd. Reprinted by permission of New Directions Publishing Corp., and David Higham Associates Ltd

Acknowledgements

By Muriel Spark, from *The Girls of Slender Means*, copyright © 1963 by Copyright Administration Ltd. Reprinted by permission of New Directions Publishing Corp. and David Higham Associates Ltd

Excerpt from *Rosencrantz and Guildenstern are Dead*, copyright © 1967 by Tom Stoppard. Used by permission of Grove/Atlantic, Inc. and Faber & Faber, Ltd

Excerpt from *Travesties*, copyright © 1975 by Tom Stoppard. Used by permission of Grove/Atlantic, Inc. and Faber & Faber, Ltd

R. S. Thomas, excerpt from 'Welsh Landscape' from *Collected Poems: 1945–1990* (JM Dent, 1993), reproduced by permission of JM Dent, an imprint of The Orion Publishing Group, London

John Wain, excerpt from *Hurry On Down* by John Wain, published by Secker and Warburg. Reprinted by permission of The Random House Group Ltd and the estate of John Wain

Timberlake Wertenbaker, excerpt from *Three Birds Alighted on a Field* from *Plays: One* (Faber, 1996), reproduced by permission of Faber & Faber Ltd

Hugo Williams, excerpt from 'Post-war British' (1994), from *Collected Poems* (London: Faber, 2002), reproduced by permission of Faber & Faber, Ltd

Excerpt from *Sexing the Cherry*, copyright © 1989 by Jeanette Winterson. Used by permission of Grove/Atlantic, Inc. and Bloomsbury Publishing Plc.

Benjamin Zephaniah, excerpt from 'The Race Industry' from *Too Black, Too Strong* (Bloodaxe, 2001), reproduced by permission of Bloodaxe Books

YORK NOTES **COMPANIONS**

Texts, Contexts and Connections from York Notes to help you through your literature degree ...

✔ **Medieval Literature**, Carole Maddern
ISBN: 9781408204757 | £10.99

✔ **Renaissance Poetry and Prose**, June Waudby
ISBN: 9781408204788 | £10.99

✔ **Shakespeare and Renaissance Drama**, Hugh Mackay
ISBN: 9781408204801 | £10.99

✔ **The Long Eighteenth Century: Literature from 1660 to 1790**
Penny Pritchard
ISBN: 9781408204733 | £10.99

✔ **Romantic Literature**, John Gilroy
ISBN: 9781408204795 | £10.99

✔ **Victorian Literature**, Beth Palmer
ISBN: 9781408204818 | £10.99

✔ **Modernist Literature: 1890 to 1950**, Gary Day
ISBN: 9781408204764 | £10.99

✔ **Postwar Literature: 1950 to 1990**, William May
ISBN: 9781408204740 | £10.99

✔ **New Directions: Writing Post 1990**, Fiona Tolan
ISBN: 9781408204771 | £10.99

Available from all good bookshops

For a 20% discount on any title in the series visit
www.yorknotes.com/companions and
enter discount code JB001A at the checkout!